LAW
BASICS
Student Study Guides

CONTRACT

FIFTH EDITION

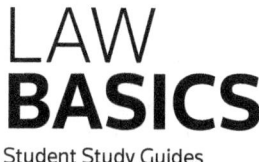

Student Study Guides

CONTRACT

FIFTH EDITION

By

Alex Gibb, LLB (Hons)
Lecturer in Law, North East Scotland College

and

Alasdair Bothwell Gordon,
LLB, BD (Hons), EdD, TQFE, LCGI
Former Lecturer in Law, North East Scotland College

W. GREEN

First Edition published in 1998
Second Edition published in 2003
Third Edition published in 2009
Fourth Edition published in 2014

ISBN 978-0-414-06505-5

Published in 2019 by Thomson Reuters,
trading as W. Green, 21 Alva Street, Edinburgh, EH2 4PS.
Thomson Reuters is registered in England & Wales, Company No.1679046.
Registered Office and address for service: 5 Canada Square, Canary Wharf, London, E14 5AQ.
For further information on our products and services, visit
http://www.sweetandmaxwell.co.uk

Computerset by W. Green.
Printed and bound by CPI Group (UK) Ltd, Croydon, CR0 4YY.

No natural forests were destroyed to make this product: only farmed timber was used and replanted.

A CIP catalogue record of this book is available from the British Library.

For orders, go to: *http://www.tr.com/uki-legal-contact*;
Tel: 0345 600 9355.

Thomson Reuters, the Thomson Reuters Logo and W. GREEN are trademarks of Thomson Reuters.

© 2019 Thomson Reuters

Crown copyright material is reproduced with the permission of the Controller of HMSO and the Queen's Printer for Scotland.

All rights reserved. No part of this publication may be reproduced, or transmitted in any form, or by any means, or stored in any retrieval system of any nature, without prior written permission, except for permitted fair dealing under the Copyright, Designs and Patents Act 1988, or in accordance with the terms of a licence issued by the Copyright Licensing Agency in respect of photocopying and/or reprographic reproduction. Application for permission for other use of copyright material, including permission to reproduce extracts in other published works, should be made to the publishers. Full acknowledgement of the author, publisher and source must be given.

FOREWORD

It was a pleasure and a privilege, some years ago, to be invited by Greens to write two of the earlier volumes in the *Law*Basics series, on *Contract* and on *Succession*, which were published in 1998 and 1999 respectively. Both of these books went on to second editions under my authorship. The *Law*Basics textbooks are now almost at the end of their third decade and their continued popularity speaks for itself.

When I wrote the original volumes, I was a lecturer at Aberdeen College, now part of North East Scotland College. I am now retired and have been away from teaching for a number of years. It is a particular pleasure to me that the authorship of subsequent editions both of *Contract* and *Succession* has been undertaken by Alex Gibb, also a lecturer at North East Scotland College. Mr Gibb has skilfully adapted, updated, improved and clarified both of these texts.

I am very pleased to commend Mr Gibb's fifth edition of *Contract Law*Basics to today's students in the expectation it will be as well received as the earlier editions and will continue to be a good and useful foundation for their studies in Scots Law.

Alasdair B. Gordon
Hamilton, South Lanarkshire
May 2019

PREFACE

Knowledge of contract law is a fundamental part of successful legal study. Contracts underpin many areas of the law, and so a sound knowledge of basic contract theory can assist greatly in the understanding and contextualising of other legal subjects.

It is in this spirit that this modest book proceeds. It is the fifth edition of an introductory book on the law of contract in Scotland, and the third edition which I have had the pleasure and privilege of being asked to update. It is always my intention when revising one of Dr Gordon's excellent works to retain the spirit and high quality of the text, whilst including necessary updates and introducing my own stylistic alterations. I have approached this project in the same manner, and hope that the resulting edition will once again assist students in gaining a solid foundation in contract law. It is also hoped, as before, that this book will be of use as a revision aid. However, it is not intended to be a substitute for the more scholarly and detailed texts available.

Due to constraints of size, a book of this nature cannot go into detailed discussion of every issue and so treatment has been concentrated on those areas that are of most fundamental importance and relevance to the student. There is a huge body of case law in this area, and an attempt has been made to include a reasonable selection of both old and new cases. The possibility of future reform has been discussed where appropriate but not covered in detail, also due to constraints of space.

Purely in the interests of word economy, the book tends to use masculine terminology but the intention is to be inclusive. Accordingly, "he" can be read as "he or she" and "his" includes "his or her" unless the context clearly indicates otherwise.

My aim has been to state the law as at 1 May 2019. Responsibility for any errors or omissions is mine alone.

Alex Gibb
Aberdeen
May 2019

CONTENTS

	Page
Foreword	v
Preface	vii
Table of Cases	xi
Table of Statutes	xxi
Table of Statutory Instruments, EU Legislation and Reports	xxiii
1. Introduction to Contracts	1
2. Agreement and Formation of Contract	7
3. Promises, Writing and Personal Bar	21
4. Contractual Capacity	29
5. Error and Misrepresentation	37
6. Illegal Agreements	57
7. Exemption Clauses in Contracts	63
8. Breach of Contract	71
9. Termination of Contract	89
10. Matters of Enforcement	97
Appendix: Sample Examination Questions and Answer Plans	109
Index	117

TABLE OF CASES

Para

Abchurch Steamship Co Ltd v Stinnes; Abchurch, The, 1911 S.C. 1010; 1911 2 S.L.T. 72 CSIH (1 Div) 10–09
Aberdeen City Council v McNeill; sub nom. McNeill v Aberdeen City Council [2013] CSIH 102; 2014 S.C. 335; 2014 S.L.T. 312 CSIH (Ex Div)..8–09
Aberdeen City Council v Stewart Milne Group Ltd [2011] UKSC 56; 2012 S.C. (U.K.S.C.) 240; 2012 S.L.T. 205 SC..10–04
Advice Centre for Mortgages Ltd v McNicoll, 2006 S.L.T. 591; 2006 S.C.L.R. 602 CSOH..3–04
Ageas (UK) Ltd v Kwik–Fit (GB) Ltd [2014] EWHC 2178 (QB); [2014] Bus. L.R. 1338 QBD 8–13
Agri Energy v McCallion [2014] CSOH 13; [2014] 1 WLUK 666; 2014 G.W.D. 5–101 CSOH 6–08
Ailsa Craig Fishing Co Ltd v Malvern Fishing Co Ltd (The Strathallan); Malvern Fishing Co Ltd v Ailsa Craig Fishing Co Ltd (The Strathallan); Strathallan, The; George Craig [1983] 1 W.L.R. 964; [1983] 1 All E.R. 101 HL..7–09
A&J Inglis v John Buttery & Co (1878) 3 App. Cas. 552; (1878) 5 R. (H.L.) 87 HL.........10–03
Albyn Housing Society Ltd v Active Sustainable Energy Systems [2016] CSOH 110; [2016] 7 WLUK 665; 2016 G.W.D. 25–458 CSOH...5–06
Alexander Philp & Co v Knoblauch, 1907 S.C. 994; (1907) 15 S.L.T. 61 CSIH (2 Div)......2–05
Allen v Hounga; Hounga v Allen [2014] UKSC 47; [2014] 1 W.L.R. 2889; [2014] 4 All E.R. 595 SC..6–03
AMA (New Town) Ltd v Law [2013] CSIH 61; 2013 S.C. 608; 2013 S.L.T. 959 CSIH (Ex Div) 8–18
AMA (New Town) Ltd v McKenna, 2011 S.L.T. (Sh. Ct) 73; [2011] 2 WLUK 866 Sh. Ct..8–18
Amin v Brown [2005] EWHC 1670 (Ch); [2005] 7 WLUK 834; [2006] I.L.Pr. 5 Ch D.....4–07
Anderson v Lambie [1954] 1 W.L.R. 303; [1954] 3 All E.R. 157 (Note) HL 5–06
Arnold v Britton [2015] UKSC 36; [2015] A.C. 1619; [2015] 2 W.L.R. 1593 SC............10–06
A Schroeder Music Publishing Co Ltd v Macaulay (formerly Instone); sub nom. Macaulay (formerly Instone) v A Schroeder Music Publishing Co Ltd [1974] 1 W.L.R. 1308; [1974] 3 All E.R. 616 HL..6–06
Attorney General v Blake [2001] 1 A.C. 268; [2000] 3 W.L.R. 625 HL..............................8–13
Avery v Bowden, 119 E.R. 647; (1855) 5 El. & Bl. 714 court of Queen's Bench................8–18
AWG Business Centres Ltd v Regus Caledonia Ltd [2017] CSIH 22; [2017] 2 WLUK 90; 2017 G.W.D. 9–131 CSIH (1 Div)...10–05
Aziz v Caixa d'Estalvis de Catalunya, Tarragona i Manresa (Catalunyacaixa) (C-415/11), EU:C:2013:164; [2013] 3 WLUK 372; [2013] 3 C.M.L.R. 5 ECJ 7–12
Balfour Beatty Construction (Scotland) Ltd v Scottish Power Plc, 1994 S.C. (H.L.) 20; 1994 S.L.T. 807 HL...8–16
Bank of Scotland v Dunedin Property Investment Co Ltd (No.1), 1998 S.C. 657; 1999 S.L.T. 470 CSIH (1 Div)..10–04
Barclays Bank Plc v O'Brien [1994] 1 A.C. 180; [1993] 3 W.L.R. 786 HL........................5–15
Barr v Crawford, 1983 S.L.T. 481; [1982] 12 WLUK 119 CSOH......................................6–02
Barr v Dunbar Assets Plc [2016] CSOH 44; [2016] 3 WLUK 567; 2016 G.W.D. 10–187 CSOH..5–15
Barry v Davies (t/a Heathcote Ball & Co); sub nom. Barry v Heathcote Ball & Co (Commercial Auctions) Ltd; Heathcote Ball & Co (Commercial Auctions) Ltd v Barry [2000] 1 W.L.R. 1962; [2001] 1 All E.R. 944 CA (Civ Div).....................................2–06
Bathgate v Rosie, 1976 S.L.T. (Sh. Ct.) 16; [1975] 1 WLUK 634 Sh. Ct............................3–02
Bennett v The Inveresk Paper Co (1891) 18 R. 975; [1891] 6 WLUK 70 CSIH (1 Div) 10–17
Bermans & Nathans Ltd v Weibye, 1983 S.C. 67; 1983 S.L.T. 299 CSIH (1 Div).............8–10
Beta Computers (Europe) Ltd v Adobe Systems (Europe) Ltd, 1996 S.L.T. 604; 1996 S.C.L.R. 587 CSOH...7–05
Bile Bean Manufacturing Co Ltd v Davidson (1906) 8 F. 1181; (1906) 14 S.L.T. 294 CSIH (2 Div)..5–18

Black v Cornelius (1879) 6 R. 581; [1879] 1 WLUK 55 CSIH (2 Div) 9–06
Black v McGregor [2006] CSIH 45; 2007 S.C. 69; [2006] 10 WLUK 172 CSIH
   (Ex Div) 8–08
Bluebell Apparel Ltd v Dickinson, 1978 S.C. 16; 1980 S.L.T. 157 CSIH (1 Div).......6–07, 8–03
Blyth & Blyth Ltd v Carillion Construction Ltd, 2002 S.L.T. 961; [2001] 4 WLUK 359 CSOH
   9–05
Blyth v Scottish Liberal Club, 1982 S.C. 140; 1983 S.L.T. 260 CSIH (2 Div) 8–08
Bogie (t/a Oakbank Services) v Forestry Commission, 2002 S.C.L.R. 278; [2001] 11 WLUK
   637 CSOH..2–02
Boston Deep Sea Fishing and Ice Co v Farnham [1957] 1 W.L.R. 1051; [1957] 3 All E.R. 204;
   [1957] Ch D 4–08
Boyd & Forrest (A Firm) v Glasgow & South Western Railway Co (No.1), 1912 S.C. (H.L.)
   93; 1912 1 S.L.T. 476 HL 5–17, 5–18
Boyd & Forrest (A Firm) v Glasgow & South Western Railway Co (1915). *See* Glasgow &
   South Western Railway Co v Boyd & Forrest (A Firm) (No.3).
British Airways Board v Taylor [1976] 1 W.L.R. 13; [1976] 1 All E.R. 65 HL 5–18
British Coal Corp v South of Scotland Electricity Board (No.1), 1991 S.L.T. 302; [1989] 12
   WLUK 365 CSOH 10–04
Brown v Neon Management Services Ltd [2018] EWHC 2137 (QB); [2018] 8 WLUK 106;
   [2019] I.R.L.R. 30 QBD 6–07
Brownlee v Robb; sub nom. Brownlee's Executor v Robb's Executrix, 1907 S.C. 1302; (1907)
   15 S.L.T. 261 CSIH (Ex Div)..10–15
Bruce & Co v Ferguson [2013] 5 WLUK 711; 2013 G.W.D. 32–640 Sh. Ct..............10–05
Budana v Leeds Teaching Hospitals NHS Trust [2017] EWCA Civ 1980; [2018] 1 W.L.R.
   1965; [2017] 12 WLUK 72 CA (Civ Div)..9–06
Burr v Bo'ness Police Commissioners (1896) 24 R. 148; (1896) 4 S.L.T. 149 CSIH
   (2 Div) 10–11
Butler Machine Tool Co v Ex–cell–o Corp (England) [1979] 1 W.L.R. 401; [1979] 1 All E.R.
   965 CA (Civ Div) 2–12
Cairns v Marianski (1850) 12 D. 919; [1850] 3 WLUK 77 CSIH (2 Div) 5–25
Cameron-Head v Cameron & Co, 1919 S.C. 627; 1919 2 S.L.T. 133 CSIH (1 Div)...........8–17
Cantiere San Rocco SA (Shipbuilding Co) v Clyde Shipbuilding & Engineering Co Ltd; sub
   nom. Cantiare San Rocco SA (Shipbuilding Co) v Clyde Shipbuilding & Engineering Co
   Ltd [1924] A.C. 226; (1923) 16 Ll. L. Rep. 327 HL 4–07, 9–14
Cargill International Trading Pte Ltd v Uttam Galva Steels Ltd [2019] EWHC 476 (Comm);
   [2019] 2 WLUK 473 QBD (Comm) 8–17
Carlill v Carbolic Smoke Ball Co [1893] 1 Q.B. 256; [1892] 12 WLUK 16 CA.............2–06
Carlyle v Royal Bank of Scotland Plc. *See* Royal Bank of Scotland Plc v Carlyle.
Carmarthen Developments Ltd v Pennington [2008] CSOH 139; [2008] 9 WLUK 399; 2008
   G.W.D. 33–494 CSOH..2–16
Carmichael v Carmichael's Executrix. *See* English & Scottish Law Life Assurance Association
   v Carmichael.
Caterleisure Ltd v Glasgow Prestwick International Airport Ltd, 2006 S.C. 602; 2005 S.L.T.
   1083 CSIH (Ex Div)..3–04
Cavendish Square Holding v Makdessi. *See* Makdessi v Cavendish Square Holdings BV.
Cawdor v Cawdor. *See* Ilona (Countess of Cawdor) v Vaughan (Earl of Cawdor).
Chapelton v Barry Urban DC [1940] 1 K.B. 532; [1940] 1 All E.R. 356 CA 2–07, 7–03
Charge Card Services Ltd (No.2), Re [1989] Ch. 497; [1988] 3 W.L.R. 764 CA
   (Civ Div) 9–03
Christie v Ruxton (1862) 24 D. 1182; [1862] 6 WLUK 157 CSIH (2 Div) 8–10
Church Commissioners for England v Abbey National Plc, 1994 S.C. 651; 1994 S.L.T. 959
   CSIH..8–03
Church of Scotland Endowment Committee v Provident Association of London; sub nom.
   Cowan (Endowment Committee of Church of Scotland)'s Trustees v Provident
   Association of London; Church of Scotland Endowment Committee v Provident
   Association of London Ltd, 1914 S.C. 165; (1913) 2 S.L.T. 412 CSIH (2 Div)...........1–06
Chwee Kin Keong v Digilandmail.com Pte Ltd [2004] SGHC 71; [2005] 2 L.R.C. 28........2–07
Clarke v Earl of Dunraven (The Satanita); Satanita, The [1897] A.C. 59; [1896] 11 WLUK 94
   HL 2–22

Table of Cases

Clea Shipping Corp v Bulk Oil International (The Alaskan Trader) (No.2); Alaskan Trader, The (No.2) [1984] 1 All E.R. 129; [1983] 2 Lloyd's Rep. 645 QBD (Comm) 8–18
Clipper Ventures Ltd v Boyde, 2013 S.C.L.R. 313; [2012] 12 WLUK 831 Sh. Ct 7–12
Cloup v Alexander (1831) 9 S. 448; [1831] 2 WLUK 88 CSIH (1 Div) 5–10
Clydebank Engineering & Shipbuilding Co Ltd v Don Jose Ramos Yzquierdo y Castaneda; sub nom. Castaneda v Clydebank Engineering & Shipbuilding Co Ltd [1905] A.C. 6; (1904) 7 F. (H.L.) 77 HL 8–17
Clydesdale Bank Plc v Black, 2002 S.C. 555; 2002 S.L.T. 764 CIH (Ex Div) 5–15
Cole v Handasyde & Co; sub nom. Cole v CH Handasyde & Co 1910 S.C. 68; 1909 2 S.L.T. 358 CSIH (1 Div) 10–13
Condor v The Barron Knights Ltd [1966] 1 W.L.R. 87; [1965] 10 WLUK 35 Assizes 9–11
Cooper v Bank of Scotland Plc [2014] CSOH 16; [2014] 1 WLUK 797; 2014 G.W.D. 6–126 CSOH 5–15
Cooperative Insurance Society Ltd v Argyll Stores (Holdings) Ltd [1998] A.C. 1; [1997] 2 W.L.R. 898 HL 8–03
Countess of Dunmore v Alexander (1830) 9 S. 190; [1830] 12 WLUK 90 CSIH (1 Div) 2–18
County Properties & Developments Ltd v Harper, 1989 S.C.L.R. 597; [1989] 3 WLUK 72 Sh. Ct 1–08
Cramaso LLP v Viscount Reidhaven's Trustees; sub nom. Cramaso LLP v Ogilvie–Grant; Cramaso LLP v Earl of Seafield [2014] UKSC 9; [2014] A.C. 1093; [2014] 2 W.L.R. 317 SC 5–19
Credential Bath Street Ltd v Venture Investment Placement Ltd [2007] CSOH 208; [2007] 12 WLUK 735; 2008 Hous. L.R. 2 CSOH 10–04, 10–08
CSC Computer Sciences Ltd v McAlinden [2013] EWCA Civ 1435; [2013] 11 WLUK 303 CA (Civ Div) 5–05
Curtis v Chemical Cleaning & Dyeing Co [1951] 1 K.B. 805; [1951] 1 All E.R. 631 CA 7–05
Cuthbertson v Lowes (1870) 8 M. 1073; [1870] 7 WLUK 96 CSIH 6–03
Dallas McMillan & Sinclair v Simpson, 1989 S.L.T. 454; [1988] 10 WLUK 267 CSOH 6–07
David T Morrison & Co Ltd (t/a Gael Home Interiors) v ICL Plastics Ltd [2014] UKSC 48; 2014 S.C. (U.K.S.C.) 222; 2014 S.L.T. 791 SC 9–09
Davis Contractors v Fareham Urban DC [1956] A.C. 696; [1956] 3 W.L.R. 37 HL 9–11
Dawson v Muir (1851) 13 D. 843; [1851] 3 WLUK 17 CSIH (1 Div) 5–09
Dawson International Plc v Coats Paton Plc (No.2); sub nom. Dawson International Plc v Coats Patons Plc, 1993 S.L.T. 80; [1991] 3 WLUK 349 CSOH 2–05
Den of Ogil Co Ltd v Caledonian Railway Co; SS Den of Ogil, The (1902) 5 F. 99; (1902) 10 S.L.T. 339 CSIH (1 Div) 8–16
Deery v Peek; sub nom. Peek v Derry (1889) 14 App. Cas. 337; (1889) 5 T.L.R. 625 HL 5–18
Demetriades & Co v Northern Assurance Co Ltd (The Spathari); Cambitsis v Norwich Union Fire Insurance Society; Borthwick v British General Assurance Co; Spathari, The; sub nom. S.S Spathari Demetriades & Co v Northern Insurance Co Ltd; Demetriades & Co v Northern Assurance Co Ltd (1925) 21 Ll. L. Rep. 265; 1925 S.C. (H.L.) 6 HL 5–22
Denny Mott & Dickson Ltd v James B Fraser & Co Ltd; sub nom. James B Fraser & Co Ltd v Denny Mott & Dickson Ltd [1944] A.C. 265; [1944] 1 All E.R. 678 HL 9–12
Diesen v Samson 1971 S.L.T. (Sh. Ct.) 49 Sh. Ct 8–13
Dingwall v Burnett, 1912 S.C. 1097; 1912 2 S.L.T. 90 CSIH (2 Div) 8–17
Director General of FairTrading v First National Bank Plc [2001] UKHL 52; [2002] 1 A.C. 481; [2001] 3 W.L.R. 1297 HL 7–12, 7–13
Donnelly v Royal Bank of Scotland Plc [2017] SAC (Civ) 1; 2017 S.L.T. (Sh. Ct) 41 Sheriff Appeal Court 9–08
Donoghue v Greater Glasgow Health Board [2009] CSOH 115; [2009] 8 WLUK 12; 2009 G.W.D. 27–432 CSOH 8–16
Dumbarton Steamboat Co Ltd v Macfarlane. *See* Macfarlane v Dumbarton Steamboat Co Ltd.
Dunlop v Higgins, 9 E.R. 805; (1848) 1 H.L. Cas. 381 QB 2–16
Dunlop Pneumatic Tyre Co Ltd v New Garage & Motor Co Ltd [1915] A.C. 79; [1914] 7 WLUK 5 HL 8–17
Earl of Orkney v Vinfra (1606) Mor. 16481; [1606] 2 WLUK 9 Court of Session 5–27

Edgar v Edgar [2014] CSOH 60; [2014] 3 WLUK 860; 2014 G.W.D. 13–236 CSOH 5–15
EDI Central Ltd v National Car Parks Ltd [2012] CSIH 6; 2012 S.L.T. 421; [2012] 1 WLUK
   406 CSIH (2 Div) 8–09
Edinburgh United Breweries Ltd v Molleson; sub nom. Edinburgh United Breweries Ltd v
   Nicolson's Trustee [1894] A.C. 96; (1894) 21 R. (H.L.) 10 HL 10–10
Effold Properties Ltd v Sprot, 1979 S.L.T. (Notes) 84; [1979] 7 WLUK 230 CSOH 2–08
Empire Meat Co v Patrick [1939] 2 All ER 85 6–07
English & Scottish Law Life Assurance Association v Carmichael; sub nom. Carmichael v
   Carmichael's Executrix, 1920 S.C. (H.L.) 195; 1920 2 S.L.T. 285 HL 10–11
Entores Ltd v Miles Far East Corp; sub nom. Newcomb v De Roos [1955] 2 Q.B. 327; [1955]
   3 W.L.R. 48 CA 2–19
Esso Petroleum Co Ltd v Harper's Garage (Stourport) Ltd [1968] A.C. 269; [1967] 2 W.L.R.
   871 HL 6–10
Esso Petroleum Co Ltd v Mardon [1976] Q.B. 801; [1976] 2 W.L.R. 583 CA (Civ Div) 5–19
Eugenia, The. *See* Ocean Tramp Tankers Corp v V/O Sovfracht.
Fenwick v Macdonald, Fraser & Co Ltd; sub nom. Fenwick v Macdonald, Fraser & Co (1904)
   6 F. 850; (1904) 12 S.L.T. CSIH (2 Div) 2–06
Ferguson v Littlewoods Pools Ltd, 1997 S.L.T. 309; [1996] 3 WLUK 441 CSOH 1–08
Ferguson v Wilson (1904) 6 F. 779; (1904) 12 S.L.T. 117 CSIH (2 Div) 5–17
Ferrier v Dods (1865) 3 M. 561; [1865] 2 WLUK 92 CSIH (2 Div) 10–17
Finnie v Glasgow & Southwestern Railway Co (1857) 20 D. (H.L.) 2; [1857] 8 WLUK 11 HL
   10–10
First Tower Trustees Ltd v CDS (Superstores International) Ltd [2018] EWCA Civ 1396;
   [2019] 1 W.L.R. 637; [2018] 6 WLUK 334 CA (Civ Div) 7–10
Fisher v Bell [1961] 1 Q.B. 394; [1960] 3 W.L.R. 919 DC 2–07
Fitch v Dewes; sub nom. Dewes v Fitch [1921] 2 A.C. 158; [1921] 6 WLUK 8 HL 6–07
Flaws v International Oil Pollution Compensation Fund, 2002 S.L.T. 270; [2001] 12 WLUK 28
   CSIH (Ex Div) 2–09
FoodCo UK LLP (t/a Muffin Break) v Henry Boot Developments Ltd [2010] EWHC 358
   (Ch); [2010] 3 WLUK 85 Ch D 7–10
Forster v Messrs Ferguson & Forster, MacFie & Alexander [2010] CSIH 38; 2010 S.L.T. 867;
   [2010] 4 WLUK 592 CSIH (Ex Div) 8–09
Forsyth v Royal Bank of Scotland Plc, 2000 S.L.T. 1295; 2000 S.C.L.R. 61 CSOH 5–15
Fortune v Fraser, 1995 S.C. 186; 1996 S.L.T. 878 CSIH (2 Div) 10–21
Foster v Craigmillar Laundry, 1980 S.L.T. (Sh. Ct.) 100; [1980] 2 WLUK 76 Sh. Ct. 5–19
Fraser & Co Ltd v Denny Mott & Dickson Ltd. *See* Denny Mott & Dickson Ltd v James B
   Fraser & Co Ltd.
Gammie v Abbey Legal Protection [2011] 12 WLUK 469; [2012] Lloyd's Rep. I.R. 322 Sh. Ct
   10–08
Gatty v Maclaine. *See* Maclaine v Gatty.
General Accident Fire & Life Assurance Corp v Hunter; sub nom. Hunter v General Accident
   Fire & Life Assurance Corp Ltd; Hunter v General Accident Corp [1909] A.C. 404; 1909
   S.C. (H.L.) 30 HL 2–06
Geys v Societe Generale; sub nom. Societe Generale (London Branch) v Geys [2012] UKSC
   63; [2013] 1 A.C. 523; [2013] 2 W.L.R. 50 SC 8–18
Gibson v National Cash Register Co Ltd, 1925 S.C. 500; 1925 S.L.T. 377 CSIH
   (2 Div) 5–20
Gillespie v Russel (1856) 18 D. 677 CSIH (1 Div) 5–20
Glasgow and Newcastle and Middlesborough Steam Shipping Co v Watson (1873) 1 R. 189;
   [1873] 11 WLUK 73 CSIH (1 Div) 2–09
Glasgow & South Western Railway Co v Boyd & Forrest (A Firm) (No.3); sub nom. Boyd &
   Forrest (A Firm) v Glasgow & South Western Railway Co (No.3) [1915] A.C. 526; 1915
   S.C. (H.L.) 20 HL 5–18
Golden Strait Corp v Nippon Yusen Kubishika Kaisha (The Golden Victory); Golden Victory,
   The [2007] UKHL 12; [2007] 2 A.C. 353; [2007] 2 W.L.R. 691 HL 8–13
Goodlife Foods Ltd v Hall Fire Protection Ltd [2018] EWCA Civ 1371; [2018] 6 WLUK 314;
   [2018] B.L.R. 491 CA (Civ Div) 7–10
Gordon Cumming v Houldsworth; sub nom. Houldsworth v Gordon Cumming [1910] A.C.
   537; 1910 S.C. (H.L.) 49 HL 10–03

Govan Rope and Sail Co Ltd v Andrew Weir & Co; sub nom. Govan Rope and Sail Co Ltd v Weir & Co (1897) 24 R. 368; (1897) 4 S.L.T. 245 CSIH (1 Div) 8–13
Gow v Henry. *See* Henry v Gow.
GPP Big Field LLP v Solar EPC Solutions SL (Formerly Prosolia Siglio XXI) [2018] EWHC 2866 (Comm); [2018] 11 WLUK 80 QBD (Comm) 8–17
Graham & Co v United Turkey Red Co Ltd, 1922 S.C. 533; 1922 S.L.T. 406 CSIH (2 Div)...8–08
Gray v Binny (1879) 7 R. 332; [1879] 12 WLUK 20 CSIH (1 Div) 5–26
Grove Investments Ltd v Cape Building Products Ltd [2014] CSIH 43; [2014] 5 WLUK 400; 2014 Hous. L.R. 35 CSIH (Ex Div)...10–05
Gunter & Co v Lauritzen (1894) 1 S.L.T. 435; [1894] 1 WLUK 44 CSOH.........................8–15
Hadley v Baxendale, 156 E.R. 145; (1854) 9 Ex. 341 Court of Exchequer........................8–16
Hamilton v Allied Domecq Plc [2007] UKHL 33; 2007 S.C. (H.L.) 142; 2007 S.L.T. 697 HL 5–20
Hamilton v Main (1823) 2 S. 356; [1823] 6 WLUK 10 CSIH (1 Div) 6–02
Harvela Investments Ltd v Royal Trust Co of Canada (CI) Ltd [1986] A.C. 207; [1985] 3 W.L.R. 276 HL 2–06
Harvey v Facey [1893] A.C. 552; [1893] 7 WLUK 139 PC (Jamaica) 2–05
Henderson v Stevenson (1870–75) L.R. 2 Sc. 470; (1875) 2 R. (H.L.) 71 HL 7–04
Hedley Byrne & Co Ltd v Heller & Partners Ltd [1964] A.C. 465; [1963] 3 W.L.R. 101 HL 5–19
Henry v Gow; sub nom. Gow v Henry (1899) 2 F. 48; (1899) 7 S.L.T. 203 CSIH (2 Div)...5–27
Herne Bay Steam Boat Co v Hutton [1903] 2 K.B. 683; [1903] 8 WLUK 9 CA 9–13
Highland Railway Co v A&G Paterson Ltd; sub nom. A&G Paterson Ltd v Highland Railway Co (1926) 26 Ll. L. Rep. 172; 1927 S.C. (H.L.) 32 HL 2–06
Highland & Universal Properties Ltd v Safeway Properties Ltd (No.2), 2000 S.C. 297; 2000 S.L.T. 414 CSIH (1 Div) 8–03
Hill v Stewart Milne Group [2011] CSIH 50; [2011] 8 WLUK 44; 2011 G.W.D. 28–611 CSIH (Ex Div) 8–17
Hislop v Dickson Motors (Forres) Ltd, 1978 S.L.T. (Notes) 73; [1974] 7 WLUK 55 CSOH..5–27
Hochster v De La Tour, 118 E.R. 922; (1853) 2 El. & Bl. 678 Court of Queen's Bench.......8–18
Hoe International Ltd v Andersen [2017] CSIH 9; 2017 S.C. 313; [2017] 2 WLUK 115 CSIH (2 Div) 10–05
Hood v Anchor Line (Henderson Bros) Ltd; sub nom. Hood v Anchor Line [1918] A.C. 837; 1918 S.C. (H.L.) 143 HL..7–04
Hostess Mobile Catering v Archibald Scott Ltd, 1981 S.C. 185; 1981 S.L.T. (Notes) 125 CSOH...8–10
Houldsworth v Gordon Cumming. *See* Gordon Cumming v Houldsworth.
Hoult v Turpie, 2004 S.L.T. 308; 2003 S.C.L.R. 577 CSOH 8–09
Household Fire & Carriage Accident Insurance Co Ltd v Grant (1879) 4 Ex. D. 216; [1879] 7 WLUK 4 CA...2–16
Hunter v Bradford Property Trust Ltd, 1970 S.L.T. 173; [1960] 3 WLUK 63 HL..............5–27
Hunter v General Accident Fire & Life Assurance Corp. *See* General Accident Fire & Life Assurance Corp v Hunter.
Ilona (Countess of Cawdor) v Vaughan (Earl of Cawdor); sub nom. Cawdor v Cawdor [2007] CSIH 3; 2007 S.C. 285; 2007 S.L.T. 152 CCSIH (1 Div) 3–02
Indigo Park Services UK Ltd v Watson [2017] 9 WLUK 46; 2017 G.W.D. 40–610 Sh. Ct..7–12
Inglis v Buttery. *See* A&J Inglis v John Buttery & Co.
Interfoto Picture Library Ltd v Stiletto Visual Programmes Ltd [1989] Q.B. 433; [1988] 2 W.L.R. 615 CA (Civ Div) 7–05
Inveresk Plc v Tullis Russell Papermakers Ltd [2010] UKSC 19; 2010 S.C. (U.K.S.C.) 106; 2010 S.L.T. 941 SC 8–09
Investors Compensation Scheme Ltd v West Bromwich Building Society (No.1); Armitage v West Bromwich Building Society; Alford v West Bromwich Building Society; Investors Compensation Scheme Ltd v Hopkin & Sons [1998] 1 W.L.R. 896; [1998] 1 All E.R. 98 HL 10–04
Ireland v Merryton Coal Co. *See* Merryton Coal Co v David Ireland & Co.
Irving v Burns, 1915 S.C. 260; (1915) 1 S.L.T. 2 CSIH (2 Div) 8–14

Jackson v Union Marine Insurance Co Ltd (1874–75) L.R. 10 C.P. 125; [1874] 12 WLUK 1 Court of Exchequer Chamber 9–13
Jacobsen Sons & Co v Underwood & Son Ltd (1894) 21 R. 654; (1894) 1 S.L.T. 578 CSIH (2 Div) 2–16
James Stuart & Co v Kennedy (1885) 13 R. 221; [1885] 11 WLUK 71 CSIH (1 Div)..........5–12
Jamieson v Watt's Trustee, 1950 S.C. 265; 1950 S.L.T. 232 CSIH (2 Div)..............................6–03
Jarvis v Swans Tours Ltd [1973] Q.B. 233; [1972] 3 W.L.R. 954 CA (Civ Div) 8–13
John Kenway Ltd v Orcantic Ltd, 1979 S.C. 422; 1980 S.L.T. 46 CSOH................................5–19
Johnstone–Beattie v Dalzell (1868) 6 M. 333; [1868] 2 WLUK 25 CSIH (1 Div)................10–14
Jones v Thurloe, 88 E.R. 126; (1722) 8 Mod. 172 Court of Kings Bench................................8–10
Kelly v Murphy, 1940 S.C. 96; 1940 S.L.T. 108 CSIH (2 Div) 1–08
Kenway Ltd v Orcantic Ltd. *See* John Kenway Ltd v Orcantic Ltd.
Krell v Henry [1903] 2 K.B. 740; [1903] 8 WLUK 20 CA...9–13
Krupp v John Menzies Ltd, 1907 S.C. 903; (1907) 15 S.L.T. 36 CSIH (1 Div).......................5–06
Kyle Bay Ltd (t/a Astons Nightclub) v Underwriters; sub nom. Kyle Bay Ltd (t/a Astons Nightclub) v Underwriters Subscribing under Policy No.019057/08/01 [2007] EWCA Civ 57; [2007] 2 WLUK 145; [2007] 1 C.L.C. 164 CA (Civ Div) 5–11
Lamonby v Arthur G Foulds Ltd; sub nom. Lamonby v Foulds Ltd, 1928 S.C. 89; 1928 S.L.T. 42 CSIH (1 Div) 8–10
Lamont v Burnett (1901) 3 F. 797; (1901) 9 S.L.T. 39 CSIH (2 Div)....................................10–11
Langstane Housing Association Ltd v Riverside Construction (Aberdeen) Ltd [2009] CSOH 52; 2009 S.C.L.R. 639 CSOH...7–09
Leggat Bros v Gray; sub nom. Leggat Bros v Moss Empires Ltd, 1908 S.C. 67; (1907) 15 S.L.T. 533 CSIH (1 Div) 9–03
L'Estrange v F Graucob Ltd [1934] 2 K.B. 394; [1934] 2 WLUK 22 KB 7–05
Lewis v Averay (No.1) [1972] 1 Q.B. 198; [1971] 3 W.L.R. 603 CA (Civ Div) 5–13
Life Association of Scotland v Foster (1873) 11 M. 351; [1873] 1 WLUK 105 CSIH (1 Div) 10–08
Littlejohn v Hawden (1882) 20 S.L.R. 5 2–08
Lloyd v Browning [2013] EWCA Civ 1637; [2013] 11 WLUK 29; [2014] 1 P. & C.R. 11 CA Civ 7–10
Lloyds Bank Plc v Bamberger, 1993 S.C. 570; 1994 S.L.T. 424 CSIH (2 Div)......................8–08
Lloyds TSB Foundation for Scotland v Lloyds Banking Group Plc [2013] UKSC 3; [2013] 1 W.L.R. 366; [2013] 2 All E.R. 103 SC 9–14, 10–04
London & Edinburgh Shipping Co Ltd v Admiralty Commissioners; Fiona, The (1920) 2 Ll. L. Rep. 342; 1920 S.C. 309 CSIH (2 Div) 9–11
London Joint Stock Bank Ltd v Macmillan; sub nom. Macmillan v London Joint Stock Bank Ltd [1918] A.C. 777; [1918] 6 WLUK 51 HL 3–06
Lord Elphinstone v Monkland Iron & Coal Co Ltd; sub nom. Lord Elphinstone v Markland Iron & Coal Co Ltd (1886) 11 App. Cas. 332; (1886) 13 R. (H.L.) 98 HL 8–17
Loudon & Co v Hunter; sub nom. John Loudon & Co v Elder's Curator Bonis (1922) 13 Ll. L. Rep. 500; 1923 S.L.T. 226 CSIH 4–05
Luminar Lava Ignite Ltd v MAMA Group Plc [2010] CSIH 1; 2010 S.C. 310 CSIH (1 Div) 10–04
Lyon & Turnbull Ltd v Sabine [2012] CSOH 178; [2012] 11 WLUK 728; 2012 G.W.D. 39–764 CSOH..5–14
Macari v Celtic Football & Athletic Co Ltd, 1999 S.C. 628; 2000 S.L.T. 80 CSIH (1 Div) 8–09
McCutcheon v David MacBrayne Ltd [1964] 1 W.L.R. 125; [1964] 1 All E.R. 430 HL 7–06
Makdessi v Cavendish Square Holdings BV; ParkingEye Ltd v Beavis; sub nom. Cavendish Square Holding BV v Makdessi; El Makdessi v Cavendish Square Holdings BV [2015] UKSC 67; [2016] A.C. 1172; [2015] 3 W.L.R. 1373 SC 8–17
Macdonald & Co v Highland Railway Co (1873) 11 M. 614; [1873] 5 WLUK 56 CSIH..8–16
Macfarlane v Dumbarton Steamboat Co Ltd; sub nom. Dumbarton Steamboat Co Ltd v Macfarlane (1899) 1 F. 993; (1899) 7 S.L.T. 75 CSIH (2 Div) 6–08
Macfarlane v Johnston (1864) 2 M. 1210; [1864] 6 WLUK 71 CSIH (2 Div) 3–02

McFeetridge v Stewarts & Lloyds Ltd, 1913 S.C. 773; 1913 1 S.L.T. 325 CSIH (2 Div).....4–03

Table of Cases

McGee Group Ltd v Galliford Try Building Ltd [2017] EWHC 87 (TCC); [2017] 1 WLUK 516; [2017] 1 C.L.C. 440 QBD (TCC) 7–09
MacGilvary v Gilmartin, 1986 S.L.T. 89; [1984] 2 WLUK 193 CSOH 5–25
Mack v Glasgow City Council [2006] CSIH 18; 2006 S.C. 543; 2006 S.L.T. 556 CSIH (Ex Div) 8–13
Mackay v Campbell, 1967 S.C. (H.L.) 53; 1967 S.L.T. 337 HL 8–07
Mackeson v Boyd, 1942 S.C. 56; 1942 S.L.T. 106 CSIH (1 Div) 9–11
M'Lachlan v Watson (1874) S.L.R. 11 549 CSIH (1 Div) 5–28
Maclaine v Gatty; sub nom. Gatty v Maclaine [1921] 1 A.C. 376; 1921 S.C. (H.L.) 1 HL ... 3–06
McLaughlin v The New Housing Association Ltd, 2008 S.L.T. (Sh. Ct) 137; [2008] 10 WLUK 773 Sh. Ct 5–12
McLaurin v Stafford (1875) 3 R. 265; [1875] 12 WLUK 77 CSIH (1 Div) 5–15
MacLeod v Kerr, 1965 S.C. 253; 1965 S.L.T. 358 CSIH (1 Div) 5–13
M'Meekin v Easton (1889) 16 R. 363; [1889] 1 WLUK 77 CSIH (2 Div) 4–09
McMillan v Caldwell, 1990 S.C. 389; 1991 S.L.T. 325 CSOH 2–08
McNeill v Aberdeen City Council. *See* Aberdeen City Council v McNeill.
McPherson v Watt (1877) 3 App. Cas. 254; (1877) 5 R. (H.L.) 9 HL 5–23
Maestro Bulk Ltd v Cosco Bulk Carrier Co Ltd; Great Creation, The [2014] EWHC 3978 (Comm); [2015] 1 Lloyd's Rep. 315; [2014] 12 WLUK 509 QBD (Comm) 8–16
Malik v Ali, 2004 S.L.T. 1280; [2004] 8 WLUK 156 CSIH (1 Div) 6–02
Marathon Asset Management LLP v Seddon [2017] EWHC 300 (Comm); [2017] 2 WLUK 594; [2017] 2 C.L.C. 182 QBD (Comm) 8–13
Marquess of Aberdeen and Temair v Turcan Connell [2008] CSOH 183; 2009 S.C.L.R. 336; [2008] 12 WLUK 725 CSOH 10–11
Mason v Provident Clothing & Supply Co Ltd. *See* Provident Clothing & Supply Co Ltd v Mason.
Mason v Liquidators of the Benhar Coal Co (1882) 9 R. 883; [1882] 6 WLUK 2 CSIH (1 Div) 2–05, 2–16
Mathieson Gee (Ayrshire) Ltd v Quigley, 1952 S.C. (H.L.) 38; 1952 S.L.T. 239 HL 1–04
Matossian v Matossian [2016] CSOH 21; [2016] 1 WLUK 606; 2016 G.W.D. 7–139 CSOH 5–26
Meikle & Wilson v Pollard (1880) 8 R. 69; [1880] 11 WLUK 19 CSIH (2 Div) 8–10
Menzies v Menzies (1893) 20 R. (H.L.) 108; [1893] 3 WLUK 44 HL 5–10
Merryton Coal Co v David Ireland & Co; Merryton Coal Co v Ireland & Son (1894) 21 R. 989; (1894) 2 S.L.T. 134 CSIH (2 Div) 8–15
Miller Fabrications Ltd v J & D Pierce (Contracts) Ltd [2010] CSIH 27; [2010] 3 WLUK 888; 2010 G.W.D. 15–283 CSIH (Ex Div) 8–18
Milner v Carnival Plc (t/a Cunard) [2010] EWCA Civ 389; [2010] 3 All E.R. 701; [2010] 2 All E.R. (Comm) 397 CA (Civ Div) 8–13
Mitchell v Caversham Management Ltd [2009] CSOH 26; [2009] 2 WLUK 711; 2009 G.W.D. 29–465 CSOH 3–06
Mitchell v Seaton Brick and Tile Co (1900) 2 F. 550; (1900) 7 S.L.T. 384 CSIH (2 Div) ... 5–06
MLS (Overseas) Ltd v Secretary of State for Defence [2018] EWHC 1303 (TCC); [2018] 5 WLUK 508; 178 Con. L.R. 197 QBD (TCC) 8–05
Montgomery Litho Ltd v Maxwell, 2000 S.C. 56; 1999 S.L.T. 1431 CSIH (Ex Div) 7–05
Morgan Guaranty Trust Co of New York v Lothian RC, 1995 S.C. 151; 1995 S.L.T. 299 CSIH 5–05
Morris v Morris [2012] 1 WLUK 102; 2012 G.W.D. 10–184 Sh. Ct 8–07
Morris–Garner v One Step (Support) Ltd; One Step (Support) Ltd v Morris–Garner [2018] UKSC 20; [2018] 2 W.L.R. 1353; [2018] 3 All E.R. 659 SC 8–13
Morrison v Robertson; sub nom. Morrisson v Robertson, 1908 S.C. 332; (1907) 15 S.L.T. 697 CSIH (1 Div) 5–13
Morton's Trustees v Aged Christian Friend Society of Scotland (1899) 2 F. 82; (1899) 7 S.L.T. 220 CSIH (1 Div) 3–02, 10–11
Muirhead v Gribben, 1983 S.L.T. (Sh. Ct.) 102; [1982] 6 WLUK 35 Sh Pr 3–02
Muirhead & Turnbull (A Firm) v Dickson (1905) 7 F. 686; (1905) 13 S.L.T. 151 CSIH (1 Div) 2–02, 10–03
Mulvein v Murray, 1908 S.C. 528; (1908) 15 S.L.T. 807 CSIH (2 Div) 6–07
Multi-Link Leisure Developments Ltd v North Lanarkshire Council [2010] UKSC 47; [2011] 1 All E.R. 175; 2011 S.C. (U.K.S.C.) 53 SC 10–04

Murray v Rennie & Angus; sub nom. Carr v Rennie & Angus (1897) 24 R. 965; (1897) 5 S.L.T. 66 CSIH (1 Div) 2–09
Nelson v The Assets Co Ltd (1889) 16 R. 898; [1889] 7 WLUK 12 CSIH (2 Div)...........2–11
Nordenfelt v Maxim Nordenfelt Guns & Ammunition Co Ltd; sub nom. Maxim Nordenfelt Guns & Ammunition Co v Nordenfelt [1894] A.C. 535; [1894] 7 WLUK 151 HL 6–08
North of Scotland Hydro–Electric Board v D&R Taylor, 1956 S.C. 1; 1955 S.L.T. 373 CSIH (2 Div) 10–08
Novoship (UK) Ltd v Mikhaylyuk; Novoship (UK) Ltd v Nikitin [2014] EWCA Civ 908; [2015] Q.B. 499; [2015] 2 W.L.R. 526 CA (Civ Div) 8–13
Ocean Tramp Tankers Corp v V/O Sovfracht (The Eugenia) [1964] 2 Q.B. 226; [1964] 2 W.L.R CA 9–11
Office of Fair Trading v Abbey National Plc; Abbey National Plc v Office of Fair Trading [2009] UKSC 6; [2010] 1 A.C. 696; [2009] 3 W.L.R. 1215 SC................7–13
Olley v Marlborough Court Ltd [1949] 1 K.B. 532; [1949] 1 All E.R. 127 CA..................7–02
O'Neill v Chief Constable of Strathclyde, 1994 S.C.L.R. 253; [1993] 11 WLUK 235 Sh. Ct...............5–03
One Step (Support) Ltd v Morris–Garner. *See* Morris-Garner v One Step (Support) Ltd.
Page One Records, Ltd v Britton [1968] 1 W.L.R. 157; [1967] 3 All E.R. 822 Ch D...........8–05
Park, Petitioners [2009] CSOH 122; 2009 S.L.T. 871; [2009] 8 WLUK 241 CSOH 2–16
Patel v Mirza [2016] UKSC 42; [2017] A.C. 467; [2016] 3 W.L.R. 399 SC.....................6–03
Paterson v Highland Railway. *See* Highland Railway Co v A&G Paterson Ltd.
Paterson Bros v Gladstone (1891) 18 R. 403; [1891] 1 WLUK 40 CSIH (1 Div)...............4–10
Patterson v Landsberg & Son (1905) 7 F. 675; (1905) 13 S.L.T. 62 CSIH (2 Div)............5–14
Patersons of Greenoakhill Ltd v Biffa Waste Services Ltd [2013] CSOH 18; 2013 S.L.T. 729; [2013] 2 WLUK 45 CSOH 10–05
Paul v Meikle (1868) 7 M. 235; [1868] 12 WLUK 41 CSIH (1 Div).........................8–10
Pearce v Brooks (1865–66) L.R. 1 Ex. 213; [1866] 4 WLUK 8 Court of Exchequer...........6–04
Petrie v Earl of Airlie (1834) 13 S. 68; [1834] 11 WLUK 117 CSIH (1 Div) 3–02
Petrofina (Great Britain) v Martin [1966] Ch. 146; [1966] 2 W.L.R. 318 CA...................6–10
Pharmaceutical Society of Great Britain v Boots Cash Chemists (Southern) Ltd [1953] 1 Q.B. 401; [1953] 2 W.L.R. 427 CA.................2–07
Phillips v Brooks Ltd [1919] 2 K.B. 243; [1919] 5 WLUK 1 KB 5–13
Philp & Co v Knoblauch. *See* Alexander Philp & Co v Knoblauch.
Photo Production Ltd v Securicor Transport Ltd [1980] A.C. 827; [1980] 2 W.L.R. 283 HL 7–09
Pollock v Macrae. *See* W&S Pollock & Co v Macrae.
Pollok v Burns (1875) 2 R. 497; [1875] 3 WLUK 11 CSIH (2 Div) 3–08, 4–06
Prenn v Simmonds [1971] 1 W.L.R. 1381; [1971] 3 All E.R. 237 HL 10–04
Proactive Sports Management Ltd v Rooney [2011] EWCA Civ 1444; [2012] 2 All E.R. (Comm) 815; [2011] 12 WLUK 2 CA (Civ Div)..................6–10
Prostar Management Ltd v Twaddle, 2003 S.L.T. (Sh. Ct) 11; [2002] 8 WLUK 219 Sh Pr..7–11
Proton Energy Group SA v Orlen Lietuva [2013] EWHC 2872 (Comm); [2014] 1 All E.R. (Comm) 972; [2014] 1 Lloyd's Rep. 100 QB (Comm) 2–02
Provident Clothing & Supply Co Ltd v Mason; sub nom. Mason v Provident Clothing & Supply Co Ltd [1913] A.C. 724; [1913] 7 WLUK 108 HL.........................6–07
Purac Ltd v Byzak Ltd, 2005 S.L.T. 37; 2005 S.C.L.R. 244 CSOH 8–09
Raffles v Wichelhaus, 159 E.R. 375; (1864) 2 Hurl. & C. 906 KB 1–04, 5–03, 5–11
McNeill v Aberdeen City Council. *See* Aberdeen City Council v McNeill.
Ranking of Hamilton of Provenhall's Creditors (1781) Mor. 6253; [1781] 8 WLUK 5 Court of Session 8–10
Regus (Maxim) Ltd v Bank of Scotland Plc [2013] CSIH 12; 2013 S.C. 331; 2013 S.L.T. 477 CSIH (1 Div)..............10–11
Regus (UK) Ltd v Epcot Solutions Ltd [2008] EWCA Civ 361; [2009] 1 All E.R. (Comm) 586; [2008] 4 WLUK 379 CA (Civ Div)............................7–10
Renfrew Golf Club v Ravenstone Securities Ltd 1984 S.C. 22; 1984 S.L.T. 170 CSOH......9–09
Rentokil Ltd v Kramer, 1986 S.L.T. 114; [1985] 6 WLUK 66 CSOH 6–07
Retail Parks Investments Ltd v Royal Bank of Scotland Plc (No.2), 1996 S.C. 227; 1996 S.L.T. 669 CSIH (Ex Div).......................8–03
Ritchie v Cowan & Kinghorn (A Firm) (1901) 3 F. 1071; [1901] 6 WLUK 48 CSIH (2 Div) 1–08

R&J Dempster Ltd v Motherwell Bridge & Engineering Co Ltd, 1964 S.C. 308; 1964 S.L.T.
353 CSIH (1 Div) 10–05
Robbie v Graham & Sibbald, 1989 S.L.T. 870; 1989 S.C.L.R. 578 CSOH 7–08
Robert Purvis Plant Hire Ltd v Brewster [2009] CSOH 28; [2009] 2 WLUK 749
CSOH 9–10, 9–14
Robertson v Anderson, 2003 S.L.T. 235; [2002] 12 WLUK 77 CSIH (Ex Div) 1–08
Robinson v Davison (1870–71) L.R. 6 Ex. 269; [1871] 5 WLUK 84 Court of
Exchequer 9–11
Robinson v Harman, 154 E.R. 363; (1848) 1 Ex. 850 Court of Exchequer 8–12
Robophone Facilities Ltd v Blank [1966] 1 W.L.R. 1428; [1966] 3 All E.R. 128 CA 8–17
Rock Refrigeration Ltd v Jones [1997] 1 All E.R. 1; [1996] 10 WLUK 142 CA
(Civ Div) 6–07
Rodger (Builders) Ltd v Fawdry, 1950 S.C. 483; 1950 S.L.T. 345 CSIH (2 Div) 8–08
Roofcare v Gillies, 1984 S.L.T. (Sh. Ct) 8; [1982] 10 WLUK 116 Sh. Pr 2–12
Royal Bank of Scotland v Greenshields, 1914 S.C. 259; (1914) 1 S.L.T. 74 CSIH
(1 Div) 5–20
Royal Bank of Scotland Plc v Carlyle; sub nom. Carlyle v Royal Bank of Scotland Plc [2015]
UKSC 13; 2015 S.C. (U.K.S.C.) 93; 2015 S.L.T. 206 SC 3–02
Royal Bank of Scotland Plc v Purvis, 1990 S.L.T. 262; 1989 S.C.L.R. 710 CSOH 5–15
Ryanair Ltd v Billigfluege.de GmbH [2010] IEHC 47; [2010] 2 WLUK 762 HC
(Ireland) 7–05
Safetynet Security Ltd v Coppage; sub nom. Coppage v Safety Net Security Ltd [2013] EWCA
Civ 1176; [2013] 10 WLUK 369; [2013] I.R.L.R. 970 CA (Civ Div) 6–07
Salaried Staff London Loan Co Ltd v Swears & Wells Ltd, 1985 S.C. 189; 1985 S.L.T. 326
CSIH (1 Div) 8–18
Salomon v Salomon & Co Ltd; Salomon & Co Ltd v Salomon; sub nom. Broderip v Salomon
[1897] A.C. 22; [1896] 11 WLUK 76 HL 1–06
Scriven Bros & Co v Hindley & Co [1913] 3 K.B. 564; [1913] 7 WLUK 27 KB 5–11
Schroeder Music Publishing Co Ltd v Macaulay. See A Schroeder Music Publishing Co Ltd v
Macaulay (formerly Instone).
Scottish Farmers Dairy Co (Glasgow) Ltd v McGhee, 1933 S.C. 148; 1933 S.L.T. 142 CSIH (1
Div) 6–07
Scottish Widows' Fund and Life Assurance Society v Buist (1876) 3 R. 1078; [1876] 7 WLUK
38 CSIH (1 Div) 10–14
Seaton Brick and Tile Co v Mitchell. See Mitchell v Seaton Brick and Tile Co.
Selkirk v Ferguson, 1908 S.C. 26; (1907) 15 S.L.T. 435 CSIH (1 Div) 5–15
Shankland & Co v John Robinson & Co; sub nom. Shankland & Co v Robinson & Co, 1920
S.C. (H.L.) 103; 1920 2 S.L.T. 96 HL 5–20
Shogun Finance Ltd v Hudson; sub nom. Hudson v Shogun Finance Ltd [2003] UKHL 62;
[2004] 1 A.C. 919; [2003] 3 W.L.R. 1371 HL 5–13
@SIPP Pension Trustees v Insight Travel Services Ltd [2015] CSIH 91; 2016 S.C. 243; 2016
S.L.T. 131 CSIH 10–05
Skerret v Oliver (1896) 23 R. 468; (1896) 3 S.L.T. 257 CSIH 8–05
Sloans Dairies v Glasgow Corp, 1977 S.C. 223; 1979 S.L.T CSIH (2 Div) 9–11
Smith v Bank of Scotland; Mumford v Bank of Scotland, 1997 S.C. (H.L.) 111; 1997 S.L.T.
1061 HL 5–15, 5–20
Smith v Eric S Bush (A Firm); Harris v Wyre Forest DC [1990] 1 A.C. 831; [1989] 2 W.L.R.
790 HL 7–08
Smith v Sim, 1954 S.C. 357; [1954] 5 WLUK 97 CSOH 5–18
Smyth v Romanes's Executors [2014] CSOH 150; [2014] 10 WLUK 528; 2014 G.W.D. 33–
642 CSOH 5–25
Spathari, The. See Demetriades & Co v Northern Assurance Co Ltd (The Spathari).
Spence v Crawford [1939] 3 All E.R. 271; 1939 S.C. (H.L.) 52 HL 5–18

Societe Generale (London Branch) v Geys. See Geys v Societe Generale.
Spook Erection (Northern) Ltd v Kaye, 1990 S.L.T. 676; [1990] 3 WLUK 37 CSOH 5–08
Steel v Bradley Homes (Scotland) Ltd, 1972 S.C. 48; 1974 S.L.T. 133 CSOH 5–08
Steuart's Trustees v Hart (1875) 3 R. 192; [1875] 12 WLUK 4 CSIH (1 Div) 5–08
Stewart v Kennedy (No.2) (1890) 15 App. Cas. 108; (1890) 17 R. (H.L.) 25 HL 5–08
Stewart (Ernest) v Stewart (Peter) (1899) 1 F. 1158; (1899) 7 S.L.T. 52 CSOH (2 Div) 6–07

Stilk v Myrick, 170 E.R. 1168; (1809) 2 Camp. 317 Assizes 3–02
Stobo Ltd v Morrisons (Gowns) Ltd, 1949 S.C. 184; 1949 S.L.T. 193 CSIH (1 div) 2–11
Strongman (1945) Ld v Sincock [1955] 2 Q.B. 525; [1955] 3 W.L.R. 360 CA 6–02
Stuart v Stuart (1869) 7 M. 366; [1869] 1 WLUK 47 CSIH (1 Div) 9–08
Stuart & Co v Kennedy. *See* James Stuart & Co v Kennedy.
Tay Salmon Fisheries Co Ltd v Speedie, 1929 S.C. 593; 1929 S.L.T. 484 CSIH (1 Div) 9–11
Taylor v Caldwell, 122 E.R. 309; (1863) 3 B. & S. 826 Court of King's Bench 9–11
Taylor v Glasgow Corp, 1952 S.C. 440; 1952 S.L.T. 399 CSIH (2 Div) 7–03
Taylor v Provan (1864) 2 M. 1226; [1864] 6 WLUK 96 CSIH (2 Div) 4–06
Teacher v Calder [1899] A.C. 451; (1899) 1 F. (H.L.) 39 HL 8–13
Thomson v James (1855) 18 D. 1; [1855] 11 WLUK 48 CSIH (1 Div) 2–17
Thornton v Shoe Lane Parking [1971] 2 Q.B. 163; [1971] 2 W.L.R. 585 CA (Civ Div) 7–02
Tsakiroglou & Co Ltd v Noblee Thorl GmbH; Albert D Gaon & Co v Societe
  Interprofessionelle des Oleagineux Fluides Alimentaires [1962] A.C. 93; [1961] 2 W.L.R.
  633 HL 9–13
TSB Bank Plc v Connell, 1997 S.L.T. 1254; [1996] 10 WLUK 137 CSOH 6–07
Uniroyal Ltd v Miller & Co Ltd, 1985 S.L.T. 101; [1982] 11 WLUK 28 CSOH 2–12
Vercoe v Rutland Fund Management Ltd [2010] EWHC 424 (Ch); [2010] 3 WLUK 187;
  [2010] Bus. L.R. D141 Ch D 8–13
Verdin Brothers v Robertson (1871) 10 M. 35; [1871] 11 WLUK 4 CSIH (2 Div) 5–06
Victoria Laundry (Windsor) v Newman Industries [1949] 2 K.B. 528; [1949] 1 All E.R. 997
  CA 8–16
Vivienne Westwood Ltd v Conduit Street Development Ltd [2017] EWHC 350 (Ch); [2017] 2
  WLUK 690; [2017] L. & T.R. 23 Ch D 8–17
Wade v Waldon; Pavilion Theatre (Glasgow) Ltd v Wade, 1909 S.C. 571; (1909) 1 S.L.T. 215
  CSIH (1 Div) 8–08
Watson & Co v Shankland (1870–75) L.R. 2 Sc. 304; (1873) 11 M. (H.L.) 51 HL 9–14
Watteau v Fenwick [1893] 1 Q.B. 346; [1892] 12 WLUK 29 QBD 4–12
Webster & Co v Cramond Iron Co (1875) 2 R. 752; [1875] 6 WLUK 24 CSIH (1 Div) 8–13
White & Carter (Councils) Ltd v McGregor [1962] A.C. 413; [1962] 2 W.L.R. 17 HL 8–18
Wick Harbour Trustees v Admiralty, 1921 2 S.L.T. 109; [1921] 7 WLUK 30 CSOH 3–02
Wilkie v Brown, 2003 S.C. 573; [2003] 5 WLUK 761 CSIH (2 Div) 8–13
Wilkie v Dunlop & Co (1834) 12 S. 506; [1834] 2 WLUK 102 CSIH (1 Div) 3–05
Wilkie v Hamilton Lodging–House Co Ltd (1902) 4 F. 951; (1902) 10 S.L.T. 163 CSIH (2
  Div) 5–06
Williamson v North of Scotland & Orkney & Shetland Steam Navigation Co, 1916 S.C. 554;
  1916 1 S.L.T. 228 CSIH (2 Div) 7–04
Wills v Strategic Procurement (UK) Ltd [2013] CSOH 26; 2016 S.C. 367; [2013] 2 WLUK
  360 CSOH 1–02
Wilson v Marquis of Breadalbane, 1990 S.L.T. 82; 1989 S.C.L.R. 48 CSIH (2 Div) 5–12
Winston v Patrick, 1980 S.C. 246; 1981 S.L.T. 41 CSIH (2 Div) 10–21
Wolf and Wolf v Forfar Potato Co, 1984 S.L.T. 100; [1983] 9 WLUK 2 CSIH (2 Div) 2–11
Wood v Sureterm Direct Ltd; sub nom. Wood v Capita Insurance Services Ltd [2017] UKSC
  24; [2017] A.C. 1173; [2017] 2 W.L.R. 1095 SC 10–06
Woodman v Photo Trade Processing Unreported July 1981 County Court 7–04
Woods Building Services v Milton Keynes Council [2015] EWHC 2172 (TCC); [2015] 7
  WLUK 820; [2015] B.L.R. 591 QBD (TCC) 8–05
Wrotham Park Estate Co Ltd v Parkside Homes Ltd [1974] 1 W.L.R. 798; [1974] 2 All E.R.
  321 Ch D 8–13
WS Karoulias SA v Drambuie Liqueur Co Ltd (No.2), 2005 S.L.T. 813; 2005 S.C.L.R. 1014
  CSOH 3–03
W&S Pollock & Co v Macrae; Macrae v W&S Pollock & Co (1922) 12 Ll. L. Rep. 299; 1922
  S.C. (H.L.) 192 HL 10–08
Wylie and Lochhead v M'Elroy and Sons (1873) 1 R. 41; [1873] 10 WLUK 12 CSIH (2 Div)
  2–09
X v BBC, 2005 S.L.T. 796; 2005 S.C.L.R. 740 CSOH 4–06
Zinc Corp Ltd v Hirsch [1916] 1 K.B. 541; [1915] 12 WLUK 79 CA 4–07

TABLE OF STATUTES

Para

UK statutes
1592 Compensation Act (c.61) 9–08
1832 Representation of the People Act ("Reform Act") (c.45) 3–02
1862 Transmission of Moveable Property (Scotland) Act (c.85) 10–15
1867 Policies of Assurance Act (c.144) 10–15
1890 Partnership Act (c.39)
    s.4(2) 4–10
    s.35 4–05
1939 Trading with the Enemy Act (c.89) 4–07
1940 Law Reform (Miscellaneous Provisions) (Scotland) Act (c.42) 8–03
1963 Stock Transfer Act (c.18) 10–15
1964 Hire-Purchase Act (c.53) 5–13
1967 Uniform Laws on International Sales Act (c.45) 2–19
1968 Trade Descriptions Act (c.29) 5–18
1971 Coinage Act (c.24) 9–03
1971 Unsolicited Goods and Services Act (c.30) 2–11
1973 Prescription and Limitation (Scotland) Act (c.52) 9–09
1974 Consumer Credit Act (c.39) 1–02, 3–03, 10–05
    s.140A–140C 5–28
1977 Unfair Contract Terms Act (c.50) 7–07, 7–08, 7–09, 7–11
    s.16 7–08
    s.17 7–09
    s.24 7–10
1979 Sale of Goods Act (c.54) 1–02, 2–22, 8–08
    s.3(2) 4–05
    s.6 5–09
    s.7 9–11
    s.8 5–12
    s.15B 10–21
    s.53A 10–21
1985 Companies Act (c.6)
    s.716 1–06
1985 Law Reform (Miscellaneous Provisions) (Scotland) Act (c.73) 3–03, 8–08
    ss.8–9 5–06
    s.8 10–05
    s.10 5–19
1988 Court of Session Act (c.36) 8–03
1990 Law Reform (Miscellaneous Provisions) (Scotland) Act (c.40)
    s.68 7–08
1991 Age of Legal Capacity (Scotland) Act (c.50) 4–02
    s.1(1) 4–04
    s.2(1) 4–04
        (4A) 4–04
    s.3(2) 4–04
1992 Cheques Act (c.32) 10–16
1995 Requirements of Writing (Scotland) Act (c.7) 3–02, 3–03, 3–04, 10–15
    s.1(2) 3–03
        (a)(ii) 3–02
        (3)–(4) 3–04
    Pt 3 3–03
1997 Knives Act (c.21)
    s.1(4) 2–07
1997 Contract (Scotland) Act (c.34) 5–18, 10–01, 10–02, 10–03, 10–21
    s.2 10–21
    s.3 10–21
1998 Late Payment of Commercial Debts (Interest) Act (c.20) 8–11

1998 Competition Act (c.41)	6–09
1998 Scotland Act (c.46)	
s.126	1–02
1999 Contracts (Rights of Third Parties) Act (c.31)	10–10
2000 Electronic Communications Act (c.7)	3–03
2000 Limited Liability Partnerships Act (c.12)	4–11
2005 Gambling Act (c.19)	1–08
s.335	1–08
2006 Consumer Credit Act (c.14)	
ss.19–21	5–28
2006 Companies Act (c.46)	4–08
ss.39–40	4–08
2010 Equality Act (c.15)	6–03
2015 Consumer Rights Act (c.15)	1–02, 6–03, 7–07, 7–08, 7–11, 7–12, 7–13, 8–08
Pt 2	7–11, 7–12
s.62	7–12
s.65	7–12
Sch.2 Pt 1	7–12
Sch.3	7–13

Acts of the Scottish Parliament

2000 Adults with Incapacity (Scotland) Act (asp 4)	4–05
2003 Title Conditions (Scotland) Act (asp 9)	10–19
2007 Adult Support and Protection (Scotland) Act (asp 10)	4–05
2012 Land Registration etc. (Scotland) Act (asp 5)	3–03
2017 Contract (Third Party Rights) (Scotland) Act (asp 5)	10–11
s.1	10–11

TABLE OF STATUTORY INSTRUMENTS, EU LEGISLATION AND REPORTS

Statutory Instruments
1999 Unfair Terms in Consumer Contracts Regulations (SI 1999/2083) 7–11
2000 Consumer Protection (Distance Selling) Regulations (SI 2000/2334) 2–21
2002 Regulatory Reform (Removal of 20 Member Limit in Partnerships etc.) Order
 (SI 2002/3203) art.2 1–06
2004 Consumer Credit Act 1974 (Electronic Communications) Order (SI 2004/3236)..3–03
2008 Consumer Protection from Unfair Trading Regulations
 (SI 2008/1277) 1–02, 2–11, 5–18
2013 Consumer Contracts (Information, Cancellation and Additional Charges) Regulations
 (SI 2013/3134) 2–21

EU Legislation
1997 Dir. 97/7 on the protection of consumers in respect of distance contracts [1997] OJ L
 144 2–21

Reports
1990 Report on the Passing of Risk in Contracts for the Sale of Heritable Property (Scot.
 Law Com. No.127) 9–11
1996 Report on Three Bad Rules in Contract Law (Scot. Law Com. No.152) 10–21
1999 Report on Penalty Clauses (Scot. Law Com. No.171) 8–17
2016 Report on Third Party Rights (Scot. Law Com. No.245) 10–11
2018 Report on Review of Contract Law: Formation, Interpretation, Remedies for Breach,
 and Penalty Clauses (Scot. Law Com. No.252) 1–02, 2–20, 8–17, 10–06

1. INTRODUCTION TO CONTRACTS

Contracts are all around us. They are part of our everyday lives. Much of the time we enter into contracts without ever pausing to reflect on the fact that we are entering into a legal relationship—one which could have very significant consequences. We purchase snacks, we travel on the bus, we make use of a range of products and services; all the time we are entering into contracts. For many, the word "contract" has connotations of large-scale transactions or long-term commitments, but, actually, these types of contracts are the exception rather than the rule. It is important to bear in mind that the "little things" involve contracts too and are in fact far more common.

1–01

HISTORY AND DEVELOPMENT

Since the earliest days of civilisation, humankind has been engaging in commercial endeavours. What began as simple exchanges of goods by barter gradually evolved over time into the often-complex transactions typical of today's economic world. Throughout history, contracts have been central to these pursuits, and for centuries the theory of business has been grounded in the concept of a contract involving binding obligations, which can be enforced by the parties to it. To put it plainly, contracts are an intrinsic part of our society, for without them the generation of wealth, and therefore economic prosperity, would not be possible.

1–02

Although they are steeped in this long history, it is worth noting that much of the development of the law relating to contracts occurred relatively recently. (Indeed, this is the case with many areas of law.) In Scotland, contract law is still largely based on common law, following the Scots law tradition of deducing legal rules from basic principles as generally accepted by society. The role of the courts has therefore been crucial in this development, with important precedents being set which were then binding on later cases. The eighteenth and nineteenth centuries saw the courts giving consideration to, and handing down judgments on, many complicated contractual disputes, and much of the case law on contract dates from this period.

In addition to this, and in particular throughout the twentieth and now twenty-first centuries, there have been major statutory inroads made into various areas relevant to contract law, such as the Sale of Goods Act 1979 and the Consumer Credit Act 1974. Following devolution and the re-establishment of the Scottish Parliament, the law of contract is placed within the legislative competence of Holyrood,[1] although there is always the possibility of Westminster passing legislation which has a "knock-on" effect on Scottish contract law. Examples from the new millennium include the Consumer Protection From Unfair Trading Regulations 2008 and the Consumer Rights Act 2015.

Indeed, in today's more complex society, the trend has increasingly been towards a higher degree of statutory or regulatory control. Integral to this process is the work of the Scottish Law Commission, whose remit is to continually review Scots law and make recommendations for reform. Issues of contract law are regularly the subject of such reviews, and in 2018 the Commission published a major report encompassing areas such as formation, interpretation and breach of contract.[2] This report has been warmly received by the Scottish Government, although the extent to which its many recommendations will be implemented is unknown.

There has also been an increase in the influence of the European Union, which has sought to harmonise many areas of law across Europe. Given the importance of contracts to business and commerce, it was perhaps inevitable that the EU would seek to increase its activities in the field of contract law, and in 2009 the European Commission published a "Draft Common Frame of Reference" for European private law (including contract). Exactly what this ongoing project will achieve remains to be seen, but suggested purposes range from the provision of a "toolbox" for the development of domestic contract law by EU Member States, to a universal "European" code of contract law which could be adopted by parties as an alternative to domestic regimes, or which could even in time become legally binding on all EU Member States.[3] Although at the time of writing the UK's future relationship with the EU is uncertain, it is fair comment to say that nearly half a century's worth of European integration has left its mark on Scotland's domestic law.[4]

In light of this tendency towards legislative measures, it is very possible that in time it will be statutes, not cases, which espouse the majority of Scottish contract law principles. Of course, it will still be necessary for the courts to make judgment on matters of interpretation, so cases will continue to be important. On this point, it is finally worth noting here that, whilst the legal systems of Scotland and England are very different from each other, there are some areas of common ground as far as contract law is concerned. As a result, although they are not binding precedents, in practice many English cases are regarded as at least highly persuasive in Scotland.

WHAT IS A CONTRACT?

1–03 A much-quoted definition of a contract is the one given by Gloag, a leading authority on the matter of Scots contract law. He opined that a contract is "an agreement which creates, or is intended to create, a legal obligation between the parties to it".[5] Whilst this certainly strikes at the heart of what a contract is, a fuller definition may be useful. One offered by MacQueen and Thomson is that a contract is

> "an agreement between two or more parties having the capacity to make it, in the form demanded by law, to perform, on one side or both, acts which are not trifling, indeterminate, impossible or illegal."[6]

The value of this latter definition is that it makes specific reference to the various basic elements that a contract must contain in order to be valid. Unless all of these elements are present, there is no enforceable contract. Of course, agreements lacking certain of these basic elements may contain *moral* obligations, and it would be wrong to suggest that moral obligations should be broken lightly, but focus here will be solely on the legal aspects. To this end, these basic elements will be discussed briefly in this chapter and then considered in greater detail throughout the remainder of the book.

Agreement

This concept is often referred to by the Latin maxim *consensus in idem* **1–04** (agreement about the same thing) and it lies at the very heart of contract law. If there is no real agreement—or the apparent agreement is in fact about different things—there is no contract. Say, for example, that Alfred owns two cars; a brand new sports car (which he has just purchased) and an old hatchback (which he wants to sell). Benny offers to buy Alfred's "car" for £5,000, with the intention of purchasing the sports car. Alfred accepts, with the intention of selling the hatchback. Is there a contract between Alfred and Benny, and if so, for what?

In fact, there is no contract at all here. Although both parties might *think* that they have entered into a contract, they have not reached an agreement about exactly the same thing. The required *consensus in idem* ("consensus" for short) is lacking. In *Raffles v Wichelhaus* (1864), a cargo was being transported on a ship called *Peerless* from Bombay to England. Unknown to both parties, at the time the contract was formed, there were two ships of the same name in Bombay harbour, one sailing in October, the other in December. In forming the "agreement", one party had meant the October ship, the other had intended the ship sailing in December. It was held that there was no consensus and thus no contract. Similarly, in *Mathieson Gee (Ayrshire) Ltd v Quigley* (1952), a firm of plant hirers offered to hire out equipment to remove mould from a garden pond. The owner of the pond thought that it was an offer to remove the silt, not merely to hire out the plant to do so, and accepted on this basis. When the hirers sued for payment, it was ultimately held that, as there was no consensus, there was no contract.

Consensus between contracting parties is achieved by concluding a valid formation process, which is the subject of Ch.2.

Formalities

As a very general rule, contracts do not require to be in writing. Agreements **1–05** made verbally are every bit as binding (in theory) as those which are written down. In fact, bearing in mind the everyday nature of contracts, most of those we enter into are entirely unwritten. However, it is often desirable to make a written record of the terms and conditions upon which a contract will proceed, particularly if those terms and conditions are lengthy or complex, so that the respective rights and obligations of the parties are clearly expressed. This is obviously very useful in the case of disputes, as the parties can provide evidence of exactly what was agreed.

For this reason, and others, the law demands that certain types of contract *are* expressed in writing in order to be binding. One of the most common examples for the legal practitioner is a contract relating to heritable property (which, broadly speaking, means land or buildings). It is easy to see why the law demands this, as heritable property tends to be of relatively high financial value, and a person's home is obviously of great importance. As a result, disputes can be very costly to resolve and the potential consequences of mistakes being made are grave. The requirement that the parties must agree terms in writing makes it less likely that problems will occur later (although, of course, the risk is not removed entirely).

Where there is a prescribed form that a contract must take, an agreement of that type that does *not* conform is potentially invalid. The law here is somewhat complicated and so will be considered separately in Ch.3.

Two or more parties

1–06 It is a basic rule of law (and common sense) that it is impossible to have a contract between fewer than two parties. In other words, you cannot have a contract with yourself. It is perfectly possible for an individual to make an agreement or "deal" with himself (for example, a New Year's resolution) but these are obviously not legal in nature and, crucially, cannot be enforced either by or against the individual. Contracts require two parties because they tend to involve reciprocal obligations (though not always, as discussed below) and there must be at least one other party so that an obligation can be enforced. In *Church of Scotland Endowment Committee v Provident Association of London Ltd* (1914) an individual attempted to enter into a contract of ground annual (a type of land rental agreement) with himself. The purported contract was held to be void on the grounds that "a man cannot by any deed constitute a debt by himself to himself".[7]

It is worth mentioning that it is possible in certain situations for the same individual person to represent two different parties to a contract. For example, someone who is a director in a company will often represent the interests of the company in contractual negotiations. Due to certain principles of company law, there is nothing (in theory at least) to prevent the director himself contracting with the company. In such a case he will be representing two parties; the company on one side, and himself personally on the other.[8] There are other situations where this might arise and some are discussed to a limited extent in Ch.4. A comprehensive coverage of the specific laws is far beyond the scope of this book but interested readers may refer to relevant texts on commercial and company law for further information.[9]

In terms of an upper limit on the number of parties, generally there is none, unless created by statute. For example, it was previously the case that no more than 20 people could enter into a partnership agreement,[10] though this provision was abolished in 2002.[11]

Contractual capacity

1–07 All parties to a contract must have the legally-recognised capability of entering into that contract. This is called having "contractual capacity". Capacity can be affected by various things, such as a person's age, mental state, or a legal status that currently applies to them. Many of these factors result in a restriction of contractual capacity. Whilst the law, in general, favours freedom, in certain circumstances it is deemed necessary to enforce such restrictions. A common motivation behind these is protection of the individual. For example, persons who are very young or seriously mentally ill lack contractual capacity because there is a risk that they will be persuaded into bad bargains, and the law assumes a responsibility to protect them from this.

Matters relating to contractual capacity are considered more fully in Ch.4.

Enforceable obligations
Finally, the agreement must create obligations that the law will recognise as being appropriate to enforce, should the need arise. Not surprisingly, the courts will not enforce agreements which are clearly illegal, criminal or immoral. In spite of the catchphrase from the criminal underworld to "put a contract out" on someone (i.e. plan an assassination), such an agreement would clearly be illegal and would not be enforced by a court of law. In Ch.6, consideration is given to contracts which are deemed to be "contractually illegal" because they are contrary to public policy, but not necessarily thought of as immoral.

1–08

There are other agreements which are perfectly legal but which the courts will not uphold. A so-called "social contract", such as a dinner date, is perfectly legal and moral—but if one party fails to turn up, the disappointed party will not be able to compel performance or seek damages. This is partly because the law favours freedom in terms of a person's social life, but also because the matter is deemed too trifling to be of concern to the courts. Social workers, counsellors and others whose role it is to provide personal or emotional support increasingly make "contracts" with their clients. These agreements are frequently in writing. They are intended to create moral obligations, so that the parties are clear as to boundaries and expectations on both sides and, as such, they have no legal significance.

It was also the case for a long time that betting and gaming wagers would not be enforced. These so-called *sponsiones ludicrae* (obligations in jest) were not illegal, yet were seen as being below the authority of the court, possibly due to the negative social stigma traditionally attached to gambling. In *Kelly v Murphy* (1940), K brought an action against M, a pools promoter, for £2,497, being the balance of prize money to which K was entitled as winner of the pool. He was unsuccessful, as the action for recovery of a gambling debt could not be entertained in Scotland. In *County Properties & Developments Ltd v Harper* (1989), a croupier made an error by giving an overpayment of gambling chips to a successful customer at a casino. The customer did not count the chips but continued playing roulette before cashing in the balance. It was held that the encashment of chips was *sponsio ludicra* and the operators of the casino could not recover their loss. In *Ferguson v Littlewoods Football Pools Ltd* (1997), a syndicate of five people completed pools coupons and passed them, with stake money, to a party who failed to pass them to Littlewoods. If the coupons had been received, a dividend of some £2.5 million would have been payable. The syndicate sought payment but the action was dismissed. They had been staking money on the chance accuracy of football forecasts, which was unenforceable in law.

However, the legal position now is entirely different. Early in the new millennium, with the social acceptability of gambling on the increase, the courts could arguably be seen to be taking a more sympathetic stance. In *Robertson v Anderson* (2001), two friends played bingo together. One of them won the national jackpot of £100,000. There was a long-standing agreement between the two parties that any winnings would be split both ways. Having established that there was such an agreement, the obvious question was whether it was enforceable. It was held that the agreement was not a gambling debt as it was collateral (connected to, but separate from) the wager itself.

In 2005, the position was put beyond doubt with the passing of the Gambling Act 2005, which came into force in September 2007. The doctrine of *sponsiones ludicrae* has now been abolished,[12] meaning that gaming contracts are enforceable. (It is important to note, however, the gambling industry is still subject to considerable statutory control.)

As a final thought here, there is an occasional problem of the so-called "gentleman's agreement" or honourable understanding. In *Ritchie v Cowan & Kinghorn* (1901), R was unable to pay his creditors, C and K, in full but arranged to pay 10s. (50p) in the £1. C and K gave him a receipt on which it stated that they were accepting his payment "in full" but added that it was understood that R would pay the balance "whenever he is able to do so". It was held that the additional words merely constituted an honourable understanding and were not legally enforceable.

---

1. Scotland Act 1998 (c.46) s.126.
2. Scottish Law Commission, *Report on Review of Contract Law: Formation, Interpretation, Remedies for Breach, and Penalty Clauses* (2018), Scot. Law Com. No.252.
3. For more information see C. Von Bar et al (eds), *Principles, Definitions and Model Rules of European Private Law: Draft Common Frame of Reference* (Munich: Sellier, 2009).
4. For an example of a Scottish case in which the Draft Common Frame of Reference was considered, see *Wills v Strategic Procurement (UK) Ltd* [2013] CSOH 26.
5. W. Gloag, *The Law of Contract*, 2nd edn (Edinburgh: W. Green, 1929), p.8.
6. H. MacQueen and J. Thomson, *Contract Law in Scotland*, 4th edn (Edinburgh: Bloomsbury Professional, 2016), p.4.
7. *Church of Scotland Endowment Committee v Provident Association of London Ltd*, 1914 S.C. 165, per Lord Dundas at [171].
8. See, e.g. the classic case of *Salomon v Salomon & Co Ltd* [1897] A.C. 22 (HL).
9. To be heartily recommended is N. Grier, *Company Law*, 4th edn (Edinburgh: W. Green, 2014).
10. Companies Act 1985 (c.6) s.716 (repealed).
11. Regulatory Reform (Removal of 20 Member Limit in Partnerships, etc.) Order (SI 2002/3203) art.2.
12. Gambling Act 2005 (c.19) s.335.

2. AGREEMENT AND FORMATION OF CONTRACT

As discussed in Ch.1, agreement lies at the very heart of contract law, and if there is no agreement, there is no contract. But how do parties actually reach an agreement? The answer lies in the process of "formation", which involves the parties undertaking some form of negotiation and settling upon (at least) the broad terms that they are willing to be bound by. Whether the contract is a simple consumer sale, or a more complex commercial transaction, the steps involved in these negotiations are, in essence, the same. 2–01

AGREEMENT

In order for there to be the required *consensus in idem*, the parties must reach an agreement only on the essential features of the contract at hand. Consequently, the parties need not reach agreement on every minute detail. What is deemed an "essential" feature varies, but in a straightforward contract of sale, the subject matter and the price are generally considered to be essential. In *Bogie (t/a Oakbank Services) v The Forestry Commission* (2002), the court held that a description of land being sold by reference to its general area and location was *not* sufficient to identify the subject matter of the contract. It seems that the courts may be more willing to find that agreement has been reached where time is a factor because the contract relates to a rapidly-changing market. In the English case of *Proton Energy Group SA v Orlen Lietuva* (2013), it was held that a contract had been concluded despite there being a range of details still to be negotiated and very informal communications between the parties. 2–02

Nowadays, many types of contract are subject to specific regulation or industry standards which outline what is to be considered an "essential" feature. Examples include employment contracts (regulated by statute) and construction contracts (governed largely by industry-accepted standard forms).

In deciding whether an agreement has been reached by the parties, the courts will tend to take an objective approach. The test is whether or not it would appear to a "reasonable man" that an agreement had indeed been reached, and the words of Lord President Dunedin in *Muirhead and Turnbull v Dickson* (1905) are often quoted:

> "commercial contracts cannot be arranged by what people think in their innermost minds. Commercial contracts are arranged according to what people say."[1]

In reaching its conclusion, the courts will consider the words and actions of the parties during negotiations. Broadly speaking, there are two stages that are crucial here to the forming of a contract: an offer must be made by one party and an acceptance must be given by the other. At the risk of stating the obvious, an offer must come before an acceptance. Equally, there can be no acceptance unless there is an offer which is capable of being accepted.

OFFER

2–03 An offer is made when one party (the "offeror") clearly indicates to another (the "offeree") the terms upon which he would be willing to be bound.

The offer may be made verbally, in writing, or by any other suitable means of communication, such as fax, text message or email. (You may remember that some contracts require to be formed in writing, explained further in Ch.3.) If the offer is communicated through any of these means, this is called an *express* offer. The offer may also be inferred from the actings of the parties, e.g. by taking goods from a supermarket shelf and presenting them at the checkout, or by getting on a bus and asking to be taken to a specific destination. In these cases the offer is not express, but is by *implication*. Regardless of how exactly the offer is made, it must signal an intention to enter into a binding contract and must outline at least the most salient details of the proposal.

Contrasting an offer with a "willingness to negotiate"

2–04 It is important to distinguish between genuine offers and certain communications that look like offers, but are not legally treated as such. There are a number of situations in which it might *appear* that someone has made an offer, when in fact they have merely indicated a willingness to negotiate. This distinction is crucial, since it is not possible to accept something that has not been offered. Whether a behaviour or communication will constitute an offer, or merely indicate a willingness to negotiate, depends on the circumstances of the case. However, certain presumptions exist regarding common commercial practices and, while these can be rebutted, compelling evidence is required.

Expressions of intention

2–05 A mere proposal to do business is not the same as an offer. In *Dawson International Plc v Coats Paton Plc* (1993), directors of CP agreed to recommend to company members that an offer from DI to buy their shares should be accepted. The recommendation was duly made but was later withdrawn when a more favourable bid was received from a third party. DI claimed that a binding contract had been entered into with CP, but were unsuccessful. Similarly, in *Mason v Benhar Coal Co* (1882), the fact that a company had proposed to issue new shares did not commit it to do so.

Even where a potential supplier of goods or services indicates the price of a commodity in advance, this will normally be taken to be merely an estimate or quotation. For example, Alison might say to Brenda that she is thinking of selling her television, which has a value of £100. If Brenda says she'll buy it for that amount, is there a contract? The answer is no, because Alison was not making an offer, she was only indicating a possible willingness to negotiate. In fact, it is *Brenda* who has made the offer here, by clearly communicating that she will buy the television for £100; it is entirely up to Alison how she wishes to respond to Brenda's offer, including refusing it and keeping the television after all.

These were broadly the facts in *Harvey v Facey* (1893). H sent a telegram to F: "Will you sell us Bumper Hall Pen? Telegraph lowest cash price." F telegraphed in reply: "Lowest price for Bumper Hall Pen £900." H then telegraphed to F: "We agree to buy Bumper Hall Pen for £900 asked by you." H received no reply to his telegram but argued that there was a valid contract. It was held that F's telegram was merely a statement of the lowest price at which he might be prepared to sell. It was not an offer to H nor was it an affirmative reply to the question in H's first telegram. ("Bumper Hall Pen" was the name of a farm in Jamaica. The case came to the Privy Council by way of appeal.)

In context, however, some communications could be taken to be a tender or a firm offer. In *Philp & Co v Knoblauch* (1907), K, a merchant, wrote to P, oil-millers:

> "I am offering today plate linseed for January/February and have pleasure in quoting you 100 tons at 41/3d usual plate terms. I shall be glad to hear if you are buyers and await your esteemed reply."

The following day, P telegraphed: "Accept hundred January/February plate 41/3d." The telegram was confirmed by letter. K then attempted to recall his original quotation by sending a telegram to that effect. It was held that K's original letter/quotation was an offer to sell and not merely a statement of the current price. A contract had been formed by P's acceptance telegram even though it did not expressly refer to the condition "usual plate terms" mentioned in the offer. K's subsequent telegram was too late to have any effect.

There are potential problems in this area since the words "offer", "estimate", "quotation" and "tender" are frequently used loosely in colloquial speech. It is a question of interpretation, of the facts and circumstances of each case, as to what the words actually mean in context.

Advertisements

An advertisement or announcement by one party that he has something for sale for which offers may be made is normally no more than an indication of willingness to negotiate. In *Paterson v Highland Railway* (1927), the fact that a railway company had announced that reduced rate tickets would be available for a particular period of time did not prevent it from withdrawing the reduction before the stated period expired.

However, there have been rare occasions where the courts have decided that particular advertisements go beyond being mere willingness to

2–06

negotiate and, in fact, are offers to the general public. The most celebrated occasion must be *Carlill v Carbolic Smoke Ball Co Ltd* (1893). CSB, through newspaper advertisements, offered to pay £100 to any member of the public who bought a patent preventative "smoke ball" and, having used it according to instructions, contracted influenza. C bought a smoke ball, used it according to instructions and, not surprisingly, failed to escape influenza. She sought payment of £100 but CSB refused payment, claiming that they had no contract with her. They submitted that the advert was no more than a willingness to negotiate and not an offer and thus could not be accepted. In all the facts and circumstances of the case, the court decided that this particular advertisement was an offer to the general public. C had accepted the offer when she bought the smoke ball and used it according to the instructions. Accordingly, there was a contract between CSB and C and she was entitled to her payment of £100.

In *Hunter v General Accident, Fire and Life Assurance Corp* (1909), a coupon policy of insurance in a diary stated that £1,000 would be paid to the representative of any diary owner killed in a railway accident within 12 months of registration with the insurance company. H sent off such a coupon to GA for the purposes of registration. Shortly afterwards, he was killed in a railway accident. GA claimed that the advertisement in the diary had not been an offer, only an indication of willingness to negotiate. H, they claimed, had merely made them an offer, which they had not accepted. There was no argument about the fact that GA had received the coupon from H. The court decided that the publication of the coupon in the diary was an offer and the return of it by H to GA was an acceptance. A valid contract had been formed and H's estate was entitled to the payment of £1,000.

Although the two cases are quite similar, in *Hunter* it was easier to show that a contract had been formed, because GA knew, and admitted they knew, of H's existence. In the case of *Carlill*, CSB had no knowledge of C as an individual. Virtually any book dealing with contract law in the UK will quote the case of *Carlill*. Nevertheless, it is a legal curiosity and somewhat of a maverick case. Today, few commercial organisations would make such undertakings as the ill-fated CSB did in the latter part of Queen Victoria's reign.

It is common in the sale of heritable property to invite offers above or around a stated figure. The seller is not bound to accept any offer that is received, even the highest. The term "fixed price" is sometimes used by sellers wishing to achieve a quicker sale, but even this constitutes no more than a willingness to negotiate, and a prospective buyer may offer a lower or higher price.

In sales by auction, the seller "exposes" the goods for sale, and the auctioneer invites offers by way of "bids". The sale is completed by the fall of the auctioneer's gavel, by which he "prefers" (accepts) the highest bid. Until that moment, the bidder may withdraw his offer. In *Fenwick v Macdonald Fraser & Co* (1904), a case involving the sale of a bull, it was held that the exposer was similarly free to withdraw his goods before the hammer fell. There is English authority in *Barry v Heathcote Ball & Co* (2001) that where there is no reserve price, the highest bid may not be rejected merely because it is not high enough. Occasionally, the so-called "referential" bid may be encountered in sealed competitive bids, such as an offer to "top" the highest bid by a stipulated amount or by a given percentage. Bids of this kind were held to be invalid in *Harvela Instruments Ltd v Royal Trust Co of Canada Ltd* (1986), a House of Lords case, unless the prospective bidders are all given reasonable notice that this method may be employed.

Invitations to treat

It comes as a surprise to many people that, generally speaking, shops do not 2–07 offer goods for sale. It is a well-established English law principle (which seems highly likely to apply in Scotland also) that by placing items for sale on display, the shop owner merely indicates a willingness to negotiate, or makes an "invitation to treat".

It is confusing, of course, when shops display signs such as "special offer" when, in fact, they are not offering anything at all. A shop owner does not have to sell any goods against his will and has an absolute right to refuse an offer to buy. In other words, the offer is not made by the seller to sell, the offer is most commonly made by the buyer to buy. In cases of this kind it has been stressed that "a shop is a place for bargaining, not for compulsory sales".[2] Having said that, a shop owner who consistently fails to honour displayed prices could fall foul of misleading price regulations, although this is more a matter of consumer protection than contract law per se.

The classic case must be *Pharmaceutical Society of Great Britain v Boots Cash Chemists Southern Ltd* (1952). Legislation required that listed poisons could only be sold under the supervision of a registered pharmacist. Such a poison had been sold in a self-service store. There was no pharmacist near the shelves where the goods were displayed but there was a pharmacist at work beside the cash desk. The question was, when did the actual sale take place? Was it when the customer took the goods off the shelf, or was it when the goods were presented at the cash desk? The court decided that the display of goods on the shelf did not constitute an offer. It was the customer who made the offer by taking the goods to the cash desk. The sales assistant, as agent for the company, accepted the offer and the contract was thus formed, under the supervision of the pharmacist. Therefore, B was not in breach of the Act.

In the subsequent case of *Fisher v Bell* (1961), a shopkeeper displayed a flick knife in his window. Beside the knife was a price ticket bearing the words "ejector knife". It was a statutory offence to sell or offer such a weapon for sale. Upon his prosecution, the shopkeeper's successful defence was that he had not sold nor had he offered to sell the weapon. He had merely indicated a willingness to negotiate, which was not a criminal offence. Subsequent legislation has tended to use expressions such as "unlawful marketing" as a catch-all provision.[3]

Difficulties of analysis can arise where no interaction is required between the buyer and seller to complete a transaction. If the goods or services can be accessed by anyone, then their availability is likely to constitute a "standing offer" which is open to acceptance. In *Chapleton v Barry Urban DC* (1940), C took a deck chair from a stack on the beach which were there on a "help yourself and pay the attendant when he comes round" basis. He was subsequently injured because the chair was defective. It was held that there was a contract between C and the District Council. The same logic could be applied to vending machines and self-service petrol pumps, though as always the circumstances can vary. It is also possible that a range of as-yet untested legal questions might arise regarding the increasingly common "self-service" checkouts installed by retailers.

Also on the issue of technology, certain other examples exist for which, at present, there are no definitive Scottish authorities. In this electronic age, perhaps the most relevant is that of online shopping. If a product is displayed as available for sale on a website, with a price clearly stated, is this an offer or an invitation to treat? If it is an offer, then it is accepted by the customer completing an order for the product and submitting payment details. This seems logical, but gives rise to a number of problems, such as availability of stock and the possibility of incorrectly-priced goods. In the Singaporean case of *Chwee Kin Keong v Digilandmail.com Pte Ltd* (2005), a seller mistakenly under-priced a product, resulting in six parties placing orders for a total of 1,600 items. In considering whether a contract existed, the court opined that a website listing *could* be an offer, but in this instance held that there was no enforceable contract as the buyers had knowingly taken advantage of the seller's mistake. It seems likely that the Scottish courts would take a similar view.

So, how is it possible to tell whether a particular statement is an offer (which can be accepted) or a mere invitation to treat (which cannot)? In fact, there are no hard and fast rules and it will depend on the facts and circumstances of each individual case. A useful rule of thumb is that if the "selling" party is publicly communicating a statement which is available for anybody to accept, that statement is likely to be an offer. If there is an element of discretion on the part of the "seller" as to whether or not to do business with the other party, then the statement is likely an invitation to treat. Thus, the deck-chair example referred to in the *Chapleton* case is categorised as an offer, whilst goods on display in a shop such as in the *Boots* case merely indicate a willingness to negotiate, or constitutes an invitation to treat.

Withdrawal of offer

2–08 An offer can be withdrawn, in most cases, at any time before it is accepted. This is an important feature of offers and the period before acceptance, when the offeror is still free to withdraw, is traditionally referred to as *locus poenitentiae* (room for repentance).

If a time limit is placed on the offer and that limit passes without an acceptance, the offer automatically lapses. If an offeror undertakes to keep his offer open for a certain time, this undertaking will be binding upon him.

This is because, in Scots law, a promise can be a binding obligation and breach of that promise could give rise to a claim for damages. (Promises are further explained in Ch.3.) In *Littlejohn v Hawden* (1882), the solicitor for the seller of an estate indicated by letter that the potential buyer had an option to purchase which would remain open for 10 days. This undertaking was held to be legally binding. If, as in *Effold Properties v Sprot* (1979), the offer simply states that it must be accepted within a certain time, this does not count as an undertaking and the offeror can still withdraw his offer. In formal written offers, it is quite common to find wording such as: "this offer, unless previously withdrawn, remains open for acceptance not later than [...]". Such wording clearly reserves the right to withdraw and puts matters beyond doubt. In *McMillan v Caldwell* (1991), it was held that a formal written offer to buy heritable property can be withdrawn verbally, provided the withdrawal reaches the offeree before he accepts.

Lapse of offer

If a stated time period expires without the offer having been accepted, it will 2–09 lapse, i.e. no longer be available for acceptance. In many cases, however, there will be no time limit stated. In these circumstances, the offer remains open for a "reasonable" time,[4] though what is reasonable depends on the facts and circumstances. Clearly there are times when it is only fair to give the second party some days to consider the offer. Equally, there are occasions when it is obvious, at least by implication, that an offer must be accepted fairly promptly, e.g. if the subject matter is raw materials which have a volatile price movement or where perishable goods are involved.

In the following two cases, the court decided that the original offer had lapsed due to the length of time, i.e. it had not been timeously accepted. *Wylie & Lochhead v McElroy & Sons* (1873): an offer to carry out certain iron work on a new building had not been "accepted" until five weeks had passed, during which time there had been a considerable rise in the price of iron. *Glasgow Steam Shipping Co v Watson* (1873): an offer made on 5 August to supply coal at 7s. (35p) per ton had not been "accepted" until 13 October, by which time coal had risen to 9s. (45p) per ton.

In contrast, the court decided in *Murray v Rennie and Angus* (1897) that an offer dated 10 June to carry out certain mason work was still open for acceptance on 21 June and that a valid contract had been formed.

Death, insanity and bankruptcy

Provided the offer has not been accepted, it will automatically lapse on the 2–10 death, insanity or bankruptcy of the offeror, unless the latter was acting purely as an agent for another party.

ACCEPTANCE

If there is no acceptance of an offer, clearly there can be no contract. An 2–11 offeree is under no obligation to accept an offer, or indeed even to respond at all. Where an acceptance *is* made, in order to form a contract it must "meet" the offer; this is called an "unqualified acceptance". If (and this is quite common) there are new terms or conditions in the so-called acceptance, no contract has yet been formed. What the original offeror has received back is confusingly called a "qualified acceptance". It is crucial to note that a qualified acceptance never concludes the process of formation of a contract. This is a rule to which there are no exceptions.

In fact, the so-called qualified acceptance is not an acceptance, as such, but a new offer. This qualified acceptance (which might more sensibly be called a counter-offer) must in turn be met by an unqualified acceptance before the parties can reach consensus and conclude formation of the contract. Some case law may help to illustrate.

Nelson v The Assets Co Ltd (1889): N wrote to A, offering to buy specific parts of a tenement property. A appeared to have accepted the offer "for our interest in the property". On an examination of the title deeds, it was discovered that A did not have a clear title to all of the property in question. N brought an action against A to deliver a valid title. In fact, there was no completed contract of sale as the "acceptance" had been qualified.

Stobo v Morrisons (Gowns) Ltd (1949): an offer was made to purchase a shop and the offer was accepted but "subject to contract". (This phrase does not have a technical meaning in Scotland, but in England it means that writing will be required to conclude the agreement.) In the circumstances of the case, the words "subject to contract" qualified the acceptance and thus there was no contract.

Wolf & Wolf v Forfar Potato Co Ltd (1984): F offered, by telex, to sell a quantity of potatoes to W, a firm of Amsterdam merchants. The offer was open for acceptance by 5pm on the following day. An "acceptance" was sent by telex from Amsterdam on the following morning, but it contained new conditions. On receipt of the telex, F telephoned W and informed them that the new conditions were unacceptable. W subsequently sent a second telex, still within the time-limit, purporting to accept the terms of the original offer. In fact, no contract existed. The first "acceptance" was a counter-offer, which killed off the original offer. The result was that the original offer was no longer capable of being accepted. The counter-offer (or qualified acceptance) from W had never been accepted by F, so the parties had not achieved consensus.

The acceptance does not require to repeat the offer word for word. It is sufficient that it shows acceptance of the offer as a whole. Like an offer, an acceptance may be either express or implied. In most cases, express acceptance is required in order to achieve consensus but sometimes it may be implied, e.g. an order for goods may not require an express acceptance, since acceptance is implied by the very act of supplying the goods. Acceptance can also sometimes be implied from a failure to reject an offer, but this is rare and can only arise if there have been similar dealings between the parties in the past. The law, in general, does not take kindly to contracts being imposed on people against their will. The unscrupulous practice of "inertia selling", whereby traders would send unsolicited goods to persons and demand payment if the goods were not returned within a specified time, was largely curbed by the Unsolicited Goods and Services Act 1971. There has since been further legislation enacted, such as the Consumer Protection from Unfair Trading Regulations 2008, under which consumers who receive unsolicited goods can keep these as if they were an unconditional gift.

The "battle of forms"
It is common for businesses when sending an order, i.e. an offer, to do so subject to their own standard pre-printed conditions. That in itself causes no major problem. The problem really begins when the second party accepts the offer on its own standard form acceptance—and the terms of offer and acceptance do not meet and may even contradict. Sometimes both sets of conditions may say that, in the event of a dispute, its terms will rule! To state the obvious, if the parties perform their respective obligations, without problem or dispute, the contents of the small print is really only academic. If, however, a dispute arises, there can be major problems, not least whether or not a contract actually exists. In fact, usually the courts decide there is basic consensus, although that may not always be entirely logical. Frequently, the terms of the contract will be those of the party who "fired the last shot".

2–12

The foundation case is *Butler Machine Tool Co v Ex-Cell-O Corp* (1979). Sellers of a machine sent their offer to sell on a standard form. It included a clause allowing the seller to increase the price if costs rose prior to delivery. The buyers sent their "acceptance" using their own standard form, containing a different set of conditions and incorporating a tear-off portion stating that the sellers accepted the buyer's standard terms. The sellers signed and returned this tear-off portion. Later, the sellers attempted to increase the price, in line with their original offer. The buyers did not consider themselves to be bound by any power to increase the price and queried whether there even was a contract. The court decided that a contract had been formed, but according to the terms of the buyers. Their purported acceptance had really been a counter-offer, which the sellers had accepted by returning the tear-off slip. The clause in the original offer, with the rest of that offer, had fallen. This decision was later followed in the Scottish case of *Uniroyal Ltd v Miller & Co Ltd* (1985), which had similar facts.

Sometimes the original offer may contain an overriding clause, stating that the terms of the offer will prevail unless the offeror consents, in writing, to any variation of these terms. The sheriff court confirmed the competence of such a clause in *Roofcare Ltd v Gillies* (1984).

Method of acceptance
A person making an offer is entitled to state the method by which the acceptance should be communicated, e.g. letter, telephone, etc. If the precise method and/or time for acceptance is stated, it must be adhered to. If no special conditions are laid down, acceptance can be given in any competent manner. Usually, it will be given in the same mode as the offer,

2–13

which is a matter of common sense rather than law.

Withdrawal of acceptance

2–14 The general rule is very simple. Once an acceptance is given, provided it is final and not qualified, it cannot be withdrawn. The parties are now in a mutually binding contract. However, under the so-called postal rules (below), there is one interesting and illogical quirk in this rule.

THE POSTAL RULES

2–15 Where parties are negotiating *entirely* by post, they do not have the advantage of being face to face, or even speaking over the telephone and they have to rely on an agent, i.e. the postal service, to convey offers, counter-offers, qualified acceptances and final acceptances. Over the years, certain common law "rules" have grown up to regulate this, not all of which are without criticism. These rules will apply in the absence of any agreement to the contrary between the parties.

Offering and accepting by post

2–16 Starting with the obvious—if an offer is posted, it must actually reach the offeree, otherwise it could not even be considered and so is of no relevance. The potential problems arise, rather, in the case of the acceptance, in particular at what point in time a posted acceptance actually achieves consensus. It might seem sensible to assume that the contract could not actually be formed until the first party receives the acceptance, but that would not be correct in law. Under the postal rules, consensus is achieved when the second party posts his acceptance.[5]

This rule is more logical than it appears. If the offeror makes his offer by post, he is, by implication, appointing the postal service as his agent. When the offeree posts his acceptance he is, in fact, placing it in the hands of the offeror's agent which is as good as placing it in the offeror's own hands. In the absence of any stipulation to the contrary, the offeror is presumed to intend the reply to be made by post.

One of the most unsatisfactory elements of the acceptance rule is that the offeror can actually be in a binding contract without being aware of it, since the acceptance could have been posted but not yet delivered. In England, it has further been decided that a contract is complete even if the posted acceptance never actually arrives,[6] though it seems unlikely that this case would be followed in Scotland.[7]

There is a further knock-on effect: if an offer is open for acceptance within a specified period, acceptance is effective if it is posted within that time limit. In *Jacobsen Sons & Co v Underwood & Son Ltd* (1894), there was an offer to buy a quantity of straw. The offer stated "for reply by Monday 6th". The acceptance was posted on the 6th but it did not arrive until the 7th. The offer had been accepted on time because the reply had been in the hands of the Post Office on the 6th. It is worth noting that this rule applies only to unqualified acceptances, and not to qualified acceptances[8] or other time-limited actions such as the exercise of options.[9]

It is quite common for parties to contract out of this somewhat tiresome rule and to state in the offer "your reply to be in my hands not later than [...]". This avoids doubt or misunderstanding.

Withdrawal of posted offer

Human nature being what it is, an offeror might post his offer and then have second thoughts and wish to withdraw it. Following on the principles outlined above, his withdrawal is only effective if it reaches the offeree before the acceptance is placed in the post.

2–17

Thomson v James (1855): J made a written offer to buy an estate from T. Some days later, T posted an acceptance. On the same day on which T posted his acceptance, J posted a letter withdrawing his offer. Both letters were delivered on the following day. In other words, J received an acceptance of the offer which he thought he had withdrawn and T received a withdrawal of the offer which he thought he had accepted. In fact, there was a binding contract since consensus had been achieved when T posted his acceptance. J was too late to withdraw his offer.

Withdrawal of posted acceptance

From the point of logic, the above rules ought to mean that once an acceptance is posted, it is irrevocable since consensus has been achieved. However, there appears to be a quirk in the law, based on the old case of *Countess of Dunmore v Alexander* (1830). A wrote to D, offering her services as a maid-servant. On 5 November, D wrote to A accepting her offer. On the 6th, D changed her mind and wrote to A withdrawing her acceptance. Due perhaps to vagaries of the contemporary postal service, A received both letters at the same time. For reasons best known to itself, the court decided that D's withdrawal of acceptance was effective; there was no contract. (If the acceptance had reached A before the recall, there would have been a contract.) Over the years, there has been much critical comment about the correctness of this decision and the law report itself is far from clear.

2–18

Scope of the postal rules

In contracts made with overseas parties, if they are made under the Uniform Laws on International Sales Act 1967, the postal rules do not apply. A contract will only be deemed to be completed when an acceptance arrives in the office of the offering party.

2–19

The postal rules do not apply to communications which, although requiring to be "sent", are deemed to be "instantaneous". It was established long ago, for example, that telex communications are not covered by the postal rules,[10] but matters are less certain with more modern technologies. It seems that the postal rules do not apply to facsimiles, and although judicial authority is scant, widespread academic opinion seems to have it that voicemails, emails and texts are likely to be similarly excluded.[11]

The future of the postal rules

2–20 The Scottish Law Commission has long been of the opinion that the postal rules ought to be reviewed. Over the past decade there has been an increase in support for their abolition and the Commission has recommended this in its *Report on Review of Contract Law*.[12] It remains to be seen whether this recommendation will be implemented, although it seems likely that this area will see reform of some sort in the near future.

DISTANCE SELLING

2–21 As a result of the European Community Directive 97/7/EC being passed, consumers became entitled to important additional protections when purchasing goods or engaging services by means of a "distance contract". These protections were first enacted under the Consumer Protection (Distance Selling) Regulations 2000, which were later replaced by the Consumer Contracts (Information, Cancellation and Additional Charges) Regulations 2013.

A distance contract is one where the "consumer" and the "trader" do not have any face-to-face negotiations. This would include traditional mail order purchases as well as electronic means such as telephone, fax, email and online. (This list is not exhaustive.) A trader is someone who acts in a commercial or professional capacity and a consumer is a party who is acting outwith any of these roles. There are a number of exceptions from regulation including business-to-business transactions and contracts for the sale of land or the provision of financial services.

The broad effect of these Regulations is that certain basic information about the trader and the terms of the contract must be supplied to the consumer. The Regulations give the consumer the right, in certain circumstances, to cancel the contract after consensus has been achieved. The consumer can, in any event, withdraw within seven working days and receive a full refund. There are common sense exceptions, such as supply of perishable goods or services which are subject to fluctuation in the financial markets. In cases where the required information has not been given by the supplier, the period is extended to three months. If the supplier does not fulfil the contract within 30 days, the consumer is entitled to a refund unless he elects to accept substitute goods or services.

IMPLIED CONTRACTS

2–22 Certain terms or conditions may be implied into a contract by statute. A clear example is a contract for the sale of moveable property, which has important statutory terms built in by the Sale of Goods Act 1979 and associated legislation. It would be unusual in the extreme, however, for a court to imply the existence of an entire contract without some overt sign by the parties that they intended to enter into a contractual relationship.

However, on occasions, it is both possible and sensible to infer that when two parties have taken certain actions, it must have been obvious that they intended to form a contract. One (admittedly rare) example is the English case of *Clarke v Dunraven* (1897) in which it was held that competitors in an amateur yacht race had, by entering into the race in terms of the club rules, contracted to pay full compensation to any competitor whose vessel was damaged in the race. Although there was no formal offer and acceptance among each of the members, the court was prepared to imply the existence of contracts.

---

1. *Muirhead and Turnbull v Dickson* (1905) 7 F. 686, per Lord Dunedin at [694].
2. G. Black, *Woolman and Black on Contract*, 6th edn (Edinburgh: W. Green, 2018), p.23.
3. See, e.g. Knives Act 1997 (c.21) s.1(4).
4. See, e.g. *Flaws v International Oil Pollution Compensation Fund*, 2002 S.L.T. 270.
5. *Dunlop v Higgins* (1848) 9 E.R. 805.
6. *Household Fire Insurance Co v Grant* (1879) 4 Ex. D. 216.
7. *Mason v Benhar Coal Co* (1882) 9 R. 883.
8. *Park, Petrs* [2009] CSOH 122.
9. *Carmarthen Developments Ltd v Pennington* [2008] CSOH 139.
10. *Entores Ltd v Miles Far East Corp* [1955] 2 Q.B. 327; *Brinkibon Ltd v Stahag Stahl* [1983] 2 A.C. 34; [1982] 1 All E.R. 293.
11. See, e.g. D. Nolan, "Offer and acceptance in the electronic age" in A. Burrows and E. Peel, *Contract Formation and Parties* (Oxford: Oxford University Press, 2010), p.65.
12. Scottish Law Commission, *Report on Review of Contract Law: Formation, Interpretation, Remedies for Breach, and Penalty Clauses* (2018), Scot. Law Com. No.252.

3. PROMISES, WRITING AND PERSONAL BAR

It is fairly obvious that a contract requires two parties and that most contracts are reciprocal. However, Scots law is somewhat unusual in that it is perfectly possible for only *one* party to be bound by an obligation—though admittedly this is rare in practice. Given how unlikely it is for someone to unilaterally commit to doing something for nothing, the law generally requires that such undertakings are put in writing. This is one of a number of situations in which, contrary to the general rule, writing is required in order to form enforceable obligations. **3–01**

PROMISES

In most contracts, both parties are debtor and creditor to one another, with each giving and taking something of value. This is usually referred to as "consideration". The tradition, in English law, is that if there is no element of consideration, the contract is not legally enforceable. In *Stilk v Mayrick* (1809), nine seamen had been engaged to sail a ship from London to the Baltic. Two of the crew deserted. The captain promised the remaining seven men that he would pay them extra wages to sail the ship home short-handed but he did not keep his word. The crew were unable to recover the extra money as there was no consideration. They were only doing what they had originally contracted to do, namely to sail the ship. **3–02**

Scots law, however, follows Roman law in this area. Consideration is not actually a requirement for an undertaking to be legally binding. An obligation to do or give something gratuitously, i.e. without asking anything in return, is as enforceable as any mutual contract. In *Morton's Trustees v Aged Christian Friend Society of Scotland* (1899), M wrote to the steering committee for a new charitable society, offering to provide pensions for 50 elderly people. He was to fund this donation by 10 annual capital payments of £100 to the Society. His offer was accepted, pensioners were appointed and M duly paid eight of the annual payments but died thereafter, with two payments outstanding. The obligation to meet these two payments was a binding contract and his trustees were liable to make the two outstanding payments.

In law, there is a general presumption against donation. In other words, it is presumed that people do not give away anything for nothing. Historically, promises would be enforceable if proven by "writ or oath", but this was abolished in 1995. Under the Requirements of Writing (Scotland) Act 1995 (RWSA) "writing" is required to constitute a gratuitous unilateral obligation, except where undertaken in the course of a business.[1] For example, in *Carlyle v Royal Bank of Scotland Plc* (2015), a verbal promise made by a bank to provide funding for a development project was held to be enforceable. A verbal promise can also become binding if personal bar operates (see below).

It appears that a true gratuitous contract, as distinct from a gratuitous unilateral obligation, is not required to be in writing. What, then, is the difference between the two? In the case of a promise, only one party, the party receiving the promise, has any right to enforce. Furthermore, it seems that a true promise does not require an acceptance to make it enforceable.[2] If it is a gratuitous contract, both parties have rights of enforcement and there will have been an offer and acceptance.

This distinction is easier to state than to apply in practice. In *Bathgate v Rosie* (1976), a child accidentally broke a shop window. His mother assured the shop owner that she would pay for the damage, but failed to do so. The sheriff held that she was obliged to pay but, perhaps wisely, did not specify whether, in his opinion, she had made a unilateral promise or entered a gratuitous contract. In *Muirhead v Gribben* (1983), a firm of solicitors assured another firm that the latter's fees would be paid if certain papers were transferred to them. This assurance was held to be contractual. An example of what looked like a promise, but was held to be a contract, can be found in *Petrie v Earl of Airlie* (1834). The Earl had not supported the Reform Act of 1832. Posters appeared accusing him of treasonable conduct. The Earl offered a reward of 100 guineas (£105) for information leading to the detection of the author and printer, the reward to be paid on their conviction. P supplied the required information but the Crown declined to prosecute. The Earl, having himself decided against a private prosecution or civil litigation, was nevertheless obliged to pay the reward to P. A clearer example of a true gratuitous contract can be found in *Wick Harbour Trustees v The Admiralty* (1921): A had undertaken to make certain ex gratia payments to W. In his judgment Lord Sands stated that it was a general principle of Scots law that

> "if a person voluntarily offers to make a payment which he is under no legal obligation to make, and the offer is accepted, that forms a binding contract."

Finally, it is worth noting that the use of certain words is not, in itself, conclusive in deciding on the status of any legal undertaking. In *Macfarlane v Johnston* (1864), a company stated by letter: "We agree to pay you, during February 1859, £100, during March 1859, £100, during April 1859, £100." In the circumstances, it was held that this was a promise, which did not have to be accepted to be valid. In other words, the legal status of the undertaking was that of a promissory note.

THE REQUIREMENTS OF WRITING

3–03 The general rule is that no special formalities are required for parties to enter into a binding contractual obligation. There are, however, exceptions to this general rule and some contracts do require writing for their constitution. Until 1 August 1995, when RWSA came into force, there were certain contracts, known as the *obligationes literis*, which required to be expressed in writing as a matter of common law, although the categories were not entirely clear. The law on how documents were validly executed was governed mainly by acts of the pre-1707 Scots Parliament, as interpreted by the courts over the years, and known by the august collective title of the "Authentication Statutes".

Under RWSA, this entire area of law was modernised. The old common law provisions disappeared, as did the Authentication Statutes. Now, a written document is required for:

(1) creation, variation or extinction of an interest in land (with the exception of leases of not more than one year's duration);
(2) gratuitous unilateral obligations, unless undertaken in the course of business; and
(3) creation of a trust where a person declares himself to be sole trustee of his own property.[3]

There are also other statutory instances where certain documents (not all of them contracts) require writing, e.g. life assurance, bills of exchange, hire purchase and credit agreements regulated under the Consumer Credit Act 1974.

Under RWSA, a document is *formally valid if it is subscribed by the granter*. In other words, a simple signature is sufficient formality, on its own, to make the document binding. Thus, most contracts to which the provisions apply only require the signatures of the parties. In the case of a basic contract, a signature is required on the last page. If the contract relates to land, any annexations also require to be signed. However, an annexation is only incorporated into any contract if it is referred to in the main document and identified on its face as being the annexation referred to. This fairly strict rule applies whether the annexation requires to be signed or not. (In practice, it is easy to overlook this requirement.)

In order for a document to be relied upon, it should also be "self-proving", for which it requires to be attested. This means that it is signed, or the signature is acknowledged, by the granter before one witness aged at least 16 (previously two witnesses were required). When a document is self-proving, its subscription is presumed valid without need for further evidence. This does not mean that such a signature is unchallengeable, e.g. if forgery were suspected. If such a problem exists, it is possible to raise an action for "reduction" of the document by the court, which has the legal effect of making it null and void. It is not easy to obtain a decree of reduction on the grounds of faulty or fraudulent execution, since the onus of proof is clearly against the party wishing to reduce. A great advantage of RWSA provisions is that even if the witness's attestation is botched, the document remains formally valid as long as there is a subscription by the granter. The courts also have a statutory power to rectify a defectively expressed document, even if probative or self-proving, under the Law

Reform (Miscellaneous Provisions) (Scotland) Act 1985. In most cases, only a self-proving document can be entered in the public registers. If a document is not self-proving, i.e. if the signature was not witnessed, an application can be made to the sheriff court to give it self-proving status should that be required.

Parties may, of course, agree between themselves that a contract will be expressed in writing. There are obviously times when such a written agreement is prudent, e.g. where the terms are particularly complex. If the parties have agreed that a written document is required then, in the absence of this, there will be no contract, even if consensus has otherwise been reached.[4]

In Ch.2, brief mention was made of electronic means of communicating offers and acceptance in contracts. The Electronic Communications Act 2000 made future provision for electronic communication to be recognised as the equivalent of a written document, including the possibility of electronic signatures. It is now the case that in a number of areas electronic communications are viewed as valid forms of writing.[5] Probably the most significant step for the current context was the introduction of the Automated Registration of Title to Land (ARTL) system, which allows the electronic registration of routine land transfers. A further example is in relation to the agreements referred to above under the Consumer Credit Act 1974, where similar provisions are now in place.[6] There continues to be statutory development in this area, and further reform seems likely in the future.

PERSONAL BAR

3–04 Personal bar is a concept which, in some ways, is easier to understand than to explain. It is based on the idea that, although the law generally exists to protect peoples' rights, there are times when the strict enforcement of a legal right might lead to an injustice. In certain situations, an individual will be "personally barred" (prevented) from enforcing a legal right that he would otherwise be entitled to rely on.

The older textbooks deal with two forms of personal bar known as *rei interventus* and homologation. These were replaced by statutory personal bar under RWSA.[7] If a contract is one which requires to be in writing, but is not (or is only partly in writing) and the party "loyal" to the defective contract (i.e. who wants it to continue—called the "first party" under RWSA) acts, or refrains from acting, with the knowledge and acquiescence of the other party (the "second party"), the latter is said to be *personally barred* from withdrawing from the contract on the grounds of lack of writing. Personal bar will only operate if the position of the first party has been materially affected by his own actings and would be similarly affected if the second party were allowed to withdraw from the contract.

Consider the following example: Clive has been renting a flat from Duncan for some time. Duncan decides that he wants to sell the flat, and

Clive is happy to buy it because he does not want to move out. The two verbally agree a price of £150,000. With Duncan's consent, Clive begins extensively redecorating the flat. However, Duncan then receives an offer of £170,000 from Edward. The question is whether Duncan is free to accept Edward's offer, since his agreement with Duncan was not expressed in writing.

On the face of it, it would seem that Duncan is free to withdraw from the agreement he made with Clive. However, this would not seem fair in light of the expense and effort that Clive has gone to on the strength of the verbal agreement they made. The relevant provisions of RWSA "bar" Duncan from withdrawing from the contract purely due to a lack of writing, provided Clive has been disadvantaged to a material extent by his reliance on the verbal agreement, and provided Duncan "acquiesced" in (knew about and accepted) what Clive was doing. So, Duncan would not be able to back out of the contract in this case.

Note that the above is an attempt to simplify what is actually a very complicated area of the law. In essence, the law is trying to strike a balance between ensuring that certain contracts are expressed in writing, whilst recognising that there is potential for individuals to "take advantage" of these rules to the detriment of the other party. Disputes are addressed by the courts on a case-by-case basis.[8] For a more recent example with some helpful judicial explanation see *The Advice Centre for Mortgages v McNicoll* (2006).

Personal bar, then, is about fairness and preventing individuals from "moving the goalposts after the game has started". It takes a number of forms, but they all adhere to this same basic principle. A number of other examples are given below.

Holding out

If a person "holds himself out" (i.e. gives the impression of himself) as being, say, of a certain age and is reasonably believed, he is personally barred from denying that he is of that age in respect of any contract that he enters while giving such an impression. In an old case of *Wilkie v Dunlop* (1834), a minor (as he was then called) booked into an inn. He gave the impression, which was reasonably believed, that he was of full age. He left without paying his bill and was sued by the innkeeper. The young man then indicated that, as he was a minor, he could not be sued for the bill (which was legally correct at the time). The court was not impressed with his argument. The minor had held himself out as being of full age and had been reasonably believed. He was personally barred from escaping his liabilities by using the defence of minority. To put it another way, he had given the impression that he was an adult and so, for the purposes of *this* contract, he would be treated as such.

Holding out could also apply in other areas of status, such as partnership or agency (explained briefly in Ch.4). If Erika says that she is the business partner of Felicity, and Felicity allows Erika to act as such, Felicity is personally barred from refusing to honour any contracts that Erika

3–05

negotiates. It does not mean that Erika has actually become Felicity's partner but, as far as third parties are concerned, the effect is the same. Of course, if Felicity did not (and could not reasonably be expected to) know of Erika's actions, she would not be personally barred.

Representation

3–06 To paraphrase the words of Lord Birkenhead in *Gatty v MacLaine* (1921), this takes place where one party, either by his words or his actions, justifies another in believing that a certain state of facts exists, and the latter party then acts on reliance on these facts to his loss. The former party is personally barred by representation from stating that the facts were different to those originally stated. Representation is similar to holding out, but relates more to facts than to the status of persons.

In *London Joint Stock Bank Ltd v MacMillan & Arthur* (1918), a clerk in the employment of M and A approached one of the partners, A, and asked him to sign a cheque for £2 for petty cash. A was in a hurry but, unwisely, signed the cheque. In fact, the cheque was blank apart from the space for figures in which were written "2 0 0"; later, the clerk put a "1" before the "2" and a "0" after it and wrote in the words "one hundred and twenty pounds". The clerk presented the cheque to the bank for payment and absconded with the money. M and A failed in an action against the bank for £118 (the difference between £120 and £2) as it was the firm and not the bank that had acted carelessly and had not taken adequate precautions to prevent forgery. The firm had acted in such a way as to justify the bank in believing that a certain state of affairs existed (that the cheque was for £120) and there was no reason for the bank to be put on its guard. The firm was personally barred by representation from stating later what the true state of affairs was, i.e. that the cheque was originally only for £2.

There can sometimes be an issue over whether a representation has been positively made, rather than it being inferred by silence or a failure to act. This was one of a range of considerations in the case of *Mitchell v Caversham Management Ltd* (2009). Here, CM were purchasing heritable property from M. A condition of the sale was that planning permission to renovate the property was to be timeously obtained by the defender. There was a delay in planning permission being granted, and M rescinded (cancelled) the contract, in accordance with its written terms. (See Ch.8 on rescission.) CM claimed, among other things, that M was barred from rescinding the contract as he had not objected to further time being required. The court did not accept that this amounted to a representation.

Acquiescence

3–07 Acquiescence takes place where a person sees his rights being invaded but takes no action to safeguard them. This lack of action leads other people to believe that he has no objection to the invasion and they make their position accordingly. He is then personally barred by acquiescence from objecting at some later date. An easy example would be failing to object to a nuisance from a neighbour's property. It is of little direct relevance to the everyday law of contract as such, but it can be important in long term continuing obligations affecting heritable property. Say Gordon owns a property that is subject to a real burden (explained briefly in Ch.10) to the effect that it can only be used as a private dwelling-house. His neighbour Harry has the right to enforce this burden. If Gordon turns the property into a hotel and Harry does not object to this, he might find later that he will be personally barred by acquiescence from enforcing his right.

Mora and taciturnity

This is closely related to acquiescence and is more relevant to the law of contract. There is no general rule that requires a person to state his objections to another party's actions, or his failure to act, immediately. Nevertheless, he should not delay unduly as he may find himself personally barred. By statute, there are prescriptive periods (see Ch.9) by which certain rights can be extinguished by a negative prescriptive period of five (in some cases, 20) years if no relevant objection is made. The effect of *mora* and taciturnity is to bar a claim, where a delay in asserting a right may have led the other party to believe that it was not going to be asserted, even when the negative prescriptive period has not run its full length. **3–08**

In *Pollok v Burns* (1875), P, a habitual drunkard, granted a bill of exchange while quite drunk. He waited six months before challenging the validity of the bill. The challenge failed on the grounds that he had not been so drunk as to be unaware of what he was doing but, in any event, by delaying for six months before making a challenge, he was personally barred on the grounds of *mora* and taciturnity.

Waiver

This is giving up a claim, or an objection, which could otherwise be made. The party who had surrendered the claim or objection would not then be able to found on it. **3–09**

Notice

Notice is perhaps the simplest form of personal bar. Party A is entitled to assume that what party B tells him is true. However, if A knows perfectly well that what B tells him is untrue, A will not be entitled to act as though he believed it to be true. In practice, there might be problems in actually proving what someone was (or was not) aware of. **3–10**

---

1. Requirements of Writing (Scotland) Act 1995 (c.5) (RWSA 1995) s.1(2)(a)(ii).
2. See *Cawdor v Cawdor*, 2007 S.L.T. 152, per Lord President Hamilton.
3. RWSA 1995 s.1(2).
4. *WS Karoulias SA v The Drambuie Liqueur Co Ltd*, 2005 S.L.T. 813.
5. RWSA 1995 Pt 3, inserted by the Land Registration etc. (Scotland) Act 2012.
6. Consumer Credit Act 1974 (Electronic Communications) Order 2004 (SI 2004/3236).
7. RWSA 1995 s.1(3)–(4).
8. *Caterleisure Ltd v Glasgow Prestwick Airport*, 2006 S.C. 602; 2005 S.L.T. 1083.

4. CONTRACTUAL CAPACITY

The basic concept of a contract is relatively simple and, as already **4–01** observed, we enter into them frequently and often with little contemplation of their legal ramifications. However, entering into a contract does have potentially significant consequences, so for this reason the law requires that the parties to a contract have "capacity", i.e. the sufficient capability of understanding the nature and consequences of what they are doing. A person's capacity can be adversely affected by factors that compromise this understanding, such as age and mental state. In addition to these, contractual capacity can also be affected by a state of affairs, such as wartime. Capacity may be limited either at common law or by statute, for various reasons, on the grounds that a party cannot, or should not be able to, enter into that contract.

CONTRACTUAL CAPACITY IN INDIVIDUALS

Children and young people
The Age of Legal Capacity (Scotland) Act 1991 (ALCSA) came into force **4–02** in September 1991. The Act was not retrospective and the basic civil and personal rights of children were not affected. The basics of the law before and after the coming into force of the Act will now be considered.

The old law
Scotland previously followed Roman law and divided young people into **4–03** two groups: pupils (girls under 12, boys under 14) and minors (girls 12 to 18, boys 14 to 18). Pupils generally had no contractual capacity and contracts were made for them by their "tutors", usually father or mother. Minors had limited capacity in that they could make contracts with the consent of their "curators", again usually father or mother. There were exceptions, e.g. if necessaries were supplied, the young person had to pay a fair price. If a minor had no parents and no curator, he enjoyed full contractual capacity. A minor in business on his own had full capacity as had a minor who was "forisfamiliated" (emancipated from his family), e.g. married and/or living away from home or serving in the armed forces. In *McFeetridge v Stewarts & Lloyds* (1913), M, a 16-year-old Irish labourer, was injured at work and accepted a compensation payment that was not over-generous. He later tried to overturn his own acceptance on the grounds of age, but was unable to do so as he was forisfamiliated. Pupils and minors could challenge contracts made on their behalf during pupillarity or minority if it could be shown that such contracts had caused them "enorm lesion" (substantial harm). The challenge had to take place not later than four years after attaining majority. This period was known as the *quadriennium utile* (useful four years). Contracts made by a minor himself

in the course of trade or business could not be challenged in this way. Rights that vested prior to 1991 are not affected but, with the progress of time, are of declining relevance.

The new law

4-04 The old division of young people under the age of majority into two separate categories disappeared and a new single tier system took its place. Young people under the age of 16 ("children") have no contractual capacity,[1] although an exception exists for "reasonable transactions" commonly entered into by persons of their age and circumstances.[2] These exceptions would include, e.g. children buying sweets or travelling on a bus. Under the old law, these transactions were all, in theory, invalid unless it could be shown that they were necessary. A positive aspect of ALCSA, therefore, is that it builds in an element of flexibility through age and circumstances, recognising that growing up is a gradual process. A nine-year-old is unlikely to be spending large sums of money, whereas a 15-year-old could have substantial spending power.

Young people aged 16 and 17 have full contractual capacity, although transactions which cause them "substantial prejudice" may be set aside on application to the court. The young person has until the age of 21 in which to apply, so the period within which the challenge may be made ranges from three to five years, depending on circumstances. The court would only set aside (declare invalid) a transaction if an adult exercising reasonable prudence would not have entered into it and it has caused, or is likely to cause, substantial prejudice to the applicant.[3] This does not imply that any contract which does not work out as well as expected can be easily set aside. Similarly, if a young person aged 16 or 17 engaged in business or trade makes a contract in that connection, it is unlikely that he will easily be able to plead substantial prejudice. Also, if a young person held himself out as being of full age and was reasonably believed, he could be personally barred. Challenges available at common law, e.g. error, fraud, facility and circumvention or undue influence are not affected.

Parties might well be ultra-cautious about entering into a transaction with any young person aged between 16 and 17, particularly if buying heritable property. Section 4 introduces a procedure for making a proposed transaction unchallengeable by judicial ratification. This is achieved by joint action under summary cause and the sheriff's decision is final. There is an element of doubt as to exactly what is meant by "proposed". It seems that judicial ratification cannot be sought retrospectively. There is no provision under the new law for any challenge to a bad bargain made on behalf of a child by a parent or guardian. A child may sue the parent or guardian for damages but could not set the bad bargain aside.

Under an amendment to ALCSA, a person under the age of 16 has the legal capacity to instruct a solicitor in connection with any civil matters where that young person has a general understanding of what it means to do so. A person aged 12 years or more is presumed to have such an understanding.[4]

Mental illness

A person experiencing mental illness will lack contractual capacity if his 4–05 illness prevents him from understanding the nature of the obligations. Any contract entered into in these circumstances will be invalid, although a person who lacks mental capacity can be made to pay a reasonable price for "necessaries".[5] It makes no difference if the other party is unaware of the mental illness, as was the case in *Loudon & Co v Elder's Curator Bonis* (1923). Traditionally, where someone was certified "insane" (an imprecise and somewhat insensitive term) they would commonly have had a curator bonis (one who has a care of goods) appointed by the court, and all contracts would be made through him.

Since the beginning of the new millennium, a number of acts have been passed with the intention of improving the law as regards adults who lack capacity—contractual capacity being just one aspect of this. The logical starting point is perhaps the Adults with Incapacity (Scotland) Act 2000, though this has since been amended.[6] Incapacity is defined as an inability through mental disorder or physical disability to act, make, communicate, understand or retain the memory of decisions. Depending on circumstances, a guardian, intromitter or intervener can be appointed and applications for appointment of a curator bonis are now incompetent. A fundamental principle of the Act is that there must be no intervention unless it is for the benefit of the adult and the outcome cannot be achieved in any other way. So far as is reasonably possible, the views of the adult must be taken into account. Furthermore, any intervention must take the least restrictive option. Thus, the Act provides for the sheriff to grant an intervention order that will permit the sale or disposal of property, including a house, without the need to go for a full guardianship order.

At common law, when a person experiences mental illness but with some lucid moments, he will be bound by contracts made during these intervals. (Given the new statutory definition of incapacity, it seems less likely for a claim that a decision was made during a lucid interval to succeed.) A person can grant a "power of attorney", appointing someone to take responsibility of his affairs should he ever lack capacity himself.

When a person who is involved in a continuing contract (e.g. a partner in a firm) subsequently becomes mentally incapable, the contract is not automatically invalidated. Thus, a partnership is not dissolved merely by the insanity of a partner, although his insanity would be a ground for the court to dissolve the firm.[7]

In law, there is a presumption of sanity. The contrary must be proved or admitted.

Intoxicated persons

Intoxication, like mental illness, is a question of fact and degree. As a 4–06 general rule, drunkenness is not a ground on which a contract's validity can be challenged unless the drunkenness has reached the stage where the person has lost his reason and could not give true consent to being contractually bound.[8]

A contract made when a person is in such a state can theoretically be challenged, but only if the intoxicated party takes steps to do so as soon as he recovers his senses and realises what he has done. Delay in taking action will likely result in his being personally barred from doing so, on the grounds of *mora* and taciturnity.[9] A classic case is *Taylor v Provan* (1864): in the course of a day, P visited T's farm and offered to buy 31 cattle, first at £13 10s. (£13.50), then £13 15s. (£13.75) and finally at £14 each. T refused to sell for less than £15. P then tried, without success, to buy cattle elsewhere. That same evening, somewhat worse for drink, P returned to T and offered him £15 per head, which was accepted. Subsequently, P claimed that he had been incapable, by virtue of intoxication, of entering the contract. As there was no evidence to show that P had been totally incapacitated by intoxication, the contract was held to be valid. Per Lord Justice-Clerk Inglis:

> "[Provan] was in such a condition from drink that he had not all his wits about him ... and if that were sufficient ground for annulling a bargain, I fear we would have plenty of reductions".

In the more recent case of *X v BBC* (2005), the pursuer sought to prevent the broadcast of a documentary in which she was depicted in an unfavourable light. One of her arguments was that she had been intoxicated when signing the "contributor's agreement" owing to the fact that she had consumed a bottle of tonic wine and 15 valium tablets. The judge, however, took the approach of assessing intoxication by observation of her actions, rather than by what she had consumed, and held that she was not sufficiently intoxicated to have lacked capacity.[10]

Enemy aliens

4–07 An alien (i.e. a person who is not a UK or Commonwealth citizen) normally has full contractual capacity in the UK during peacetime. However, the position is quite different in the case of an enemy alien. Such a person only emerges in times of actual war. If there is a state of war between the UK and another country, anyone who voluntarily resides or carries on business in that country, or in territory occupied by it, is counted as an enemy alien.[11] It does not matter what his original nationality is; he could even be British. It is illegal to make contracts with him and any existing contracts are considered void, at least during the period of hostilities.[12]

At the end of the war, certain of the parties' rights may revive, although the original contract probably will not be performed. *Cantiere San Rocco v Clyde Shipbuilding and Engineering Co Ltd* (1923): an Austrian company had, in May 1914, entered into a contract with a Scottish company for the supply of marine engines for £11,550, to be paid by instalments. The Austrians paid the first instalment of £2,310 in May 1914. Some work was done but the contract could not be taken further due to the outbreak of war. After the war, the Austrians brought an action for repayment of the instalment they had paid. They could not, strictly speaking, recover this money under the law of contract, as the original contract no longer existed. They were, however, entitled to recover the instalment by "restitution" on the principle of *causa data causa non secuta* (consideration given, but consideration not followed).

In the English case of *Amin v Brown* (2005), the issue of what constitutes an "enemy alien" in modern times was given extensive consideration (although not directly in relation to contractual capacity). The conclusion reached was that the conflict between the UK and Iraq did not constitute "war" in a legal sense, and therefore an Iraqi national was not precluded from enforcing her rights before a UK court.

CONTRACTUAL CAPACITY IN BUSINESS ORGANISATIONS

Corporate bodies
Corporate bodies are sometimes referred to as artificial, juristic or non- **4–08** natural persons, i.e. they are recognised in law as persons who have capacity to contract, but they are obviously not "people" in the normal sense of that word. The capacity of the body will vary according to its constitution.

If it was constituted by Royal Charter, the Charter itself may provide which types of contract may be formed. In practice, such a body would be able to enter into any contract not expressly forbidden. In the case of a body set up by statute, provision will be found in the relevant statute and, possibly, in delegated legislation. In the previous two examples, if such a body purports to do something not permitted under its constitution, it is said to be acting ultra vires (beyond the powers). Contracts that are ultra vires are void and cannot be made valid even with the consent of all members of the body.

The most common form of corporate body is the limited company. Historically, a company was bound by the "objects" of the company (the reason for the formation of the company and what its ongoing purposes and powers were) as set out in its memorandum of association. So far as third parties are concerned, the doctrine of ultra vires is now only of historical interest in the case of registered companies. The Companies Act 2006 now clearly states that any outside party contracting with a company need not be concerned about its capacity to contract.[13]

Because corporate bodies are non-natural persons, contracts must be made on their behalf by "agents" (see below) such as directors, office bearers or managers. It is important to note that the capacity of the agent is irrelevant to the capacity of the corporate body; it is a well-established principle that an agent cannot increase the capacity of the person he is acting on behalf of.[14]

Unincorporated bodies
Unincorporated bodies, such as many clubs, associations and churches, do **4–09** not have a separate personality in law from those who make them up.

(There is an important exception to this rule in the case of Scottish business partnerships, for which see below.) An unincorporated body cannot make contracts or be sued in its own name, only in the name of its trustees or office bearers. Thus, the capacity of an unincorporated body is nil, although from a practical point of view, the capacity of its office bearers is what matters. When three office bearers signed a promissory note "on behalf of the Reformed Presbyterian Church, Stranraer", they were personally liable, since the church was an unincorporated body and totally lacked contractual capacity.[15]

Partnerships

4–10 In Scotland, a partnership ("firm") has a distinct legal personality of its own, even although it is not incorporated.[16] A partner in a firm is the agent both for the firm and for his fellow partners. Every partner is liable jointly and severally for all the debts of the firm. Thus, an unpaid creditor, after he has first sued the firm and not received full satisfaction, can sue any one of the partners for the full outstanding debt. This partner is then entitled to claim pro rata (proportionate) relief from the other partners.

The acts of the partners in carrying on the usual business of the firm are binding on that firm, provided they are within its normal scope and objects and also provided there is nothing to put a third party on his guard (i.e. raise suspicion). A partner in a business firm has implied authority to borrow money in the firm name, again provided there is nothing to put a prospective lender on his guard. In *Paterson Bros v Gladstone* (1891), the firm of P, builders and joiners, had three partners, R, W and J. W took full charge of finance. R took out a loan and granted security in the firm name through G, a moneylender, at 40 per cent interest. R then misappropriated the loan. The firm was not liable to repay G since the loan had been granted in suspicious circumstances. A business firm could easily have obtained a regular loan at a much lower rate of interest. G (the third party) was a moneylender, well experienced in financial matters. He ought to have been put on his guard.

Limited liability partnerships

4–11 The Limited Liability Partnership Act 2000 created a new legal body, the limited liability partnership (LLP). An LLP is a legal person, separate from its members, combining the organisational flexibility of a traditional partnership but allowing limited liability for its members. Contractually, an LLP has the capacity to contract as if it were a natural person. It would do so through its members, as agents for the LLP.

Agents

4–12 An agent is a person who has been authorised by another (the "principal") to act on his behalf in forming contracts with third parties. The agent will not wish to be a party to the contract but will bring the principal and the third party into a contractual relationship. As mentioned above, the capacity of an agent cannot exceed that of his principal.

An agent may be said to have *actual* authority and this actual authority may be either express or implied. A third party is entitled to presume that an agent has the normal powers that an agent in his position would usually have, unless there is something to put him on his guard. In the latter case, the third party cannot be said to be acting in good faith until he satisfies himself on this matter. So, provided an agent is acting within the normal area of authority of a person in his position, he can bind his principal contractually, even although the principal may not have authorised what he has done. This is always subject to the third party having acted in good faith.

There can even be times when an agent has been expressly forbidden from forming certain contracts or has had some unusual restriction placed on his authority—and yet, he can still contractually bind his principal. Provided the agent acts within the normal scope of an agent of his type and the third party has no knowledge of the restriction, or is not put on his guard, the agent can bind his principal. This is called *apparent* or *ostensible* authority. The agent has no authority at all; he only appears to have it. Although the contract between the agent and the third party is valid, the agent may still be liable in damages to his principal for disobeying his clear instructions. In *Watteau v Fenwick* (1893), the manager of a public bar was instructed not to buy supplies for use in the bar. This was an unusual restriction. A cigar salesman, who knew nothing of this arrangement, came into the bar and, in good faith, sold the manager a quantity of cigars for resale. The bar owner refused to pay for them, claiming that the manager had no authority to buy such supplies. Since the third party (the cigar salesman) had no notice of the restriction and there was nothing to put him on his guard, the contract was valid. The bar manager had acted within his ostensible authority. His principal, the bar owner, was contractually bound.

---

1. Age of Legal Capacity (Scotland) Act 1991 (c.50) (ALCSA 1991) s.1(1).
2. ALCSA 1991 s.2(1).
3. ALCSA 1991 s.3(2).
4. ALCSA 1991 s.2(4A), inserted by the Children (Scotland) Act 1995 (c.36) Sch.4 para.53(3).
5. Sale of Goods Act 1979 (c.54) s.3(2).
6. See, e.g. the Adult Support and Protection (Scotland) Act 2007 (asp 10).
7. Partnership Act 1890 (c.39) s.35.
8. Erskine, I, 3, 16.
9. See, e.g. *Pollock v Burns* (1875) 2 R. 497, explained in Ch.3.
10. The action to prevent broadcast did, however, succeed on other grounds.
11. Trading With the Enemy Act 1939 (c.89) s.2.
12. See, e.g. *Zinc Corp Ltd v Hirsch* [1916] 1 K.B. 541.
13. Companies Act 2006 (c.46) ss.39–40.
14. *Boston Deep Sea Fishing and Ice Co Ltd v Farnham* [1957] 3 All E.R. 204.
15. *McMeekin v Easton* (1889) 16 R. 363.
16. Partnership Act 1890 (c.39) s.4(2).

5. ERROR AND MISREPRESENTATION

When a contract is formed, the parties to it may be completely unaware of any relevant legal requirements. As a result, they may have a contract which is *ex facie* (on the face of it) perfectly valid but which, in some way, is defective. This might be due to an issue already discussed in previous chapters, such as Cheryl being unaware that Deborah lacks capacity, or Eddie being unaware that the contract to sell his house to Frank should be in writing. Another commonly encountered problem is where one party makes a mistake (an "error") during contractual negotiations and agrees to something that he may not have, had he known the truth. This problem can become even more serious if this error was due to misrepresentations made by the other party. **5–01**

VALIDITY OF CONTRACTS

Depending on the form of the defect, the contract may turn out to be "void" or "voidable". The distinction between these is crucial and they will now be separately examined. **5–02**

Void "contracts"
Basically, a contract is void if, for any reason, the element of consensus is lacking. Strictly speaking, it is illogical to refer to a "void contract", since there is no contract and there never has been. For reasons of brevity, however, it is convenient to use this term. **5–03**

Lack of true consent may arise in a number of situations. It might be that one or both of the parties lacks capacity (as discussed in Ch.4) or that there is a misunderstanding about the subject matter of the contract.[1] If an apparently valid contract is void, for whatever reason, it has no legal effect and must be treated as though it has never existed. The contract (obviously) cannot be enforced by the courts.

Third parties may also be affected if a contract is void. Even if third parties act in good faith (honestly) and without knowledge of its nullity, they cannot acquire any rights through a void contract. A simple example would be stolen goods, which can never be the subject of a valid contract; no matter how many times they change hands, stolen goods remain the property of their original owner.

For example, in *O'Neil v Chief Constable of Strathclyde* (1994), one car was exchanged (bartered) for another car which turned out to have been stolen. The car that had *not* been stolen was sold to a third party who took it in good faith and paid a fair price. The court held that because one stolen car had been involved, the original contract of barter was void. The third party could not acquire rights to the non-stolen car. (However, it would be open for the third party to sue the seller he had dealt with.)

37

Voidable contracts

5–04 If a defect in a contract does not strike at the root of the agreement and does not, therefore, remove the basic consensus, the contract is not void, merely voidable. (A contract could also be voidable because of some defect in its formation, e.g. if a contract for the sale of a house is not in writing, as explained in Ch.3.) If a contract is voidable, it is valid until steps are taken to have it "avoided", which basically means cancelled.[2] The parties therefore have two options: either they can ignore the defect and treat the contract as fully binding, or one of them can use the defect as a means of setting the contract aside.

A particularly important point to note is the different position of third parties when compared with void contracts. If goods, property or rights which have changed hands under a voidable contract are subsequently transferred to a third party, that third party does acquire ownership of them, so long as he has acted in good faith and for value and, at the time of transfer, the original contract has not been avoided. To put it simply, a third party can acquire rights when the "original" contract was voidable, but can never acquire rights when the original contract was void. (This distinction is explained in greater detail below.)

The right to cancel a voidable contract may be lost in certain cases, such as where the parties cannot restore each other to their former positions, known as restitutio in integrum (entire restoration). As indicated above, a third party cannot be required to give up goods acquired in good faith and for value. This has a further important knock-on effect; if the third party has acquired goods in such a manner, the original voidable contract can no longer be set aside. Personal bar may also operate to prevent the contract being avoided.

THE EFFECT OF ERROR ON CONTRACTS

5–05 Either party (or both parties) to a contract may have entered into it under some form of error and this may well affect the validity of the contract. In the first instance, errors can be divided into two distinct categories: errors of law and errors of fact.

An error as to law could arise where one or other of the parties was in error in relation to his rights (or his obligations) or to the legal effect of the contract. The general rule is that an error as to law does not affect the validity of a contract, as summarised by the well-known legal maxim *ignorantia juris neminem excusat* (ignorance of the law is no excuse). In the English case of *CSC Computer Sciences Ltd v McAlinden* (2013), CSC awarded pay increases to certain employees in the mistaken belief that they were under a legal obligation to do so. It was decided that the employees were entitled to retain these pay increases in spite of the employer's error.

It is, however, worth noting that it *might* be possible in some cases to recover money that has been paid over erroneously, as per the decision in *Morgan Guaranty Trust of New York v Lothian RC* (1995). Such a claim for "repetition" (repayment) is not strictly part of the law of contract, rather it is available as an equitable remedy known as the *condictio indebiti*, under the rules of unjustified enrichment.

An error as to fact arises when one or both of the parties are mistaken as to some fact connected with the contract, e.g. the price of the goods. Error as to fact is much more relevant for present purposes, as it can affect the validity of a contract in different ways. What follows hereafter is an examination of the legal effect of errors of fact in different situations.

ERROR OF EXPRESSION

Errors of expression can arise where there is no doubt what both parties meant but, owing to a clerical error of a third party, the written contract is not expressed in the terms originally agreed by the parties. In *Anderson v Lambie* (1954), the owner of an estate, of which a farm formed part, agreed to sell only the farm. Due to a mistake by his solicitor, the entire estate was conveyed to the buyer. As the disposition (the deed which conveys heritable property) did not give effect to the original agreement, the court reduced the disposition so that a new one, which would only include the farm, could be recorded in its place.

5–06

Krupp v John Menzies Ltd (1907) is a case that perpetuates an unfortunate clerk's arithmetical error. K was the manager of a hotel, owned by J. At the time of her appointment there was a verbal agreement that, in addition to a basic salary, she would be paid 1/20th of the net annual profit of the hotel. A clerk was instructed to draw up a written agreement and he was given an old contract, referring to another hotel, to use as a style. In this old contract, the manager's share was shown as 1/10th of the net annual profits, but the clerk was told to halve this amount in the case of K's contract. The clerk was unable to calculate 1/2 of 1/10th and, by mistake, he inserted the figure of 1/5th in K's contract. After working for J for some years, K sued for payment of her share of the profits, claiming 1/5th as expressed in the written contract, rather than the 1/20th which had originally been agreed verbally. J was allowed to bring evidence to show what the original agreement between the parties had actually been.

In some ways, this type of error is not so much an error of fact as a defect in the way in which the contract is expressed. At common law, there is equitable power to deal with such situations by reducing the written document entirely, as demonstrated in the cases above. This can only take place after an action of reduction. There is a more simple statutory procedure to rectify documents that fail to express what the parties intended.[3] In practice, the statutory procedure is more usual than the common law action of reduction and tends to be less expensive. Another advantage of the statutory procedure is the power given to the court to change the wording of a document. At common law, the court can basically uphold or reduce a document (or parts of it) but cannot change it. A statutorily rectified document is, to all intents and purposes, counted as though it had always been in its rectified state. There is protection for third parties who have acted in good faith in reliance on the document in its original state.

Error of expression can also occur when a person expresses an offer in terms which he did not intend and the incorrect offer is accepted, e.g. quoting a lower price than intended. If the person accepting the offer knows that there is a mistake, the contract is probably void. If he does not know of the mistake, the position is less clear and all one can say is that the contract could be voidable in some circumstances. In *Seaton Brick & Tile Co Ltd v Mitchell* (1900), a contractor was held to be bound by a tender that had been based on his own miscalculations. However, in *Wilkie v Hamilton Lodging-House Co Ltd* (1902), a joiner offered to do certain work at "schedule rates" but undercharged his total bill through a miscalculation that was obvious on the face of the document; he was entitled to charge the full amount. (This matter is also considered under "unilateral error", below.)

If there is a faulty transmission of an offer, there will be no contract if the message delivered is substantially different from the original. In these days of fax and email, such problems are less common than they were when telegrams were sent down land-lines in Morse code. In *Verdin Bros v Robertson* (1871), an order made by telegram was incorrectly transmitted, with the result that the goods (and invoice) were sent to the wrong address. It was held that there was no consensus and thus no contract.

ERROR OF INTENTION

5–07 For there to be an error of intention, one or both of the parties must be mistaken as to the nature or subject matter of the contract which they are entering. This area can be divided into three aspects: (1) unilateral error; (2) common error; and (3) mutual error (incidental and essential). Common error and mutual error are sometimes said to be forms of "bilateral" error; this is a somewhat misleading term as it could be taken to imply that both parties must be in error, which, as will become clear, is not always the case.

Unilateral error

5–08 The general rule is that if the error is of one party only, this does not affect the validity of the contract. So, if a person with full contractual capacity freely and willingly pays more for something than it is worth or sells something for less than its true value, the contract cannot be set aside on these grounds alone.[4]

The situation is different, however, if the person was persuaded to enter the contract by fraud or misrepresentation (see below). In *Stewart v Kennedy* (1890), S agreed to sell heritable property to K, but because the property was subject to an entail (a restriction on its sale), the contract was "subject to the ratification of the court". S thought this phrase meant that the court would decide if the price was fair and reasonable, which was not so. The court held that this error on S's part would only be a ground for reducing the contract if it could be shown that the error was induced (caused) by the other party. In *Spook Erection (Northern) Ltd v Kaye* (1990), a business mistakenly believed that a property it was selling was subject to a 990-year lease, whereas it was only for 90 years. As there was no misrepresentation, the contract was valid.

Unilateral error could also be relevant where the other party *knew* that a mistake had been made and was prepared to take unfair advantage. In *Steuart's Trustees v Hart* (1875), a seller of land believed that it was burdened with an annual feu-duty[5] of £9.75, whereas the true amount was 15p, making the capital value of the land considerably greater. The buyer knew the correct amount of feu-duty and also knew of the seller's mistake. The court reduced the contract of sale.

It is a somewhat different matter if one side makes a mistake but the other party genuinely does not know of it. In *Steel's Trustee v Bradley Homes* (1972), one party agreed in writing to receive an interest payment on money but, unknown to the other party, had intended to request payment from two years earlier than the agreement provided. The contract stood.

Common error

Common or shared error can arise when both parties have made the *same* **5–09** mistake about a matter of fact. If the error is material (very important), the contract will be void. A statutory example is where there is a contract of sale of specific goods (e.g. a particular painting) which, unknown to the seller, have perished at the time the contract is made. In such circumstances, the contract is void.[6]

However, if the common error is really just a matter of opinion, as distinct from a genuine error of fact, the contract will be valid. In *Dawson v Muir* (1851), M sold certain vats to D for £2. Both parties were of the opinion that they were only of scrap value. Subsequently, it was found that they contained white lead, valued at £300. M wished the contract to be set aside but, as there was no error of fact, the contract stood.

Mutual error

This refers to a situation where, for reasons good or bad, the parties have **5–10** misunderstood one another. Each party thinks consensus has been achieved, but each has a different perception of what has been agreed. In such a situation, the courts will look at the terms of any written contract or the prior negotiations in reaching a judgment.

If the misunderstanding does not go to the heart or "root" of the contract, it is deemed "incidental".[7] Incidental errors do not prevent basic consensus and therefore the contract will stand (unless the error was induced by misrepresentation, in which case the contract may be voidable). In *Cloup v Alexander* (1831), the manager of a company of French comedians hired an Edinburgh theatre "for their performances". The comedians subsequently discovered that it was illegal for them to present their performances in that particular theatre. They were still obliged to pay the rent. The error in this case was a secondary or collateral issue, namely what kind of act could be put on in the theatre. The essential part of the contract was the hire of the building, which had been done without any reference to the kind of act which was to be performed. Furthermore, there had been no misrepresentation on the part of the owners of the theatre.

If the misunderstanding is material, and goes to the root of the contract, it is deemed "essential".[8] An essential error will render the contract void, as there is no true consensus. Per Lord Watson in *Menzies v Menzies* (1893), an error is essential "whenever it is shown that, but for it, one of the parties would have declined to contract." Traditionally, essential error occurs in five possible situations, although these should not be regarded as exhaustive.

Subject matter

5–11 This arises when the parties believe they are in agreement as to which item or service forms the subject matter whereas, in fact, they have different things in mind.[9] In *Scriven v Hindley* (1913), a bidder at an auction sale put up a bid for a barrel which he thought contained hemp. In fact, it contained considerably cheaper tow. The bidder was not bound by the contract.

More recently, in *Kyle Bay Ltd v Underwriters* (2007), a misunderstanding about the way in which an insurance settlement would be calculated was deemed insufficient to void the contract because the true subject matter was not "essentially and radically different" from what the party in error believed.

Price

5–12 The fact that a price has not been fixed does not make a contract void as a matter of course. If it has not been fixed (or some clear reference system put in place to ascertain the price) this usually means that the parties are still at the pre-contract stage of negotiation. However, it is possible for both parties to think that a price has been fixed whereas, in fact, they have different prices in mind. In such circumstances, the contract will be void. In *McLaughlin v The New Housing Association Ltd* (2008), the parties had different understandings as to the statutory calculation to be used to fix the price in a "right to buy" house purchase and the contract was reduced.

If one party has already performed under the contract, there may be practical problems where the goods have been consumed or are in such a condition that it is impracticable to return them to their original owner. If the goods cannot be returned, the courts have power both at common law and by statute[10] to fix a reasonable price. In *Stuart & Co v Kennedy* (1885), the parties were at cross purposes as to how an order for stone was to be priced, which only became evident once the stone was in place. The contract was void, but it was not practicable to dig up the stone, and so the buyer had to pay the market price. A similar solution was applied in *Wilson v Marquis of Breadalbane* (1859), where there was a genuine misunderstanding about the price of cattle.

Identity
In many cases, it matters little with whom a party actually contracts. **5–13**
However, there are times when identity can be of the essence of a contract. There are certainly cases where *delectus personae* (choice of person) applies. Common sense indicates that if Geraldine wants her portrait painted by Harriet, she need not accept a portrait painted by somebody else instead. But what if the identity of the parties is not relevant to the contract? If one party makes an error in this situation, does this make the contract void? Perhaps, as the following cases demonstrate.

In *Morrisson v Robertson* (1908), a con-man named Telford (T) introduced himself to M, a cattle dealer, fraudulently claiming to be the son of Wilson of Bonnyrigg, a dairy farmer of good credit, who was known to M. T, alias Wilson, also claimed that he had been given authority by his father to buy two cows from M on "the usual credit terms". M was totally deceived and gave the cows to T without hesitation, on the basis of Wilson of Bonnyrigg's good standing. T had no intention of paying for the cows. He sold them on to a third party, R, who bought in good faith and for value. When M realised that he had been tricked, he made enquiries and found that the cows were in R's possession. T had disappeared by this time and there was no immediate prospect of raising an action against him. M sued R for the return of the cows. The court decided that the original contract between M and T was void because of the error in M's mind as to the true identity of T. The latter had never owned the cows and so he could not pass ownership to R, the third party, even though R had acted in good faith. The cows still legally belonged to M, who was entitled to recover them. R was entitled to sue T for return of his money.

This case should be contrasted with *MacLeod v Kerr* (1965). K advertised his car for sale. A con-man named Galloway (G), who told K his name was Craig, responded to the advertisement and agreed to buy the car. He wrote out a cheque for the required amount and signed it "L Craig". K gave G the registration document and G drove the car away. When K presented the cheque it was dishonoured by the bank, as it was from a stolen chequebook and the signature was a forgery. The police were informed. A few days later, G, now giving his name as Kerr, sold the car to Gibson, a garage proprietor, who bought in good faith. G was subsequently arrested and convicted of criminal charges. The question now to be resolved was the ownership of the car. MacLeod, the procurator fiscal, raised an action of multiplepoinding to allow the civil courts to decide on the matter. K argued that there had been essential error of identity, which made the original contract void. If he had succeeded in such a submission, the car would still have belonged to him. However, the court held that the car belonged to Gibson, the third party. The original contract between K and G had not been void, merely voidable. When the contract was formed, there was no error in K's mind as to the identity of the person with whom he was contracting: it was the man in front of him, whether he called himself Galloway or Craig. This was not a case of essential error as to the identity of the party, so *Morrisson v Robertson* was not applied. Even although the original contract had been voidable through induced incidental error, it could no longer be set aside because the third party (Gibson) had acquired rights.

In two English cases involving identity, contracts were held to be voidable. In *Phillips v Brooks* (1919), a trickster visiting a jeweller's shop claimed to be Sir George Bullough. The shop owner checked a directory and found that there was such a person at the address given and allowed the trickster to take away a ring on credit. In *Lewis v Averay* (1971) a con-man obtained credit by claiming to be the actor Richard Greene (best remembered for his role as "Robin Hood") and by producing a Pinewood Studios card.

However, a more recent English case perhaps demonstrates a different approach. In *Shogun Finance Ltd v Hudson* (2004), a rogue purchased a car on hire-purchase using a stolen driving licence in the name of Patel. The finance company conducted a credit check on the name given and approved the sale. The next day, "Patel" sold the car to H, who bought it in good faith and for value. When the fraud came to light and the dispute went to court, H argued that he had obtained a good title to the car. This was based on the Hire Purchase Act 1964, which protects a bona fide third party who purchases a car that is still subject to a hire-purchase agreement. However, ultimately the House of Lords held by a 3:2 majority that the original contract was void, as the finance company had only intended to contract with the *genuine* Mr Patel, on whom the credit check had been satisfactory. Therefore, no rights could be transferred to H, who had to return the car.

Quantity, quality or extent

5–14 Some authorities take the view that this is really just another example of error as to the subject matter (above) rather than a distinct category of its own. However, even if there is consensus regarding subject matter, there can still be an error made relating to the quantity, quality or extent of that subject matter. In *Patterson v Landsberg & Son* (1905), P bought from a London dealer certain items of jewellery, which appeared to be antique. They were actually reproductions, a fact which the seller disguised. The contract was void, as there had been a crucial error made as to the quality of the goods.

It would be less relevant, of course, if two parties made the same mistake. In the more recent case of *Lyon & Turnbull v Sabine* (2012), both parties to the sale of a table believed it to be an antique, when instead it was a reproduction. The contract stood, the case being distinguished from *Patterson* on the grounds that there had been no misrepresentation by the seller. The result of this was akin to that of common error (as explained above).

Nature of the contract

5–15 It seems that this kind of error can only arise in the case of a written contract. For example, someone might sign a document that he did not intend to, or in a way in which he did not intend, such as signing as a witness only to find that he was a party to the deed. Where the document concerns a gratuitous obligation (see Ch.3), error as to its nature justifies reduction. In *McLaurin v Stafford* (1875), a party thought he was signing a will, when in fact he was signing a disposition; the document was reduced. Similarly, in the more recent *Edgar v Edgar* (2014), a disposition was reduced on the grounds that the party signing it thought it was a loan agreement.

However, in normal transactions, the law is not generally sympathetic to individuals who, without being induced by misrepresentation, sign solemn undertakings and subsequently claim not to have fully understood them. This has long been the case; in *Selkirk v Ferguson* (1908), an action of reduction failed after a party signed a contractual document believing it to be identical to an earlier draft, when in fact a material alteration had been made. This same principle can still be seen in operation in recent decisions. In *Barr v Dunbar Assets Plc* (2016), a businessman sought reduction of a document he had signed as personal guarantor of a business debt, claiming he believed he was signing as a joint guarantor; his action failed.

Although the courts are unwilling to overturn clear written agreements, it appears that they are willing to reduce certain agreements where there is a lack of good faith towards spouses who agree to act as guarantor, or "cautioner" to use the precise term. It is fair to say there has been considerable judicial development of this particular area. In *Royal Bank of Scotland Plc v Purvis* (1990), a wife acted as cautioner for money lent by R to her husband and signed a formal document accordingly. R subsequently raised an action against the wife for payment of all sums due. The wife claimed that she had signed the cautionary obligation at the request of her husband, that it had not been explained to her and that she was unfamiliar with commercial terms. She claimed that the document was void on the grounds of essential error as to its nature. The court held that, since the wife knew she was signing a document in favour of a bank which gave rise to obligations, it could not look into what was in her mind when she signed. Accordingly, she was thus bound by it.

A different approach was taken in the later case of *Smith v Bank of Scotland* (1997). Here, a wife was persuaded by her husband to sign a standard security over their matrimonial home in favour of the bank, effectively acting as cautioner for her husband's debt. The House of Lords held that a bank is under a duty to advise a cautioner spouse (or indeed anyone in a similarly intimate relationship) to take independent advice. This decision appeared to bring Scots law "into line" with a previous English decision, *Barclays Bank Plc v O'Brien* (1994), and is as clear an example as one might find of the courts creating new law.

However, judicial response to the *Smith* case has been somewhat mixed, with subsequent decisions keeping the scope of the good faith duty very narrow. In *Forsyth v Royal Bank of Scotland Plc* (2000), it was held that the bank had no duty to advise a cautioner spouse where it had reasonable grounds to believe that she already had access to a solicitor, and in *Clydesdale Bank Plc v Black* (2002), the duty was held to have been satisfied where the lending bank had followed current best practice. In the more recent case of *Cooper v Bank of Scotland Plc* (2014), there was no evidence that the bank had taken any steps at all to warn a spouse of the potential consequences of signing a standard security. It was held that they had not satisfied the good faith duty and the security was reduced.

MISREPRESENTATION

5–16 It could be said that misrepresentation is really just part of error. It is fairly obvious that, in at least some of the cases considered above, the "misunderstanding" between the parties arose from the conduct or statements of one party to the other. If one party makes such a statement to another, and that statement is false, this is called a misrepresentation.

Misrepresentation can have at least two effects on a contractual situation. First, if the misrepresentation induces an error on the part of the other party, the validity of the contract might be affected as outlined above. Secondly, if the party making the misrepresentation did so either fraudulently or negligently, the misled party might also have the right to claim damages.

There are, then, three distinct types of misrepresentation: (1) innocent; (2) fraudulent; and (3) negligent. Although it might be inferred from the paragraph above, it is worth clarifying that innocent misrepresentation does not give rise to a claim for damages, whilst the other two forms potentially do.

Innocent misrepresentation

5–17 If a person makes a false statement, honestly believing it to be true, the misrepresentation counts as innocent—provided there is no negligence. If this innocent misrepresentation induces an essential error, the contract may be void. If an incidental error is induced, the contract may be voidable. However, before a contract can be reduced on the grounds of innocent misrepresentation, the misrepresentation must have been more than merely trivial and must have been relied on by the party misled, inducing him to enter the said contract. In addition, the party wishing to reduce must be in a position to give restitutio in integrum (entire restoration to the original position). If this is not possible, the contract will generally have to stand.

In *Ferguson v Wilson* (1904), W, an engineer in Aberdeen, advertised for a partner to join him and invest in what he called an "established business". F replied to the advertisement and, in the course of negotiations, W was very optimistic about future business prospects. Encouraged by W's enthusiasm, F agreed to become his partner and invest in the business. F soon found that W's optimism about the state of the business had been misplaced. He raised an action to reduce the partnership agreement on the grounds of essential error, which he claimed was induced by W's fraudulent misrepresentation of the overall position of the firm. The court held that there had been misrepresentation and restitutio in integrum was possible, so the partnership agreement was set aside. However, the court felt that there had been no fraud, merely innocent misrepresentation, so no damages were awarded.

In *Boyd & Forrest v Glasgow & South Western Railway Co* (1912), B, contracting engineers, agreed to build a new stretch of railway track for G. The price was fixed by B at £243,000 based on data provided by G, especially particulars of test borings taken along the proposed route. B subsequently found that the information with which they had been supplied was materially inaccurate, making the work much more difficult and expensive than they had contemplated. It turned out that the original test borings, and the figures produced from them, had been the work of independent surveyors and were accurate. However, G's own engineer disagreed with some of the figures and had altered them. He had done so with the best of intentions because he honestly believed that they were inaccurate. Despite many problems, B completed the track but at a cost of £379,000, more than £100,000 above the contract price. B sued G for damages on the grounds that, having been supplied with misleading information, they had been induced to enter the contract by fraudulent misrepresentation. The House of Lords decided that there had been no fraud since G's engineer had altered the figures only because he honestly believed them to be inaccurate. If there had been any misrepresentation at all, it was innocent and thus no damages could be awarded.

Fraudulent misrepresentation

Like innocent misrepresentation, fraudulent misrepresentation may induce error, making the contract void or voidable. If the error is essential, the contract is void, otherwise it is voidable. "Trade puffs" or *verba jacantia* (words thrown about) are allowed some degree of latitude in practice, since few people take claims such as "good value" or "superior quality" too seriously. However, the Consumer Protection from Unfair Trading Regulations 2008[11] do provide certain criminal sanctions where there is material misdescription of goods or services.[12] There are similar provisions regulating potentially false or misleading statements about heritable property made by solicitors, estate agents or property developers.

Where a statement of opinion—which turns out to be wrong—is made in the course of business and, in context, is reasonably relied on, it may count as a misrepresentation, though it is more likely to be counted as negligent than fraudulent. A statement of pure future intention such as "I am hoping to expand my business over the next five years" is not a misrepresentation since, as a pure future statement, it is neither true nor false. If, however, a future statement relies on some present fact and is unreliable, it is not "pure" and may count as misrepresentation. In *British Airways Board v Taylor* (1976), an airline knowingly overbooked certain flights, but confirmed to a customer that there was a seat on a particular plane. This was held not to be a pure future statement. Even allowing for likely cancellations, the airline knew that it could not guarantee a seat.

As stated above, a victim of fraud is potentially entitled to damages since fraud is a delict (a "civil wrong"). It may also be criminal, but need not be

5–18

for damages to be claimed. At common law, the *acti quanti minoris* (very loosely meaning "something off the price") probably did not form part of Scots law. This interpretation meant that defective property could not be retained by the "innocent" party *and* the price be reduced by the damages claimed. The contract had to be cancelled and the property returned before the claim for damages could be entertained. This rule was formally abolished by the Contract (Scotland) Act 1997. In any event, the courts seemed to take a more lenient view in the case of fraud. Even before the 1997 Act, the deceived party could sue for damages even if he did not wish to reduce the contract. In *Smith v Sim* (1954), Sim advertised a public house in Montrose for sale and, through his solicitors, supplied certain figures about the turnover to Smith. Relying on these figures, Smith bought the business. He subsequently raised an action for damages claiming that the figures were fraudulent. He was entitled to proceed with his action and it was not necessary for him to rescind before doing so.

The rule regarding restitutio in integrum has also not been applied quite so strictly in the case of fraud. In *Spence v Crawford* (1939), S, a director of a private company, attempted to reduce a contract for the sale of shares to C, a fellow director, on the grounds of fraudulent misrepresentation. Although it was difficult for S to give exact restitutio in integrum, because of a change in value of the shares due to C's subsequent actions, a cash readjustment could achieve the equivalent of restitutio.

Misrepresentation is not fraudulent unless it was known to be untrue and conscious dishonesty must be proved. Mere carelessness is not fraud, but it may amount to negligence. *Bile Bean Manufacturing Co v Davidson* (1906) gives a classic example of fraud. B advertised "Bile Beans" as being manufactured from secret ingredients, known only to Australian Aborigines until discovered by a famous explorer. These claims were found to be totally fictitious. D was able to claim damages for fraudulent misrepresentation.

The most famous case in this area is probably *Derry v Peek* (1889). The directors of the Plymouth, Devonport and District Tramways Company issued a share prospectus stating that the company had the right to use steam power in its trams. D bought shares in the company on the strength of that statement. In fact, the company was only entitled to use steam power if it was issued with a Board of Trade certificate. The Board declined to issue such a certificate. D failed in his action for damages against the directors of the now insolvent company since the statement had been made in the honest belief that it was true, even although the directors had not taken all reasonable care to check their statements. The law on company prospectuses was changed by statute shortly afterwards and is now governed by the companies acts. It has been suggested that one of the effects of this case was to raise the civil burden of proof of fraud to virtually the equivalent of criminal proof.

Reference is made above to the 1912 case of *Boyd & Forrest*. In fact, the contractors were not finished with their litigation. Having lost their first action, B raised a second action—*Boyd & Forest v Glasgow & South*

Western Railway (1915)—this time for reduction of the original contract on the grounds that G's innocent misrepresentation made it voidable. If B had succeeded in reducing the contract, the track could obviously not have been torn up. However, B would have been able to claim the actual cost of the railway and at least would not be making a loss. The House of Lords was not convinced that there had been any misrepresentation. Even if there had been, B's claim failed. B had not proved that the alleged misrepresentation had actually induced them to enter the contract. Furthermore, having continued to work on the track, even after discovering the inaccuracy of information, B had personally barred themselves. Finally, even if the contract was voidable, it could not be reduced, because restitutio in integrum was impossible.

Today, few contractors would give a fixed price on a large undertaking such as laying a rail track. Furthermore, it is at least possible, if a similar situation did arise at the present time, that G could be sued for damages on the grounds of negligent misrepresentation.

Negligent misrepresentation
This is an area of law which has developed over time and is, in fact, still developing. One of the potentially confusing elements is the crossover between the law of delict and the law of contract. Negligence, i.e. failure in a duty of care, is a delict which can give rise to damages. There need not be any dishonesty involved and usually there is not. A representation is negligent if the person making it failed to take reasonable care in making the representation and he was under a legal duty to do so.

Hedley Byrne & Co Ltd v Heller & Partners Ltd (1964): HB were advertising agents who were asked by Easipower Ltd (E) to arrange their advertising. HB enquired into the financial soundness of E by requesting their own bank to write to H&P, bankers to E. H&P stated that E were financially stable enough to honour the contract. The letter from H&P was headed: "Confidential. For your private use and without responsibility on the part of this Bank". In reliance on the information contained in the letter, HB placed advertisements. Shortly afterwards, E went into liquidation, leaving HB with a substantial loss. It was clear, from subsequent enquiries, that E had been in considerable financial difficulties when H&P had made their reassuring statement. HB sued H&P for damages on the grounds of negligent misrepresentation. The case established that bankers do owe a duty of care in answering such enquiries where it is clear that recipients rely on them. However, no damages were due in this particular case because of the express provision that the information was given "without responsibility".

The above case really only dealt with the civil wrong or delictual aspects, but the basic principle was extended to contractual matters in the case of *Esso Petroleum Co v Mardon* (1976). M wished to take the tenancy of a filling station owned by EP. An experienced sales representative of EP stated that by the third year of operation the through-put of petrol should be around 200,000 gallons a year. M relied on this information and entered into the tenancy agreement. He did not make the profit anticipated. When EP sued him for sums due, M counterclaimed on the grounds that EP's negligent misrepresentation had induced him to enter the contract. M's counterclaim was successful; a duty of care was owed by EP.

This case was subsequently applied in two Scottish cases: *Kenway v Orcantic Ltd* (1980), where a ship did not have the carrying capacity claimed and *Foster v Craigmiller Laundry Ltd* (1980), where there was an untrue statement that a factory was free from asbestos.

By statute, it is provided that damages for negligent misrepresentation are recoverable in Scotland.[13] This provision was relied upon in the case of *Cramaso LLP v Viscount Reidhaven's Trustees* (2014), where it was held that damages could be claimed as a result of negligent misstatements made regarding the population of a grouse moor.

Silence or concealment as misrepresentation

5–20 When parties enter a contract, they normally do so after negotiating "at arm's length". Neither party is going to volunteer information unless he has to. Say, for example, that Ian is negotiating with Jerry to purchase an antique painting. He offers to buy the painting for £200, a price which is acceptable to Jerry. If Ian knows that he already has a buyer lined up who will pay £500 for the same painting, he does not need to disclose this to Jerry.

As a general rule, contracting parties are expected to see to their own interests and satisfy themselves. This is sometimes expressed in the maxim *caveat emptor* (let the buyer beware). Although beyond the scope of this book, a buyer frequently has important statutory protection, particularly when purchasing as a consumer. What follows is basically the common law position.

If a direct question is put, it must be answered truthfully, otherwise the reply could count as fraudulent misrepresentation. Problems can arise, however, when nothing is said. Can silence count as misrepresentation? In *Gillespie v Russel* (1856), G, a land owner, sought to cancel a lease of mineral rights he had given to R. Apparently, R had known that the land in question contained a particularly valuable seam of coal, but G had been unaware of this fact at the time he gave over the lease. The lease was held to be valid as the concealment of such information by R was not fraud; he was merely seeing to his own interests. In *Royal Bank of Scotland v Greenshields* (1914), G undertook to act as cautioner for an individual whose bank account was overdrawn. RBS did not disclose that this customer also owed them other sums. G would not have acted as cautioner if he had known about the additional debt. G's caution was held to be valid, RBS having no duty to disclose the other debt. (It has already been discussed above that, following the decision of *Smith v Bank of Scotland* (1997), banks owe a duty of good faith towards a cautioner who is in an intimate relationship with the debtor.)

There can, however, be cases in which silence is, in fact, a subtle form of misrepresentation. *Gibson v National Cash Register Co* (1925): G ordered two new cash registers from NCR. He was actually supplied with two second-hand machines, reconditioned to look like new. This was clearly fraudulent.

The courts have also more recently been influenced by English judicial decisions to the effect that there *might* sometimes arise a positive "duty to disclose" in commercial relationships. In *Hamilton v Allied Domecq Plc* (2007), H agreed to undertake a joint business venture with AD. It was H's understanding that a certain product strategy (suggested by him) would be followed, but this did not in fact happen. The venture failed, and H claimed that AD had misrepresented their intentions by allowing him to believe that his strategy would be followed. The House of Lords acknowledged that, in limited circumstances, a failure to speak could give rise to liability in delict, but decided that there had not, in this case, been any misrepresentation.

A further problematic area is where parties are "economical with the truth". In fact, half-truths can be every bit as misleading as complete untruths. A second-hand car dealer might truthfully tell a prospective customer that a particular car has been "thoroughly checked". But if nothing had been done to cure the many faults discovered by the check, the assurance would be worthless. In *Shankland v Robinson* (1920) the seller of a machine stated to a prospective purchaser that it was not going to be requisitioned by the government. In fact, it was requisitioned when the parties were still negotiating, but the seller failed to inform the prospective buyer—a subtle form of misrepresentation.

Contracts not subject to the "arm's length" rule
Having established the general "arm's length" rule, there may be occasions 5–21
where parties to a contract *do* require to make full disclosure to one another. In other words, they do not merely contract at arm's length. Contracts which are not subject to the arm's length rule fall into two main categories.

Contracts uberrimae fidei *(of utmost good faith)*
These are contracts of so-called utmost good faith, insurance or partnership 5–22
being the two generally accepted categories. This is no mere academic matter as, in all insurance contracts, the policy will be voidable if the party insured has failed to disclose some material fact which might affect the risk being undertaken by the insurer, even if the insurer did not ask a specific question relating to it. This is powerfully illustrated by the case of *The Spathari* (1925). D, a Greek ship broker, resident in Glasgow, bought the SS Spathari, a Finnish ship at Hull, with the intention of selling her to a syndicate of Greeks at Samos. At the time, Greek vessels had great difficulty in getting insurance due to poor safety records. D came to an arrangement with B, a Glasgow ship broker, that the ship would be transferred into B's name, that the latter would register and insure her, ostensibly as owner, until the voyage to Samos was complete. On the voyage to Greece, the Spathari sank. The insurance company was entitled to refuse payment on account of B's failure to disclose a material fact, namely the "Greek" element of the boat, even though that element might appear somewhat tenuous.

Contracts involving a fiduciary relationship

5–23 These are contracts where the parties stand in a relationship of trust to one another, e.g. parent and child, agent and principal, solicitor and client. Common sense would indicate that such parties do not normally contract with each other as strangers. Solicitors have strict professional rules about making contracts with clients outwith the provision of normal professional services. *McPherson's Trustees v Watt* (1877): W, an advocate in Aberdeen, arranged for a trust, to which he was solicitor, to sell four houses to his brother. W did not disclose that his brother had already agreed to resell him two of the houses at a favourable price. W should have made full disclosure to the trust about the true nature of the transaction. The contract of sale was void.

OTHER FACTORS AFFECTING VALIDITY

5–24 In the following situations, the validity of the contract is affected because the consent of one of the parties has been improperly obtained.

Facility and circumvention

5–25 A contract can be reduced where the party misled is not necessarily lacking in mental capacity, but is suffering from weakness of mind due to old age or ill health, i.e. there is a "facility". Circumvention is the motive to mislead, falling short of actual fraud. If both factors are present and the party misled suffers some kind of harm or loss as a result of the contract, it is voidable.

A classic and somewhat melodramatic case is *Cairns v Marianski* (1850), where F, an elderly man, living with a daughter and son-in-law, M, transferred property to the son-in-law. After F's death, C, his other daughter, successfully had the transfer documents reduced. There was evidence that F had been under the "command and control" of M. Similarly, in *MacGilvary v Gilmartin* (1986), M, the executor of his late mother's estate, successfully raised an action to reduce a deed which she had signed transferring heritable property to his sister. When she signed the deed, the mother was severely depressed, due to the death of her husband and the daughter had taken advantage of this situation. By contrast, in *Smyth v Romanes' Executors* (2014), an action for reduction failed because there was no clear evidence of circumvention.

Undue influence

5–26 A contract is voidable if one person is in a position to influence another and abuses this position to induce this other party to make the contract to his disadvantage. Although similar to facility and circumvention (and indeed often pled as an alternative), there is no need to prove that the weaker party was subject to any weakness of mind. In *Gray v Binny* (1879) a father left an estate to his son by will. His mother persuaded the son (with the help of the family solicitor to whom she owed money) to transfer the estate to her. The transfer was subsequently reduced. The mother and the solicitor had taken advantage of the son's ignorance as to his rights and of the fact that he had confidence in them.

Undue influence is most likely to occur in fiduciary relationships, such as doctor to patient or solicitor to client. There is no set list, so in theory it could take place in any relationship where there is an element of confidence. A useful (and recent) summary of the relevant principles can be found in *Matossian v Matossian* (2016), in which the relationship was that of child to elderly parent.

Force and fear
Generally, if a contract is entered into because of force or fear it is void **5–27** through lack of true consent. The threats may be physical or mental, e.g. "blackmail", and could be made in respect of a near relative as well as to the victim himself. In *Gow v Henry* (1899), a threat to dismiss a workman from his post, without just cause, counted as force and fear. However, a threat to do something legal, such as pursuing a legitimate debt, or asking a dishonest employee to resign rather than call in the police, is not force and fear. In the very old case of *Earl of Orkney v Vinfra* (1606), the Earl commanded V to sign a contract. V refused, but then did so when the Earl threatened to kill him. The contract was void. In *Hunter v Bradford Trust Ltd* (1977), two sisters in financially embarrassed circumstances came to an arrangement with a property company over the sale by roup (auction) of certain heritable property. On the night before the roup, a director of the company discovered that the signed agreement did not reflect what he thought the terms of the contract were. He refused to proceed with the sale until the sisters signed a new agreement. After prolonged discussion well into the night, the sisters signed the new agreement, which was less favourable to them than the first. They were not successful in their attempt to have the second agreement reduced. In *Hislop v Dickson Motors (Forres) Ltd* (1978), a cashier was accused by her employers of embezzling certain funds. She admitted the accusation and agreed to try to repay the money. She voluntarily handed over her car and a blank bank deposit account withdrawal form. The employer subsequently discovered that she also had a current account. Two representatives of the employing company went to her house and after heated words, she gave them a blank signed cheque, with which they withdrew the current account balance. At her trial, the charge against the cashier was "not proven". In a subsequent civil action, she was unsuccessful in attempting to have the delivery of the car and the deposit account withdrawal form set aside. However, the signature on the blank cheque was set aside on the grounds that her consent had been vitiated by force and fear.

Extortionate terms
The general rule is that a contract is neither void nor voidable merely on the **5–28** grounds of being a poor bargain. In *M'Lachlan v Watson* (1874), M took a 10-year lease of a Glasgow hotel under an arrangement that could not, by

any standards, have been considered to be anything other than a poor bargain and which included payment of an annual "bonus" of £600 to W. M died four years into the lease but his widow was unsuccessful in her attempts to have the lease reduced.

However, there are undoubtedly times when parties are not negotiating from equal bargaining positions, which might result in someone accepting disadvantageous terms purely due to a lack of alternatives. There are statutory protections in place regulating this (see Ch.7), but mention can usefully be made here of consumer credit agreements. Under statute, the court has power to re-open and alter or set aside any credit agreement if it deems there is an unfair relationship between the parties.[14] There are few set rules laid down as to what "unfair" means, but factors which the court might take into account are: the terms of the agreement; the conduct of the creditor; and any other matter relating to the debtor or creditor. Of particular relevance is the interest rate applied, which cannot be extortionate; perhaps the most prominent example of this is the often controversial "high-cost short-term credit" (often referred to as "payday loans"), which have been the subject of recent regulation.[15]

SUMMARY OF FACTORS AFFECTING VALIDITY[16]

Error
5–29
1. Of law—no effect on the contract.
2. In transmission—no contract.
3. Of expression—reduction at common law or statutory rectification.
4. Of intention:
    (a) unilateral—contract valid;
    (b) common—contract void, but only if error is essential and refers to facts, not merely opinion; or
    (c) mutual—contract valid if error is collateral, but void if essential.

Misrepresentation
5–30
1. Fraudulent and negligent—contract voidable if misrepresentation is collateral and void if the misrepresentation is essential; damages in either case, but in delict rather than contract. Contract cannot generally be set aside if: third parties have acquired rights in good faith and for value; restitutio in integrum is not possible; or personal bar has operated.
2. Innocent—as above, but no damages.

Force and fear
5–31 Contract void.

Facility and circumvention and undue influence
5–32 Contract voidable.

1. As was the case in *Raffles v Wichelhaus* (1864) 2 Hurl. & C. 906, explained in Ch.1.
2. Commonly encountered synonymous terms include "set aside" and "reduced".
3. Law Reform (Miscellaneous Provisions) (Scotland) Act 1985 (c.73) ss.8–9; for a more recent case see *Albyn Housing Society Ltd v Active Sustainable Energy Systems* [2016] CSOH 110.
4. This rule finds one exception in the case of gratuitous contracts.
5. A fee payable by the occupier of land.
6. Sale of Goods Act 1979 (c.54) s.6.
7. Also known as *error concomitans* (collateral error).
8. Also known as *error in substantialibus* (error in the substantials).
9. Reference can again be made to *Raffles v Wichelhaus* (1864) 2 Hurl. & C. 906.
10. Sale of Goods Act 1979 (c.54) s.8.
11. Consumer Protection from Unfair Trading Regulations 2008 (SI 2008/1277).
12. This area was formerly regulated by the Trade Descriptions Act 1968 (c.29).
13. Law Reform (Miscellaneous Provisions) (Scotland) Act 1985 (c.73) s.10.
14. Consumer Credit Act 1974 (c.39) ss.140A–140C, inserted by the Consumer Credit Act 2006 (c.14) ss.19–21.
15. For more information see the Financial Conduct Authority website: *http://www.handbook.fca.org.uk* [Accessed 22 May 2019].
16. Reproduced from D. Field and A. Gordon, *Elements of Scots Law*, 2nd edn (Edinburgh: W. Green, 1997).

6. ILLEGAL AGREEMENTS

A contract must be lawful, both in its objects and in the way it is performed. **6–01** If either of these elements are not satisfied, the courts will not enforce the agreement. Such agreements are known as *pacta illicita* (illegal agreements), although that title is somewhat misleading. It need not necessarily be illegal, in the sense of being criminal, to set up such agreements, but the courts will not enforce them nor will they award damages in the event of breach. Some of these agreements would more properly be termed "unenforceable".

GENERAL PRINCIPLES

The first general principle to consider is ex turpi causa non oritur actio (no **6–02** action arises out of an immoral situation) and it is the duty of the judge to take notice that it is an illegal agreement. In *Hamilton v Main* (1823), H sought to set aside a promissory note for £60 which he had granted to M in payment of an account for his stay at M's public house for a seven-day period. During that period, H had, in company with a prostitute, consumed a vast quantity of wines and spirits in a drunken orgy. The promissory note was unenforceable in law. In *Malik v Ali* (2004), A financed the purchase of a house, which was put into M's name. A lived in the house on the understanding that if the money was not repaid, ownership would be transferred to him. In fact, the whole arrangement was designed to assist M in securing a visa for her fiancé; the court accepted the possibility that the agreement between M and A could be a *pacta illicitum* and therefore unenforceable.

Another maxim in this area of law is in *turpi causa melior est conditio possidentis* (in an immoral situation, the position of the possessor is the better one). Thus, the loss is allowed to lie where it falls, e.g. a person pays money for an illegal drug, which is then not supplied. He will not be able to take legal steps to recover the money from the drug dealer. In *Barr v Crawford* (1983), a woman was informed that the chances of her taking over the licence of a public house from her late husband were not good. She paid out over £10,000 in bribes in an attempt to secure the transfer. She later sought to recover the bribe money, but her action was dismissed.

However, when the parties are not *in pari delicto* (equally at fault), the court may assist the party who is less blameworthy. In the English case of *Strongman v Sincock* (1955), architects had promised builders that they would obtain necessary building licences. They failed to do so, which made the completed building illegal. The builders were successful in their claim for damages against the architects.

STATUTORY ILLEGALITY

6–03 An Act of Parliament can place a limit on the freedom of a person to make a contract. Sometimes it may even declare a certain type of contract to be illegal, and therefore void. In either case, any such contract would be unenforceable.

However, the courts may give effect to rights which arise under the contract, to prevent one party from gaining an unfair advantage over another. In *Cuthbertson v Lowes* (1870), C sold L two fields of potatoes at £24 per Scots acre. Under the weights and measures acts, this contract was void, as imperial measures had become obligatory. L took delivery of the potatoes but did not pay the full price. C sued for the balance. Even though the contract could not be enforced by the court, C was entitled to the market value of the potatoes at the time of harvesting. By contrast, in *Jamieson v Watt's Trustee* (1950), W requested J, a joiner, to carry out certain work. Under the Defence Regulations 1939, this required a licence. J applied for a licence to carry out work valued at £40, knowing that the total cost would be higher. When he tendered an account of over £114, he was not entitled to claim the amount in excess of the licence figure. More recently, in *Allen v Hounga* (2014), it was held that being an illegal immigrant did not bar a worker from enforcing her employment rights.

Similarly, illegality of a contract will not necessarily prevent a party from recovering money paid in anticipation of performance. In *Patel v Mirza* (2016), M asserted that he had access to "insider" information which would soon influence the price of shares in the Royal Bank of Scotland. P paid M a substantial sum of money so that M could use this information for the benefit of both men, which constitutes a serious statutory offence. In time the expected inside information was not in fact forthcoming, so M never used P's money, although he failed to return it. In a lengthy dispute which was subject to much judicial consideration and ultimately decided by the Supreme Court, P succeeded in reclaiming the money.

In Ch.7 it will be demonstrated that it is illegal for parties to attempt to contract out of certain statutory provisions, such as those under the Consumer Rights Act 2015. Various forms of discrimination on the grounds of gender, race, disability and other characteristics are also prohibited by statute, by virtue of the Equality Act 2010.

ILLEGALITY AT COMMON LAW

6–04 A contract is illegal at common law if its purpose is criminal (e.g. to commit a murder), fraudulent (e.g. to swindle a third party), or immoral. In *Pearce v Brooks* (1886), a firm of coach builders agreed to hire out a specially constructed brougham carriage to a prostitute. The firm knew that she intended to use the carriage to ply her trade around the streets of London. She failed to pay the carriage hire, but the sum could not be recovered in court as the purpose of the contract was immoral.

AGREEMENTS CONTRARY TO PUBLIC POLICY

Public policy, like public morality, is notoriously difficult to define, **6–05** particularly in a complex modern society. Some agreements are clearly against public policy, such as contracting with an enemy alien or interfering with the administration of justice. Less easy are contracts that seek to restrict a person's freedom to work or to trade, e.g. upon termination of employment. Such restrictions might be legitimately motivated and reasonable in their terms, but the legal system has historically been reluctant to limit commercial freedom. A range of such agreements will now be considered.

Covenants in restraint of trade

A covenant in restraint of trade, also known as a "restrictive covenant", is **6–06** a contractual term which seeks to restrict a person's freedom to work or his freedom to carry on in business. The very general common law rule is that such conditions are void, unless it can be shown that the restrictions are reasonable both for the parties to the contract and for the public. The courts will also want to be convinced that the parties are contracting on equal terms.[1]

Certain types of agreement have been the subject of extensive common law development, of most relevance being employment contracts and contracts for the sale of a business.

Agreements between employers and employees

A restrictive covenant seeks to prevent an employee from working in **6–07** competition with his former employer in the future. This may be part of the employee's contract of employment and normally will only take effect when, for whatever reason, the employment comes to an end. Even if the employee is wrongfully dismissed, the restrictive covenant may still apply.[2] The covenants are probably most common in service industries or in businesses where there are trade secrets or sensitive information.

The courts do not generally take kindly to an individual being unreasonably restrained and such an agreement will not be enforced unless the employer can show that he is protecting his legitimate interests. In addition, the terms of the covenant must be reasonable in protecting this interest. When assessing reasonableness, the courts will consider factors such as the type of business, location, area of operations, and the status of the employee within the business.

For example, it is legitimate for an employer to protect his customer base, so a covenant may be upheld where it is likely that customers will be enticed away to a rival business by the outgoing employee.[3] It is also the case that former employees can be prevented from actively canvassing customers.[4] However, it is not legitimate to prevent fair competition, so a covenant that seeks to do this will be unenforceable.

Two similar, yet contrasting, cases might help to illustrate the delicateness of this balance. In *Fitch v Dewes* (1921), an outgoing solicitor's clerk who was well-known to the firm's clients was prevented from becoming engaged in a rival business within seven miles of his former employer's office. On the other hand, in *Dallas McMillan & Sinclair v Simpson* (1989), a 20-mile radius was deemed wider than necessary to protect the interests of a firm of Glasgow solicitors, due partly to the very dense population of the area.[5] Also of interest is the older case of *Stewart v Stewart* (1899), where a radius of 20 miles from Elgin *was* held to be reasonable and enforceable, but of course this is a far more thinly populated area.

It is also well-established that an employer is entitled to protect his trade secrets. A classic example is *Bluebell Apparel v Dickinson* (1980). D was taken on as a management trainee by B, manufacturers of "Wrangler" jeans. Within a few months, D was in sole charge of one of B's Scottish factories. Shortly afterwards, he intimated that he was leaving to take up a position with a rival jeans manufacturer, Levi Strauss & Co. The court held that the two-year worldwide restriction in his contract was enforceable, as both companies operated on a worldwide basis and D was in possession of trade secrets that would be of value to a business competitor.

A trade secret need not necessarily refer to a secret technical process. It could refer to any confidential information and would have to be a matter of proof in particular circumstances. In *TSB Bank Plc v Connell* (1997), the business of a bank—including the identities of customers, their banking arrangements and their family and financial circumstances—was included in this category.

The courts do not have power to change an agreement into which parties have voluntarily entered. Either the agreement stands or it falls. Anyone thus seeking to impose a restrictive covenant ought to bear this in mind. If the restrictive covenant is set aside by the court, it falls entirely and leaves no protection for the party who originally imposed it. *Empire Meat Co v Patrick* (1939): P was the manager of a butcher's shop. He was well known to the regular customers who came mainly from within a one-mile radius of the shop. On first taking up his employment, P had agreed that he would not set up business nor work for another butcher within a five-mile radius of his employer's premises. This restriction was too great and thus entirely unenforceable. A one-mile radius would have been acceptable but the court had no power to change the agreement.

There is yet a further complication. What if there are, say, two parts to the agreement, one of which seems reasonable and the other does not? Does the entire agreement fall? Provided the two parts are severable, i.e. capable of being separated and standing on their own, the court may be prepared to allow one part to stand but to delete ("blue pencil") the other part. However, as explained above, the court will not substitute a reasonable restriction for an unreasonable one. *Mulvein v Murray* (1908): Mulvein owned a footwear business, employing Murray as a travelling salesman. Murray had signed an agreement that he would not: (1) sell to or canvas any of Mulvein's customers; nor (2) sell or travel in any of the towns or districts traded in by Mulvein, for one year after leaving his employment. The first provision was reasonable but the second provision was not. The reasonable part of the restriction was severable (i.e. it could stand on its own) and thus enforceable. The other restriction was void.

Agreements between the buyer and seller of a business
When a purchaser buys the goodwill of a business, he will usually insist that **6–08** the seller binds himself not to set up in competition within a certain area and/or time. The courts are more willing in these cases to enforce the agreement, but the test of reasonableness will still apply. The agreements must not cover a longer period of time, nor a wider area of operations, than is necessary.

A famous case is *Nordenfelt v Maxim Nordenfelt Guns and Ammunition Co Ltd* (1894). N, the owner of a cannon manufacturing business sold it to M and agreed not to engage in the making of cannon anywhere in the world for 25 years. As the business was quite unique and customers so few—namely governments—the restriction, considering all the facts and circumstances of the case, was neither too wide nor contrary to the public interest. By contrast, in *Dumbarton Steamboat Co Ltd v MacFarlane* (1899), M was a partner in a carrier's business, that traded in the Glasgow area. The business was sold to D, who insisted that M agree not to carry on a similar business anywhere in the UK for a period of 10 years. A restriction affecting the entire UK was too wide, since D's area of operation was restricted to Glasgow and the West of Scotland. As in the case of employers and employees, the court had no power to vary or rewrite the agreement.

These two cases demonstrate that the question is very much one of degree and circumstances in each instance. A more recent case providing some useful modern commentary is *Agri Energy v McCallion* (2014), in which a five-year restriction covering the whole of Scotland was held to be reasonable and enforceable.

Joint agreements between manufacturers or traders
These types of agreement involve manufacturers and traders working **6–09** together to regulate markets and prices. Although not unknown in common law, these "cartels" are mainly regulated by statute and delegated legislation to protect the interests of the public. Until relatively recently they were perfectly legal and not uncommon in business. (More mature persons may also remember resale price maintenance, when the prices of the same goods in all shops were identical.)

Considerable water has flowed under the legal bridge in this area, the current law being found in the Competition Act 1998 and a range of EU legislation. Competition law is a subject in its own right and as such is beyond the scope of this book.

***Solus* agreements**
These are agreements between the supplier of goods and the distributor or **6–10** retailer under which the retailer sells only one brand of goods, in return for special discounts or privileges. Such *solus* (alone, only) agreements are

quite common but, if challenged, must again meet the reasonableness test. The relative bargaining position of the parties might also be taken into account.

In *Petrofina (GB) v Martin* (1966), M purchased a garage, which was the subject of a *solus* agreement with P. M made new arrangements with P to the effect that, in return for rebates, he would supply only P's petrol and oil. The agreement was to last for 12 years or until such time as M had sold 600,000 gallons of petrol, whichever was the longer period. M discovered that he was trading at a loss and, as a result, formed a limited company and came to an arrangement with Esso. P tried to enforce the original agreement but it was found to be unreasonable and invalid for a number of reasons, two of them being: (1) the 12-year period was too long; and (2) the restriction obliged him to carry on his business, even though it was running at a loss. As in other restrictive agreements, there is the possibility of more than one restriction being imposed. If these are severable (as explained above) the court may uphold one restriction and reject the other. In *Esso Petroleum Co Ltd v Harper's Garage (Stourport) Ltd* (1968), a 21-year *solus* agreement in respect of one filling station was set aside, whereas another agreement for four-and-a-half years between the same parties—but in respect of a different filling station—was upheld.

Finally of relevance here are sole service agreements, under which one party agrees to provide services exclusively to another. Again, these are common, but must meet the reasonableness test if challenged. In *Proactive Sports Management Ltd v Rooney* (2011), footballer Wayne Rooney entered into an eight-year agreement with P for the exclusive use of his image rights. After five years R purported to terminate the agreement and was sued. It was held that the agreement was unenforceable, since it imposed very substantial restrictions on R's commercial freedom. Also relevant to the decision was the fact that R was only 17 years old when he signed the agreement and neither he nor his parents had taken legal advice before doing so.

---

1. See, e.g. *Schroeder Music Publishing Co Ltd v Macaulay* [1974] 3 All E.R. 616.
2. It should be noted that this is not a settled point; compare, e.g. *Rock Refrigeration Ltd v Jones* [1997] 1 All E.R. 1 with *Brown v Neon Management Services Ltd* [2018] EWHC 2137 (QB).
3. *Scottish Farmers Dairy Co (Glasgow) Ltd v McGhee*, 1933 S.C. 148.
4. *Rentokil Ltd v Kramer*, 1986 S.L.T. 114; *Safetynet Security Ltd v Coppage* [2013] EWCA Civ 1176.
5. Similar reasoning was applied to the city of London in *Mason v Provident Clothing & Supply Co Ltd* [1913] A.C. 724.

7. EXEMPTION CLAUSES IN CONTRACTS

At an early stage in this book it was emphasised that, before anyone can **7–01** claim that a contract—and, thus, a binding obligation—exists, there must be *consensus in idem*. This means that both parties are in one mind as to the essential elements which make up the main terms and conditions of the obligation from the outset.

Sometimes, one of the two parties will try to bring conditions into the contract of which the other party has no knowledge—or, if he does know about them, does not quite understand or realise their significance. This is particularly prevalent where one party has greater bargaining power than the other, and might attempt to incorporate an exclusion or limitation of his liability by using phrases such as:

"PERSONS ENTER THESE PREMISES AT THEIR OWN RISK."

"THE MANAGEMENT ACCEPTS NO RESPONSIBILITY FOR ARTICLES LEFT IN THIS CLOAKROOM."

"IN THE EVENT OF ANY DAMAGE OCCURRING TO THIS ITEM WHEN IN CONTROL OF THE COMPANY, LIABILITY SHALL BE RESTRICTED TO £100 PER ITEM."

These terms are often displayed prominently at the party's place of business, but sometimes they are not so clearly brought to the attention of the party to be bound by them. A particular issue arises when such conditions are printed, or referred to, in a document or on a "ticket" that is issued after an agreement has already apparently been reached.

Where a clause attempts to free the party entirely from liability, it is called an exclusion clause. Where a clause attempts to place a limit on the amount of damages that will be claimable, it is called a limitation clause. The rules regulating these two types of exemption clause are largely the same; whether or not the clause is enforceable depends partly on whether attention has been properly drawn to it before the contract is agreed, and partly on the nature of the exemption itself.

ATTEMPTS TO IMPOSE POST-FORMATION CONDITIONS

It is a well-established principle of common law that additional conditions **7–02** cannot be added after the contract has been formed, unless there is the consent of both parties. In *Olley v Marlborough Court Ltd* (1949), Mr and Mrs O made a hotel booking. On the wall of their room was a notice "THE

PROPRIETORS WILL NOT HOLD THEMSELVES RESPONSIBLE FOR ARTICLES LOST AND STOLEN". Mrs O left her fur coat in the room, locked the door and gave the key to the hotel receptionist. A thief obtained the key and stole the coat. The hotel company unsuccessfully attempted to rely on the notice on the wall to exclude them from liability. They could not do so, since the condition was not known to Mr and Mrs O until after the contract had been formed and was not part of it.[1]

The issuing of a ticket

7–03 When a ticket is issued upon payment for goods or services, it can be intended either as a receipt for money paid or it may be a voucher to claim property or services, e.g. uplifting goods from a dry cleaner or handing over a cinema ticket. Quite often, the ticket will have conditions printed on it, or it may refer to conditions published elsewhere. Sometimes there will be no ticket, but a notice may be displayed on business premises that is intended to be a written exemption clause in an otherwise unwritten contract. Sometimes the clause will appear both on a ticket and on a notice.

For a condition printed on a ticket to be essential to, or an integral part of, the contract, the ticket itself must be *more* than just a voucher or receipt. It will usually be recognised that a ticket is an integral part of contracts of carriage (e.g. a train journey) or deposit (e.g. left luggage) and the courts would expect a reasonable person to be aware that such contracts are normally subject to published conditions.

If the ticket is not an integral part of the contract and is merely a receipt or voucher, conditions printed on it will not generally be binding. In *Chapelton v Barry UDC* (1940), conditions excluding liability were not binding on a man who had hired a deck chair on the beach and had been injured as a result of using it. The ticket was, in the circumstances of the case, taken to be only a receipt and words printed on it were not part of the contract. *Taylor v Glasgow Corp* (1952): T went to a public baths for a hot bath. She paid at the entrance kiosk and received a ticket that she had to hand over to the attendant as a voucher. On the front of the ticket were the words "FOR CONDITIONS, SEE OTHER SIDE". On the back were words excluding G from liability for any damage to property or personal injuries. T knew that there was printing on the back of the ticket but did not read it. T alleged that, due to the negligence of a bath attendant, she was allowed to fall down some stairs, causing her injury. She sued G for damages. G unsuccessfully attempted to rely on the exclusion clause on the back of the ticket. The ticket was merely a voucher or receipt to show what service T had paid for and to give entry to the appropriate part of the baths. The exclusion clause was not part of the contract.

Was attention adequately drawn to the condition?

7–04 Where conditions are prominently displayed, and can be read by the other party before entering the contract, the conditions will be deemed to be incorporated whether the other party actually read them or not.[2] Where conditions are printed, or referred to, on a ticket, their existence must be adequately brought to the attention of the other party, even if the ticket is integral to the contract. If attention is not adequately drawn to the conditions, the contract itself is still valid but the conditions on the ticket are not binding. In *Henderson v Stevenson* (1875), S bought a ticket for a voyage from Dublin to Whitehaven. On the back of the ticket was printed:

"THE COMPANY INCURS NO LIABILITY WHATEVER IN RESPECT OF LOSS, INJURY, OR DELAY TO THE PASSENGER OR TO HIS OR HER LUGGAGE, WHETHER ARISING FROM THE ACT, NEGLECT OR DEFAULT OF THEIR SERVANTS OR OTHERWISE".

S did not read this condition and the clerk who issued the ticket did not draw his attention to it. The steamer was wrecked off the Isle of Man due to the negligence of the company's servants. S's claim for damages was successful. The condition had not been imported into the contract of carriage. There was no reference on the front of the ticket to the condition on the back. S's attention had not been adequately drawn to the condition and he was not bound by it.

In *Williamson v North of Scotland Navigation Co* (1916), conditions had been printed on the front of a steamer ticket but in the smallest typeface known. These conditions had not been validly incorporated into the contract. By contrast, in *Hood v Anchor Line* (1918), operators of a shipping line successfully incorporated an exclusion clause into a contract when it was handed to a passenger in an envelope clearly asking passengers to read the information on the enclosed ticket. The exclusion clause was printed legibly on the front.

Acceptance of conditions
If a person actually signs in acceptance of conditions, he is presumed to have read and accepted them (unless misrepresentation took place). In *L'Estrange v Graucob* (1934), L bought—for use in her café—a coin-operated cigarette machine from G and signed a purchase agreement containing certain conditions in small print. These conditions exempted G from liability if the machine did not work. As L had signed the agreement, she was bound by it. She had failed to read the exclusions properly but they had not been misrepresented to her nor concealed from her. The same would apply to the signing of a ticket; being asked to sign in this way is not common but it can still happen occasionally, e.g. at a dry cleaners, if the material of items taken in for cleaning cannot be identified by its label.[3]

7–05

Sometimes, conditions are appended to an item, or supplied in an accompanying document upon delivery. Again, these must be adequately drawn to the attention of, or accepted by, the other party. This is particularly important if they are unusual or overly onerous. *Interfoto Picture Library Ltd v Stiletto Visual Programmes Ltd* (1988): S, an advertising agency, required period photos of the 1950s. On 5 March 1984, S telephoned IPL, a commercial photographic library, to enquire if it had anything suitable.

The same day, IPL dispatched 47 transparencies, packed in a jiffy bag, with a delivery note. At the top right-hand corner of the note the date of return was clearly stated as 19 March 1984. At the foot of the document under the heading of "Conditions" there were nine conditions in four columns. Condition two read:

"All transparencies must be returned to us within fourteen days from the date of delivery. A holding fee of £5 plus VAT will be charged per day for each transparency retained by you longer than the said period of fourteen days."

S did not actually use the transparencies and forgot about them. They were not returned until 2 April 1984. An invoice then followed for holding charges of £3,783.50. The court dismissed this claim, although it awarded a *quantum meruit* payment (i.e. a sum in recognition of the service actually provided). This case was followed in Scotland in *Montgomery Litho Ltd v Maxwell* (2000).

Opening the "shrink wrap" of an item might also be held to constitute acceptance of conditions, provided notice of them is visible through the wrapping, even if the detail of them is not.[4] It is very common now for online transactions to require the purchaser to click a box confirming acceptance of "terms and conditions", a hyperlink to which is almost invariably provided. These "click-wrap" agreements likely have the equivalent effect of a signature, regardless of whether the buyer actually follows the hyperlink or not. In *Ryanair Ltd v Billigfluege.de GmbH* (2010), it was held that continued use of a website constituted implied acceptance of the clear and unambiguous terms and conditions.

Implied acceptance

7–06 Sometimes, even though no notice is given of a specific exemption, a person may still be bound by it because he is aware of it due to previous dealings between the parties. However, before allowing this, the courts would have to be convinced that the previous dealings had been consistent. *McCutcheon v David MacBrayne Ltd* (1964): McC sought damages in respect of his car which had been lost when MacB's ferryboat sank on a trip from Islay to Tarbert. His brother-in-law, McS, had arranged the shipment of the car. Both men had, in the past, sent items by MacB's ferry. In principle, MacB required shippers to sign a so-called "risk note", which excluded MacB from certain liabilities. In previous dealings, both McC and McS sometimes had, and sometimes had not, signed such notes. In the case of the present contract, only a receipt had been issued to McS and no risk note had been signed by him. The wording of the exclusion clause containing in risk notes was also published in MacB's office and on Islay pier. The court was not convinced that there had been a consistent course, as risk notes had sometimes been signed and sometimes not. Thus, the clause was not part of the contract in question and McC was entitled to compensation for his lost car.

THE NATURE OF THE EXEMPTION

Whilst incorporation of exemption clauses is regulated by common law, statutory rules exist regarding the nature and extent of the exemption itself. The effect of this is that, even if an exemption has been properly incorporated under common law, it might still be deemed ineffective under statute. The Unfair Contract Terms Act 1977 (UCTA) set up this statutory regime, although subsequent legislation has further reformed it. Significantly, protections relating to consumers in this regard are now contained within the Consumer Rights Act 2015 (CRA). 7–07

Unfair Contract Terms Act 1977
The title of this Act is somewhat misleading, as it does not cover all unfair contract terms, only exemption clauses. Prior to October 2015, UCTA applied to all types of contracts, but due to CRA coming into force it no longer applies to consumer contracts. Therefore, its modern relevance is mainly in terms of contracts between businesses. 7–08

The scope of UCTA is broad. "Business" is defined so as to include companies, partnerships, sole traders, professionals, local authorities and government departments. Essentially, it does not include individuals who act in a personal or private capacity. Many types of contract are covered, including sale and hire of goods, employment and the supply of services, and contracts for entry to premises. Certain contracts are, however, excluded from the Act. These include insurance and contracts for the transfer of an interest in land; although, as regards the latter, in practice UCTA is often invoked in respect of contracts tangential to the sale of land, such as for the conducting of surveys.[5]

A condition in a contract to which UCTA applies is void if it purports to exclude or limit liability for death or personal injury. For all other exemptions regarding breach of duty, the condition shall have no effect unless it is "fair and reasonable".[6] Note that only the exemption is voided; the contract itself remains valid, provided it can continue without the offending clause.

Standard form contracts
It is common for businesses to contract subject to their own standard terms and conditions. It is also common for these to exclude or limit the extent to which the business will be liable for breach of contract or non-performance. Often these are not subject to negotiation, and the other party must simply "take or leave" the proposal. Any such term which seeks to exclude or restrict liability for breach or non-performance is subject to a similar "fair and reasonable" test.[7] 7–09

The above only applies where standard terms have been imposed by one party on the other; if parties who are both in business elect to sign contracts "at arm's length", they will generally be bound by them. In *Photo Production Ltd v Securicor Transport Ltd* (1980), S agreed to provide security inspection at a factory. One of their employees criminally started a fire in the factory, resulting in a loss of £615,000. The factory owners sued for damages. S relied on a clause in its standard conditions that excluded liability in most situations. The clause clearly covered acts such as that of S's employee; S were not liable.[8] Similarly, UCTA offers no protection where parties have agreed to contract on industry-wide standard terms, as is common in the construction and oil and gas sectors.[9]

The "reasonableness" test

7–10 The burden of proving that a term is fair and reasonable in its context lies with the business that is seeking to rely on it. In determining fairness, the court will have regard to all relevant circumstances, including: the facts known to the parties at the time the contract was made; the relative bargaining strengths of the parties; the financial resources of the parties; and whether cover could have been obtained through insurance.[10]

In practice, where the parties are both businesses and are of similar bargaining power, the courts will tend to enforce the exclusion.[11] This may even be the case where there are other problems with the contract, such as misrepresentations having been made.[12] Nowadays most businesses take out insurance cover to protect themselves against the risks to which they are subject.

Consumer Rights Act 2015

7–11 Part 2 of this Act deals with unfair contract terms and replaces certain sections of UCTA. It also entirely replaces certain subsequent legislation, such as the Unfair Terms in Consumer Contracts Regulations 1999.

CRA only applies to consumer contracts, i.e. where one party is a "trader" acting in the course of a business, and the other is a "consumer" acting as an individual. Historically, judicial interpretation of what constitutes a "consumer" has been somewhat narrow: for example, in *Prostar Management Ltd v Twaddle* (2003) it was held that a professional footballer was not a consumer for the purposes of the contract with his agent.

Protection under CRA

7–12 CRA reaffirms the position that a trader cannot exclude or limit liability for death or personal injury caused by negligence.[13] Although not contained within Pt 2, it is also worth noting here that traders cannot exclude liability under the statutory implied terms in consumer contracts.

The essence of the other relevant provisions is to apply a "fairness" test to contract terms. A term which is deemed "unfair" is not binding on the consumer, but the contract will be binding provided it can continue without the unfair term. A term is deemed to be unfair if

> "contrary to the requirement of good faith, it causes a significant imbalance in the parties' rights and obligations under the contract to the detriment of the consumer".[14]

A case decided under the older Regulations, but which still serves as a leading case considering "fairness", is *Director General of Fair Trading v First National Bank Plc* (2001). Here, the allegedly unfair term was one which permitted a lender to enforce interest charges for an extended period, specifically after the debtor had been granted additional time to pay by the court. In determining that this was *not* an unfair term, the House of Lords held that the requirement of "good faith" was simply one of fair and open dealing, and that "significant imbalance" would only be established where it was so weighted in favour of the trader so as to tilt the parties' rights and obligations significantly in his favour. More recently, in *Aziz v Caixa d'Esalvis de Catalunya* (2013), the European Court of Justice held that "significant imbalance" would primarily be established where the consumer had been denied an advantage otherwise available under national law, and that "good faith" required the trader to demonstrate a reasonable assumption that the consumer would have agreed to the term in individual negotiations.

An indicative (but not exhaustive) list of contract terms that might be considered unfair include: exclusions of liability for the trader's non-performance; a right of the trader to dissolve the contract where the consumer has no such right; and the imposition of disproportionate sums in the event of the consumer's non-performance.[15] In *Clipper Ventures Ltd v Boyde* (2013), it was held that a cancellation clause requiring compensation to be paid at a "sliding scale" which increased as the time for performance approached was *not* disproportionate and therefore not unfair.

Indeed, the claim that disproportionate sums have been imposed has been brought into issue perhaps more often than under any other heading. In recent times, it has been argued in respect of several cases in which consumers sought to challenge charges imposed by privately-operated car parks. It is common when such facilities are provided for there to be an initial period during which the car park may be used freely or at little cost, but where continued use after the initial period attracts a charge. Often, these charges are (arguably) very high, far exceeding what one might expect to pay for extended-use parking facilities, and are framed more in the way of penalties than legitimate charges. Despite arguments as to their fairness being put forward by consumers, to date the courts have been unwilling to deem such arrangements unfair.[16]

Enforcement of CRA
Whilst a challenge under CRA can be litigated directly by an aggrieved consumer, it is also possible for complaints to be considered by certain regulatory bodies, who may then take action to prevent the use of unfair terms.[17] Historically, this was the remit of the Office of Fair Trading, as illustrated by the *First National Bank* case discussed above, and the infamous "banking charges" cases which followed.[18] Under CRA, the remit for this is primarily that of the Competition and Markets Authority, which has extensive powers of investigation and enforcement.

7–13

1. A similar principle was applied to automatic car parks in *Thornton v Shoe Lane Parking Ltd* [1971] 2 Q.B. 163.
2. *Woodman v Photo Trade Processing*, Exeter County Court, reported in *Which?*, July 1981; although in this case the conditions were held to be unenforceable on other grounds.
3. *Curtis v Chemical Cleaning and Dyeing Co* [1951] 1 K.B. 805.
4. *Beta Computers Ltd v Adobe Systems Ltd*, 1996 S.L.T. 604.
5. See, e.g. *Smith v Eric S Bush (A Firm)* [1990] A.C. 831; *Robbie v Graham & Sibbald*, 1989 S.L.T. 870; and the Law Reform (Miscellaneous Provisions) (Scotland) Act 1990 (c.40) s.68.
6. UCTA 1977 s.16.
7. UCTA 1977 s.17.
8. See also, *Ailsa Craig Fishing Co Ltd v Malvern Fishing Co Ltd*, 1982 S.C. (HL) 14.
9. See, e.g. *Langstane Housing Association Ltd v Riverside Construction (Aberdeen) Ltd*, 2009 S.C.L.R. 639 and *McGee Group Ltd v Galliford Try Building Ltd* [2017] EWHC 87 (TCC).
10. UCTA 1977 s.24.
11. See, e.g. *Regus (UK) Ltd v Epcot Solutions Ltd* [2008] EWCA Civ 361 and *Goodlife Foods Ltd v Hall Fire Protection Ltd* [2018] EWCA Civ 1371.
12. *Food Co UK LLP (t/a Muffin Break) v Henry Boots Developments Ltd* [2010] EWHC 358 (Ch.), approved by *Lloyd v Browning* [2013] EWCA Civ 1637; but contrast *First Tower Trustees Ltd v CDS (Superstores International) Ltd* [2018] EWCA Civ 1396.
13. CRA 2015 s.65.
14. CRA 2015 s.62.
15. CRA 2015 Sch.2 Pt 1.
16. See, e.g. *Indigo Park Services UK Ltd v Watson*, 2017 G.W.D. 40–610; for an alternative (though as yet similarly unsuccessful) ground for challenge see Ch.8.
17. CRA 2015 Sch.3.
18. *Office of Fair Trading v Abbey National Plc* [2010] 1 A.C. 696.

8. BREACH OF CONTRACT

Once a contract has been correctly formed, and is free from any problems affecting its validity, the parties must carry out (or "perform") their obligations. Fortunately, the majority of contracts are performed uneventfully but, unless human nature changes radically, there will always be some defaulters. When one of the parties to a contract fails to carry out his side of the obligation, he will be considered in breach of contract, unless the reasons for his non-performance are recognised as valid in law (considered in Ch.9). **8–01**

BREACH AND REMEDIES

In practice, breach can arise in three different ways: (1) total non-performance; (2) partial performance; or (3) defective performance. This is important because it might have a bearing on the rights that can be exercised by the other party. Taking a simple example, say that Isabelle agrees to buy four tons of granite chippings from Jenni. Isabelle pays the agreed price, but Jenni either (1) doesn't deliver, (2) delivers only half the ordered amount, or (3) delivers limestone chippings instead of granite. In any of these situations, Isabelle would have a right to seek a "remedy", i.e. something that would redress the imbalance that had been created. However, exactly what Isabelle would be entitled to do would differ according to the circumstances. **8–02**

The "innocent" party (Isabelle in the example above) has access to various remedies and other defences measures against the "party in breach" (Jenni). The main remedies and defensive measures are: specific implement and interdict; rescission; retention; lien; and action for payment. In addition, the innocent party will often have a right to claim damages for any losses suffered as a result of the breach. These issues will now be examined in turn.

SPECIFIC IMPLEMENT AND INTERDICT

In Scots law (unlike some other jurisdictions), it is an innocent party's basic right to ask the court for a decree to make the party in breach fulfil the terms of his obligation under the contract. If the action is in the positive, i.e. to make the party in breach do something, the court may award a decree *ad factum praestandum* (for the performance of an act) which means, quite literally, that the party must specifically implement his contractual obligations. If the action is in the negative, i.e. to stop the party in breach from doing something he agreed not to do, the court may award a decree of interdict; this would be appropriate, for example, to prevent breach of a restrictive covenant.[1] **8–03**

The differences between the two can be well illustrated with some contrasting cases. In *Retail Park Investments Ltd v Royal Bank of Scotland Plc (No.2)* (1996), RBS were tenants to RPI under a 25-year lease for the purpose of providing retail banking. With seven years left to run on the lease, RBS wished to vacate the premises, leaving only cash-dispensing machines in place. RPI successfully sought specific implement compelling RBS to keep the branch open, the court holding that the provision of cash machines was not sufficient to satisfy the terms of the lease.[2]

Interdict, on the other hand, can never be used to enforce a positive obligation. In *Church Commissioners for England v Abbey National Plc* (1994), AN closed a branch office, which constituted a breach of their lease with C, the landlords. C sought an interim interdict (a short-term measure preventing further breach) to preserve their position until an action for specific implement could be raised. The court refused, holding that this was an inappropriate remedy, since it would indirectly compel positive performance. It was observed, however, and is worth noting here, that the court has wide power under the Court of Session Act 1988 to make various orders enabling a pursuer to be restored to his position prior to the wrongful act.

If the party in breach wilfully fails to obey the decree, whether it be positive or negative, further sanctions can be imposed by the court, such as a fine or even imprisonment, though in practice the court rarely takes these draconian steps. If there is apparent non-compliance, the court will expect an explanation but will listen to reason and normally give sufficient time to allow the party in default to put matters right.[3]

Under Scots law, specific implement is, in theory, the primary remedy to which an innocent party is entitled in the case of breach of contract. In practice, it is not a particularly common remedy, largely because of the practical difficulties often encountered in compelling someone to act. In addition, the court will *not* grant a decree *ad factum praestandum* if it would be unjust or inappropriate to do so. The following are the main areas where the courts do not consider specific implement to be a suitable remedy.

Obligations to pay a sum of money

8–04 Historically, it was possible for someone who failed to pay his debts to be imprisoned, though this has long been viewed as contrary to public policy. Since a debtor in default of a court decree could find himself liable to imprisonment, it follows that it would be similarly unacceptable to enforce a purely monetary debt in this manner.

Moreover, it is possible for a creditor to enforce payment by simpler and more effective processes, such as an action for payment (see below) and through the law of diligence (debt recovery).

Contracts involving personal relationships

8–05 It is important not to confuse these with the "social arrangements", discussed in Ch.1. Contracts involving personal relationships are very different, as they are certainly enforceable, though not by this particular remedy. It is perhaps easier to illustrate the concept than explain it; relevant examples are contracts of employment and partnership.

For instance, if Ken and Lionel are business partners, and Lionel does not wish the partnership to continue, common sense indicates that there is nothing to be gained by Ken taking Lionel to court and trying to force the issue. In *Skerret v Oliver* (1896), a minister of a presbyterian church had been suspended from office. He asked the court for a decree *ad factum praestandum* to force the church to reinstate him, but this was held to not be an appropriate remedy. Similarly, in the English case of *Page One Records Ltd v Britton (t/a The Troggs)* (1967), the manager of a pop group was unable to keep his post by court action as the members of the group had lost confidence in him. (Under employment legislation, an employee who has been unfairly dismissed may, occasionally, be awarded reinstatement by an industrial tribunal. The common law position, however, is as above.)

A modern example arising from a slightly different context can be found in *Woods Building Services v Milton Keynes Council* (2015). Here, MKC had conducted a tender process in which WBS was an unsuccessful bidder. However, it was later determined that the process had been flawed, and that WBS actually *should* have been successful. WBS claimed, therefore, that MKC should be ordered to award them the contract. It was held that such an order would only be made in exceptional circumstances, and would not be an appropriate remedy in this case.[4]

Where the subject matter has no intrinsic value

In many contracts, the subject matter has no special significance in itself **8–06** compared to others of an identical type. A common example is a commodity sold by weight, such as flour or sugar. Whilst these obviously have a monetary or *market* value, they lack *intrinsic* value because one bag of a certain weight is indistinguishable from another bag of exactly the same weight.

Since a suitable replacement for such goods can often be easily obtained elsewhere, the appropriate remedy for the innocent party would be to rescind (call off) the contract (see below). A damages claim would also be appropriate if, for example, the innocent party had been required to pay a higher price for the replacement, or had otherwise incurred expense due to the breach.

Although perhaps self-evident, it is worth emphasising that an action *ad factum praestandum* would be appropriate if the contract concerned a specific item such as a unique painting. Subject matter such as this is said to have a *pretium affectionis* (price of affection), i.e. a value in itself beyond its mere market price.

Obligations that are illegal or impossible

It was mentioned in Ch.1, and discussed at some length in Ch.6, that the **8–07** courts will not enforce an illegal obligation. Logic dictates, therefore, that specific implement is inappropriate in such a situation. The same principle applies where the decree could not be lawfully enforced, e.g. if the party in breach is outwith the jurisdiction of the Scottish courts.

It is also self-evident that an obligation which is impossible to perform cannot be enforced. Occasionally, the courts may be willing to refuse decree if, whilst not being literally impossible, performance would cause hardship to the defender out of all proportion to the benefit of the pursuer. In can be observed, however, that this is rarely applied in practice.[5]

A potential problem arises where an agreement is perfectly legal, and possible, when it is made, but circumstances later change so that the obligations *become* illegal or impossible. Such obligations similarly cannot be enforced by specific implement, and indeed there are other implications for the contract of such a situation arising (see Ch.9).

RESCISSION

8-08 The innocent party may, in certain circumstances, bring the contract to an end without going near a court of law. Clearly, if such a remedy was too widely available, it would favour "hotheads" who would be happy enough to call off a contract for the slightest and most trivial of reasons.

Rescission means the justifiable cancellation of a contract. The verb of rescission is "rescind", although sometimes, particularly in the area of contracts to buy and sell heritable property, the verb used is "resile". The two verbs appear to mean the same thing.

For rescission to be appropriate, the breach must be "material" (very significant) and go to the root of the contract. What exactly will be considered material is not always an easy issue, and will be judged according to the facts of the case. A refusal to perform obligations is one classic example that can be considered a material breach even if the party felt justified in his refusal. In *Blyth v Scottish Liberal Club* (1983), a club manager was held to be in breach after refusing to carry out certain tasks in the honest, but mistaken, belief that they were not part of his duties.

Refusal to perform is called "repudiation". When faced with repudiation, the innocent party can rescind and claim damages or, if he believes that there is still life in the contract, he might choose not to rescind. This is a somewhat complicated matter, and is further considered under "Anticipatory Breach", below.

Rescission must be exercised with care. An inappropriate rescission itself counts as a repudiation and can give rise to a claim in damages by the other party, i.e. the party originally in breach! In *Wade v Waldon* (1909), Wade, a famous comedian, better known by his stage name "George Robey", contracted with Waldon to appear in one year's time at a Glasgow theatre. A clause in the contract provided that Wade was to confirm his appearance 14 days before the performance and also to supply publicity material. He failed to do either. Waldon called off the entire contract, although Wade was more than willing to appear at the theatre as agreed. Wade *was* in breach of contract, but it was not a material breach and could not justify rescission on Waldon's part. The essence of the contract was Wade's appearing on stage, which he had always been willing to do. Waldon was thus liable in damages, as he had repudiated the contract.

In any contract, both parties are bound to perform their respective obligations. The implication is that one party cannot insist on performance by the other if he himself is not willing to carry out his part of the agreement. An employee is entitled to pay for duties performed but if he chooses to take an afternoon off, without permission, he cannot expect to be paid for it. In *Graham v United Turkey Red Co* (1922), a contract of agency dated in 1914 provided that G was to sell only cotton goods made by UTR, in return for payment on a commission basis. From 1916 onwards, G sold goods made by other manufacturers and was thus in breach of contract. G was only entitled to commission up to 1916, i.e. up to the time when he himself was still keeping faith with his obligation, but not for the period thereafter.

There is a further complication. Although rescission does not necessarily terminate a contract in its entirety, if the innocent party rescinds, he may then be prohibited from enforcing performance of any part of the contract. In the case of *Lloyds Bank Plc v Bamberger* (1994), the innocent party rescinded a contract and then sought certain interest payments, as specified in the contract, from the defaulting party. This was not possible since the innocent party had rescinded the contract and could not now seek to invoke the interest clause; it is worth noting, however, that the specific wording of the clause was critical to the judgement. Indeed, provisions are often built in to a contract which keep certain parts of it alive, even if the material parts are rescinded. This is now standard practice in contracts for heritable property, though careful draughtsmanship is required and a successful claim is still not guaranteed. In *Black v McGregor* (2006), the would-be buyer of a house failed to pay the agreed purchase price, resulting in the seller rescinding the contract and claiming interest payments. The relevant clause stipulated that interest would be payable from the date of rescission until the date of resale, however when the seller raised the claim the house had not yet been resold. The seller's claim failed, since the provisions of the clause had not been satisfied.

Clearly, one of the problems in this whole area is knowing when a breach of contract is material. Parties may agree between themselves at the outset which breaches would count as material. In some cases, it will be clearly implied. Common sense dictates that a wedding dress would normally be required by a bride in time for her wedding. In such a case, it is said that *time is of the essence* of the contract. Usually, however, time is not of the essence unless expressly stated to be so or circumstances, such as the involvement of perishable goods, make it clear that it is implied. In contracts for the sale of heritable property, payment of the purchase price on the date of entry is not of the essence at common law. *Rodger (Builders) Ltd v Fawdry* (1950): F agreed to sell land to R, with entry at 11 November. R failed to pay at the date of entry. A fortnight later, F warned R that the agreement to sell would be at an end unless payment was made in full by

28 November. Payment was not made on the 28th and F immediately agreed to sell the same subjects to B. It was held that F was not entitled to rescind merely because of a delay in payment.

This does not mean that parties are expected to wait indefinitely for contracts to be performed. The normal practice is to issue a "warning" to the other side and, frequently, impose a reasonable time limit for performance. As shown in the previous case, that time limit *must* be reasonable. Again, on a point of standard practice regarding the sale of heritable property, it is now common for the seller to state that time is of the essence as regards payment in full at the date of entry.

Particular problems can arise where the breach is one of several stipulations, as in *Wade v Waldon* (above), or involves defective performance. Just how defective does performance have to be to count as a material breach? At common law, that is not always easy to answer. Sometimes statutory provisions may give guidance, such as those in the Sale of Goods Act 1979 and the Consumer Rights Act 2015.

In contracts of lease it is common to find an *irritancy* or termination clause that allows the landlord to irritate, i.e. end, the lease in the event of specified breaches by the tenant. There were cases in the past where the remedy had been abused, resulting in statutory regulation. Under the Law Reform (Miscellaneous Provisions) (Scotland) Act 1985, the landlord's right to irritate cannot be exercised unless the tenant is given at least 14 days written notice in the case of a monetary breach. In the case of non-monetary breach, the court will only confirm the irritancy if the landlord has acted in a reasonable manner.

RETENTION

8–09 Retention is the withholding of payment of a monetary debt (or other contractual obligation) until such time as the other party performs his obligation in full, e.g. a tenant may wish to withhold his payment of rent until the landlord carries out his legal duty to put the house in a habitable condition. There are some restrictions as to when this measure can be used since, as a general rule of law, a debtor cannot refuse to pay a debt simply because he has another claim against the creditor. Retention, like lien (below), is not so much a remedy as a defensive measure.

Perhaps the most important restriction placed on retention is that, generally, it can only be exercised when the obligation being withheld is reciprocal (or "counterpart") to the obligation not being performed. There has been much judicial commentary on this issue in recent times, with the result that the legal position seems to have shifted somewhat.

Historically, the consequence of this principle was that one party could not withhold payment due under *one* contract because *another* contract had been breached, or because there was a debt of some other kind due. (Although this situation could always be remedied under the concept of compensation, on which see Ch.9.) Moreover, it was also the case that, where a contract involved a range of obligations, failure to perform one obligation by one party did not necessarily justify the withholding of any and all obligations by the other.

A good illustration of this was *Macari v Celtic FC* (1999), which came to court after M was dismissed as manager of Celtic Football Club over his failure to comply with a residence obligation in his contract. M argued that he was justified in retaining performance because, previously, CFC had breached their implied obligation of trust and confidence towards him as their employee. The court held that M was *not* justified in doing this, as the residence obligation was not a counterpart of the trust obligation.

However, it was soon observed that the decision in *Macari* was potentially problematic,[6] and indeed subsequent judicial treatment has been mixed.[7] A different approach was taken in *Forster v Ferguson & Forster* (2010), where it was held that a firm of solicitors were not required to make pension payments to a partner who had embezzled money from the firm, despite arguments from the pursuer that his obligation to act with utmost good faith was not counterpart to the firm's obligation to honour his pension rights. This position was developed further in *Inveresk Plc v Tullis Russell Ltd* (2010), where it was commented that *all* obligations relating to the same transaction should, at least as a starting point, be viewed as reciprocal to one another unless there is a clear indication to the contrary, and held that obligations under two separate contracts *could* be considered counterparts if they related to the same transaction.[8]

On the other hand, in the more recent decision of *McNeill v Aberdeen City Council* (2013), it was held that an employer continued to be bound by an obligation of trust and respect even after breach of contract by an employee. The decision was justified by the suggestion that only "substantive" obligations of the contract were counterpart to each other, which seems to disagree with earlier recent cases. It is perhaps fair to say that this is a complex area, which is continually developing.

LIEN

Lien (pronounced "lean") is the withholding of property which would **8–10** normally be delivered to the other party. There are two kinds of lien: general and special. The special lien is by far the more common, and is much more restrictive in scope.

In outline, a special lien allows a person who has done work on the moveable property of another, or has not been paid the purchase price of goods, to retain possession of that property until he has received the payment due. Say, for example, that Kerry takes her car to Lynne's garage for repairs. If Kerry cannot pay the bill once the repairs are complete, Lynne can retain possession of the car until payment is made. This is exercising a right of lien against these "special" (specific) goods.

A general lien, on the other hand, is a much broader right. It allows the holder of the property to retain possession in respect of any obligation that is due, even those relating to another transaction. Further, it may also allow retention of property not directly related to the transaction itself. One of the earliest established examples of such a right is that exercised by innkeepers, who have a right of general lien over a guest's belongings, pending payment of the hotel bill.[9]

The categories of trades and professions who enjoy a right of general lien are very narrow, and the court do not seem to favour any extension to them. A solicitor's right of lien is well established, being traced back to the old case of *Ranking of Hamilton of Provenhall's Creditors* (1781). This allows a law agent to, say, retain title deeds and share certificates in his possession until a client had paid his professional account for drawing up a new will. *Paul v Meikle* (1868): Mrs D bequeathed certain heritable property to her son. The will had been drawn up by M, Mrs D's solicitor, who was also her creditor in respect of unpaid professional fees extending over many years. M was entitled to retain the will until his fees were paid. (In practice, it is nowadays relatively simple to defeat a lien over a document if it is of a type where a duplicate or certified copy can be obtained.) However, in *Christie v Ruxton* (1862), it was held that the lien did not cover cash advances made by a solicitor to his client. It seems that an accountant does not enjoy a right of general lien, although it is well established that he has right of special lien.[10] A banker has a general lien on bills of exchange, cheques and promissory notes belonging to a customer, provided these have come into his possession in the course of banking transactions. This general lien does not extend to articles left with the bank for safe keeping.

It must be noted that lien is purely a possessory right. The holder is not the owner and cannot treat the property as his own, i.e. he cannot sell it, even if the purpose is to pay the money owed. Furthermore, the property must be in the relevant legal possession of the party wishing to exercise lien; it is not enough that the property is simply under this party's control. This is strictly applied in cases of special lien. In *Hostess Mobile Catering v Archibald Scott Ltd* (1981), S sold H a piece of catering equipment, but the item was not paid for in full. When it was returned to S for repairs under guarantee, S unsuccessfully attempted to exercise a right of lien to encourage payment, since their possession (to effect repairs) was not relevant to the breach (non-payment of the item).

A further point worth noting is that a special lien can only be exercised against property belonging to the party who owes the obligation. In *Lamonby v Foulds* (1928), a garage owner was not entitled to exercise lien over a lorry which the defaulting customer held under a hire-purchase agreement. On the other hand, it may be possible for a general lien to extend to property owned by a third party. In *Bermans & Nathans Ltd v Weibye* (1983), an innkeeper was held to have legitimately exercised lien over hired costumes that had been left by defaulting guests.

Although it is only a defensive measure, lien is common in practice and highly persuasive in making payment forthcoming. It is particularly useful where the innocent party does not wish to rescind or where it would be pointless to do so because he has, in fact, performed his part of the contract.

ACTION FOR PAYMENT

Although some legal textbooks might convey a different impression, the most common breach of contract is non-payment of money. As explained above, specific implement would not be an appropriate remedy for pursuing a money debt. A short delay in payment is not necessarily a material breach, and it is sometimes a fine line between delay in payment and actual non-payment. Thus, rescission must not be exercised too hastily. In any event, it would normally be inept to rescind a contract unless restitutio in integrum (restoration of parties to their original position) were possible. Where the contract price is unpaid but goods have been delivered or services performed, the creditor can recover payment by means of a court action. Most such actions are undefended. The creditor would then be able to enforce his decree by diligence. 8–11

Under an action for payment, only the debt itself may be claimed, plus interest, although a claim for consequential losses may also be available. The calculation of interest can be agreed between the parties, although various statutory provisions also exist to regulate this in certain circumstances. For example, the Late Payment of Commercial Debts (Interest) Act 1998 gives rights to businesses to charge interest on late payment of money debts due by other businesses or by bodies in the public sector.

DAMAGES

Damages are a compensatory remedy which are available to an innocent party in addition to any other remedies claimed. The purpose of damages is simple: to compensate the innocent party for his loss and to place him in the position he would have been in had the contract been fully performed— in so far as money alone is capable of doing this.[11] There are a number of principles to be applied by the court in assessing a damages claim; these will now be considered in turn. 8–12

Calculating damages
In determining what damages (if any) might be available, loss is a logical starting point. Generally, if no loss is suffered by the innocent party, no damages can be claimed.[12] Whilst these losses will, of course, most often be financial, it is also possible to claim damages for mere trouble and inconvenience. In the oft-cited case of *Webster v Cramond Iron* (1875), damages were awarded for breach of contract despite no financial loss being proven, though it should be emphasised that these were "nominal". More recently, in *Mack v Glasgow City Council* (2006), M took action against her landlords for their alleged failure to maintain her rented property. M was successful in her damages claim based on the trouble and inconvenience she suffered as a result of the flat's damp problem. Indeed, the courts are showing an increasing tendency to award substantial damages 8–13

even in the absence of quantifiable financial loss being proven, e.g. due to the disappointment caused when a wedding photographer fails to appear on the arranged day,[13] or when a holiday fails to match the reasonable expectations of the holidaymaker.[14]

The amount of loss actually suffered must be carefully calculated, since in Scotland damages are designed to compensate the innocent party rather than to punish the party in breach.[15] Although some legal systems do allow "punitive" damages, this is not generally the case in this country. That said, in one very unusual English case the House of Lords were willing to take a somewhat different approach. In *Attorney-General v Blake* (2001), B, a British spy who had defected to the Soviet Union, was sued by the Crown as being (among other things) in breach of his employment contract. B had published a very profitable account of his time as an intelligence agent, and the Crown sought to recover damages. Instead of applying the usual compensatory principles, the court allowed damages to be calculated based on the gains B had made by publishing his memoirs. (Note that this is a different concept again to punitive damages.) The court made it clear that this was an exceptional case and that damages of this kind would not be readily available.[16]

Also worthy of mention here is the so-called "Wrotham Park" calculation of damages, whereby the sum payable is determined by assessing what the party in breach would have had to pay in order to be released from his obligations. The term is derived from the leading case, *Wrotham Park Estate Co Ltd v Parkside Homes Ltd* (1974), in which P had purchased land, any development of which had to be approved by W. P built and sold houses on the land in breach of this restriction and W sued. The court held that a proper measure of damages was the sum which W might have reasonably required in return for granting approval. Judicial reception of this decision has been decidedly mixed, although recent authorities have positively applied the approach.[17] It worth noting, however, that the Supreme Court recently disapproved of the term "Wrotham Park damages" as being overly confusing, preferring the term "negotiating damages" to describe the same concept.[18]

There might be some difficulty in assessing exactly what position the innocent party would have been in had the contract been fully performed. The general principle is that the innocent party's position as a result of the breach is compared to the position he would have been in had the contract been properly performed and damages are then calculated accordingly.[19] It is usual for this assessment to be made as at the time of the breach itself, but the courts have occasionally shown willingness to take into account events that happen *after* the breach. In the English case of *Golden Strait Corp v Nippon Yusen Kubishka Kaisha* (2007), a contract for a ship charter contained a clause that the charter could be terminated if war broke out between various named countries. In December 2001, the charterers, N, repudiated the contract by returning the ship to the owners, G. G claimed damages calculated according to the remainder of the charter period, which was due to run until December 2005. However, in March 2003 war broke out between the UK, US and Iraq, an event which would have allowed N to terminate the charter without penalty. The House of Lords decided (by a 3:2 majority) that this post-breach event should be taken into account and held that G's damages should be calculated according only to the period December 2001 to March 2003, i.e. the period during which N had no legitimate grounds for termination.[20]

Causation

Damages can only be recovered for losses actually caused by the breach of contract. In other words, there must be a proven link between the breach and the loss incurred. In *Irving v Burns* (1915), B, secretary of a picture-house company, engaged I to carry out certain plumbing work, although B had no authority to do so. I performed his part of the contract but received no payment, since the company had become insolvent. I then sued B for damages since, at common law, an agent is said to "warrant his authority" and it was now clear that B had been given no authority to form the contract. I's action was unsuccessful. He had undoubtedly suffered a loss and B had undoubtedly breached his warranty of authority. However, the one had not been directly caused by the other; even if the contract had been properly formed, I still would have received no payment since the company was insolvent. He was thus no worse off as a result of B's conduct.

8–14

Duty to mitigate loss

The innocent party is expected to take reasonable steps to minimise his loss, i.e. to keep it as low as possible, otherwise his claim for damages could be restricted to the amount he could have claimed if he had taken such steps. Thus, if a party is not supplied with goods, but then delays purchasing suitable replacement goods elsewhere until the price has risen, his claim for damages will be restricted. These were essentially the facts in *Ireland v Merryton Coal Co* (1894), where a wholesaler failed to honour an agreement to supply coal to a retailer over a period of four months. In claiming damages, the retailer failed in his efforts to claim damages at the current market price of coal, which had risen during the supply period.

8–15

It should be noted that the innocent party is only expected to take "reasonable" steps to minimise his loss. He does not have to take extraordinary steps. Thus, in *Gunter v Lauritzen* (1894), L had agreed to sell a cargo of Dutch hay to G. The latter intended to resell the hay in consignments to his customers. L failed to supply goods of the required quality but when he was sued for damages, claimed that G could have obtained the goods elsewhere and that he had not minimised his loss. In fact, the commodity was in very scarce supply and could only have been obtained by buying in small amounts from various suppliers throughout the country. The court found that minimisation of loss did not require such an onerous demand. The innocent party was only required to take reasonable steps.

Remoteness of loss

8–16 Losses that are caused by a breach of contract can be very far-reaching, but common-sense dictates that a limit must be placed on the liability of the party in breach. As a general rule, only loss that is a foreseeable result of the breach of contract can be claimed. Damages in that case are referred to as "general" or "ordinary" damages. If there are special or "knock-on" circumstances that lead to an unusual or special loss, the party in breach is not held liable (i.e. to pay "special" damages) unless he knew of the special circumstances at the time the contract was formed. The basic effect is that a party in breach of contract will not normally be liable for all the consequences of the breach.

This basic principle is often referred to as the "rule in *Hadley v Baxendale*", after the English case which established it.[21] H's flour mill was at a standstill because the cast-iron crankshaft from a steam engine had fractured. The broken crankshaft had to be sent from the mill in Gloucester to a foundry at Greenwich, to be used as a pattern for a replacement. B, a carrier, was given the task of transporting it. He was told that it was a crankshaft for a mill but he was not made aware that, on account of the broken crankshaft, the mill was at a standstill. Most mills normally kept a spare. B was negligent and caused a delay in delivering the new crankshaft. He was in breach of contract because he had undertaken to complete his work within two days. However, H was not entitled to claim special damages for the loss of profits when the mill was at a standstill because these special circumstances had not been properly explained to B when the contract was formed. Thus, this special loss of profit was beyond what the carrier could have been expected to foresee.

The rule was later applied in a leading Scottish case, *Balfour Beatty Construction (Scotland) Ltd v Scottish Power Plc* (1994). B were constructing a concrete aqueduct to carry the Union Canal over a by-pass. This required a long "continuous pour" of concrete. Work on the first stage was almost complete when the electricity supply failed. As a result, the first stage had to be entirely demolished. B claimed special damages of over a quarter of a million pounds against S. In the House of Lords, B lost their case. It would have required a high degree of technical knowledge of the construction industry on the part of S for them to have foreseen the results of an interruption of the electricity supply.

Some further case law may help to illustrate how the courts have interpreted this rule in practice. It is fair to say that it is applied strictly in most instances.

Macdonald v Highland Railway Co (1873): confectionery for the celebration of the coming of age of Lord Macdonald on the Isle of Skye was sent by rail from Inverness via Dingwall and Strome Ferry. The cartons containing the confectionery were clearly marked "PERISHABLE", thus clearly bringing the railway company's attention to the special circumstances of the contract. Due to the company's negligence, the cartons were held up at Dingwall. When eventually they reached Skye, the celebration was past and the confectionery had perished. The railway company were liable for all the loss because the special circumstances, i.e. that the goods were perishable, had been clearly brought to their notice at the time the contract was formed.

Den of Ogil Co Ltd v Caledonian Railway Co (1902): the *Den of Ogil*, a steamship of 4,000 tons lying at Plymouth, had broken one of her pistons. A replacement had been cast at Port Glasgow and was sent by passenger train to Plymouth. The railway company were informed that the carriage was urgent and that delay would cause detention of the ship. However, they were not informed that it was such a large ship, which had 57 crewmen on board, nor were they told that the casting was a piston. There was a delay of some three or four days in delivery. The ship owner sued the railway company for damages, including outlays and loss of profits. The railway company were liable for general damages in respect of the part of the outlays caused by the delay, but not for special damages in respect of the loss of profit.

Victoria Laundry v Newman Industries (1949): N agreed to supply a boiler to V, who required it to expand their business and to permit them to take up a large government contract. The boiler was delivered late, by which time the government contract had been lost. As N had no way of knowing about the government contract when they agreed to supply the boiler, they were only liable for ordinary or general damages for the foreseeable loss of business and not for any special damages in respect of the lost contract.

Donoghue v Greater Glasgow Health Board (2009): a contractor was engaged to resurface a path on premises operated by G. Despite the contract stating that asphalt should be used, the path was resurfaced with gravel, resulting in a nearby flight of stairs becoming slippery due to loose stones. D, an employee of G, slipped on the stairs and was injured. G claimed that the contractor should be liable to indemnify them against D's claim, since the accident would not have occurred had it not been for their breach of contract. The court held that the loss associated with D's claim was too remote to be recoverable.

Maestro Bulk Ltd v Cosco Bulk Carrier Co Ltd (2014): M had chartered a ship from C. The charter was for an unspecified period, but the contract stipulated that 20 days' notice ought to be given by M before return of the ship. M gave only six days' notice. C claimed that, had M given sufficient notice, they would have been able to charter the ship to another client at a higher fee and therefore that M was liable for the lost income. It was held that this was not an appropriate measure for damages.

LIQUIDATED DAMAGES

In the cases considered so far, the courts have been required to assess the quantum (amount) of damages to be paid when a breach of contract has taken place. Parties can, however, agree at the outset how much will be paid as damages in the event of a breach. This is particularly common in

8–17

contracts involving building or contracting work, e.g. to cover loss incurred through delays in completion. This form of damages is called liquidated damages and is perfectly legitimate and enforceable provided it is a genuine pre-estimate of loss. Confusingly, such a provision in a contract is often called a "penalty clause". This is an unsatisfactory title since, as demonstrated above, damages for breach of contract are intended to be compensatory, not penal.

In assessing whether such a clause is enforceable, the actual name given to it is unimportant; what matters is its actual effect. If it is clear that the clause is intended to punish rather than to compensate, then it is invalid and unenforceable; the burden of proof seems to sit squarely on the party wishing to challenge the clause.[22] Where the clause is invalid, the court would have to assess damages using the usual criteria. On the other hand, where there is a valid liquidated damages clause, whatever it may actually be called, the amount recoverable by the innocent party is restricted to that amount even if the actual loss is larger or smaller than the sum specified. So, in some cases it might be preferable for the innocent party if the clause is invalid.[23]

The concept of liquidated damages is an old one and has long been supported by the court in appropriate circumstances. As Lord Diplock stated in *Robophone Facilities v Blank* (1966), there seems to be

"no reason in public policy why the parties should not enter into so sensible an arrangement under which each knows where they stand in the event of a breach."

The court's willingness to enforce can be illustrated with reference to some historical cases. *Lord Elphinstone v Monkland Iron & Coal Co* (1886): tenants in a mineral lease had undertaken to level and soil-over deposits of slag by a certain date under a "penalty of £100 per imperial acre for all ground not so restored". The sum was liquidated damages, not a penalty and was enforceable; in other words, it was a genuine pre-estimate of loss. *Cameron-Head v Cameron & Co* (1919): in a contract between a firm of timber merchants and the proprietor of an estate, the former bought standing timber on the understanding that the wood was to be cleared by April 1918 under a "penalty of 10s. per day until such is done". By April 1919, the wood had still not been cleared. An action was raised for a year's "penalty". The "penalty" of 10s. (50p) per day was a reasonable pre-estimate and enforceable.

Very rarely there could be circumstances in which it is impossible to give a genuine pre-estimate of loss. If this is so, any sum agreed on by the parties will be accepted as liquidated damages, even if in normal circumstances it would appear penal. *Clydebank Engineering and Shipbuilding Co v Castaneda* (1904): Clydebank, by two contracts, undertook to supply four torpedo-boat destroyers to the Spanish Government. The contract included a clause: "The penalty for late delivery shall be at the rate of £500 per week for each vessel not delivered ... in the contract time". All vessels were delivered many months late. The Spanish Government brought an action against Clydebank for £75,000, calculated in accordance with the "penalty" clause. Clydebank claimed that this provision was penal and thus unenforceable. The remainder of the Spanish fleet had by now been sunk by the Americans off the coast of Cuba. It was accepted that the sum of £500 per week was liquidated damages as it had been impossible to give an accurate pre-estimate of loss at the time the contracts were formed.

In distinguishing between penalty clauses and genuine liquidated damages clauses, the courts have very often had regard to the principles famously set out by Lord Dunedin in *Dunlop Pneumatic Tyre Co v New Garage and Motor Co* (1915). These can be summarised as follows:

1. The use of the words "penalty" or "liquidated damages" is not conclusive in itself.
2. The essence of a penalty is a deterrence for breach; the essence of liquidated damages is a genuine pre-estimate of loss.
3. Whether a sum is a penalty or liquidated damages is a question judged at the time of the formation of the contract, not at the time of the alleged breach.
4. In making such a judgement the following four tests may assist:
    (a) if a sum is clearly extravagant, it will be held to be a penalty;
    (b) if a sum is greater than that which should originally have been paid, it will be held to be a penalty;
    (c) if the same single lump sum is payable on the occurrence of several different situations, it will be presumed to be penal (though this can be rebutted);
    (d) the fact that it is difficult or impossible to make a precise pre-estimation of loss is not in itself an obstacle to a sum being liquidated damages.

These guidelines became the generally accepted approach and were applied consistently in subsequent cases for around a century. However, during that time a number of potential problems came to light, especially given the general increase in complexity of commercial transactions. The Scottish Law Commission (among others) recognised that the area was in need of reform.[24]

More recently, the UK Supreme Court established a new test in the conjoined cases of *Cavendish Square Holding v Makdessi* and *Parking Eye Ltd v Beavis* (2015). In *Cavendish*, the relevant provision was a non-competition clause in a contract for sale of a business, breach of which by the seller would result in the forfeiture of future payments totalling $44 million. In *Parking Eye*, the provision was a condition imposed upon users of a privately-operated car park whereby failure to vacate after two hours would incur a charge of £85.

The court held that the main question to be considered now is whether the clause constitutes a primary obligation of performance under the contract, or a secondary obligation which is exorbitant, unconscionable, or imposes a detriment on the party in breach which is out of all proportion to the interests of the innocent party. If the clause is deemed to be the latter, it will be a penalty and therefore unenforceable. In both *Cavendish* and *Parking Eye*, the Supreme Court upheld the clauses.[25]

It was observed in the decision that in regard to a straightforward damages clause, Lord Dunedin's tests would usually be "perfectly adequate" to determine its validity. However, emphasis was also placed on the innocent party's legitimate interests going beyond mere compensation, e.g. the right to incentivise performance of the contract. This seems at odds with Lord Dunedin's opinion that the essence of a penalty is a deterrence for breach.

Following the *Cavendish* and *Parking Eye* decisions, the Scottish Law Commission held a further consultation on penalty clauses, although decided against recommending legislative reform at this stage.[26] An English case decided since is *Vivienne Westwood Ltd v Conduit Street Development Ltd* (2017). Here, C leased a retail premises to V, agreeing a concession whereby V would pay a reduced rent for the first five years, with a review thereafter in line with market conditions. The contract stipulated that in the event of breach by V, the concession could be terminated and a higher rate of rent applied retrospectively. V failed to pay rent in June 2015, resulting in C claiming that the higher rate was payable. The court held that this caused a disproportionate detriment to the tenant and therefore constituted an unenforceable penalty clause. It seems that for now, this is an area that will continue to be developed through the courts.[27]

ANTICIPATORY BREACH

8–18 It might seem strange for a party to a contract to claim a remedy for breach until a breach had actually occurred. However, it is possible that one of the parties could indicate in advance of performance, by his words or actions, that he does not intend to fulfil his obligations. This is known as anticipatory breach.

For example, Miles, a pop singer, forms a contract with Norman, a promoter, that he will perform at a concert on 16 July. On 1 May, Miles intimates to Norman that he will not be appearing; in other words, he will be in breach of contract come 16 July. What remedies are open to Norman? In fact, Norman would have a choice. He could treat this as a repudiation of the contract by Miles and could thus rescind (as explained above) on the grounds of material breach, and claim damages. Or, he could wait until the time of performance and see what actually happened. In the latter case, there is no rescission and the contract is kept alive. If Miles does actually appear at the concert, there is no breach of contract. If he does not, breach has occurred and Norman can rescind and sue for damages. (It perhaps should be clear that if the contract is rescinded in May, the damages payable will be much less than if the contract is kept alive and the breach subsequently takes place on 16 July.)

For an anticipatory breach to take place, the refusal to give performance must be definite. If one party merely expresses doubts about his ability to perform, that is not anticipatory breach. If, in such circumstances, the other party then attempts to rescind, that party could well find himself being sued for damages.[28]

A controversial question is whether or not the innocent party should be able to disregard the anticipatory breach altogether, by performing his side of the bargain and then claiming the contract price. In *White & Carter (Councils) Ltd v McGregor* (1962), W supplied street litter bins to local authorities on condition that W could sell advertising space on the bins. One of W's representatives called at M's garage to arrange a new advertising contract which was to last for three years. Terms were agreed with the garage manager and the contract was duly formed. Later in the day, M telephoned W to cancel the contract. W chose to ignore this purported cancellation. They duly prepared the advertisements and displayed them for the three-year period. W were held to have been entitled to proceed with the contract and to sue for the contract price, even although M had already intimated that he would not perform his side of the obligation.

It has to be said that the above case is not without its critics and, although a House of Lords appeal on a Scottish case, the verdict was by a 3:2 majority. It has been pointed out that there is a paradox in the decision, since the pursuers were able to overcome the normal principle of minimisation of loss as they were suing for a money debt and not for damages.[29]

The English courts have shown a marked reluctance to follow this decision,[30] but the Scottish courts continue to do so.[31] The approach was recently affirmed in *AMA (New Town) Ltd v Law* (2013), where it was stated that the innocent party should be able to enforce the contract "unless circumstances render it impossible, or in exceptional circumstances, wholly unjust."[32] What is meant by "exceptional" would be for the courts themselves to decide in any particular case.

A party choosing to "sit it out" may still be taking a certain risk. In *Avery v Bowden* (1855), the owner of a ship who waited for the expiry of a 45-day period during which the defendant was supposed to be loading a ship, although the latter had already admitted he could not do so, received an unpleasant surprise when the Crimean War broke out. The cargo port was Odessa and the contract was terminated on the grounds of supervening illegality. This concept is discussed in more detail in the next chapter.

---

1. As was the case in *Bluebell Apparel v Dickinson*, 1978 S.C. 16; 1980 S.L.T. 157, explained in Ch.6.
2. The position is different in England (*Co-operative Insurance Society Ltd v Argyll Stores (Holdings) Ltd* [1998] A.C. 1) but was confirmed as the correct approach in Scotland in

Highland and Universal Properties Ltd v Safeway Properties Ltd, 2000 S.L.T. 414.
3. See the Law Reform (Miscellaneous Provisions) (Scotland) Act 1940 (c.42).
4. The same principle was applied in *MLS (Overseas) Ltd v Secretary of State for Defence* [2018] EWHC 1303 (TCC).
5. For unsuccessful attempts with useful commentary see *Mackay v Campbell*, 1966 S.C. 237 and *Morris v Morris* [2012] 1 WLUK 102.
6. See, e.g. W. MacBryde, "The Scots Law of Breach of Contract: A Mixed System in Operation" (2002) 6(1) Edin. L.R. 5–24.
7. Of particular interest are the judgments of Lord Drummond Young in *Hoult v Turpie*, 2004 S.L.T. 308 and *Purac Ltd v Byzak Ltd*, 2005 S.L.T. 37.
8. This decision was followed in *EDI Central Ltd v National Car Parks Ltd* [2010] CSOH 141, which was later affirmed by the Inner House on other issues: [2012] CSIH 6.
9. See, e.g. *Jones v Thurloe* (1722) 8 Mod. 172.
10. *Meikle & Wilson v Pollard* (1880) 8 R. 69.
11. This passage paraphrases the famous opinion expressed by Baron Parke in *Robinson v Harman* (1848) 1 Ex. 850.
12. *Wilkie v Brown*, 2003 S.C. 573.
13. *Diesen v Samson*, 1971 S.L.T. (Sh. Ct) 49.
14. *Jarvis v Swan Tours* [1973] 1 All E.R. 71; *Milner v Carnival Plc (t/a Cunard)* [2010] EWCA Civ 389.
15. *Teacher v Calder* (1898) 25 R. 661.
16. For a somewhat recent example see *Novoship (UK) Ltd v Mikhaylyuk* [2014] EWCA Civ 908.
17. See, e.g. *Vercoe v Rutland Fund Management Ltd* [2010] EWHC 424 (Ch.) and *Marathon Asset Management LLP v Seddon* [2017] EWHC 300 (Comm).
18. *One Step (Support) Ltd v Morris-Garner* [2018] UKSC 20.
19. *Govan Rope and Sail v Weir* (1897) 4 S.L.T. 245.
20. See also *Ageas (UK) Ltd v Kwik-Fit (GB) Ltd* [2014] EWHC 2178 (QB).
21. *Hadley v Baxendale* (1854) 9 Ex. 341.
22. *Hill v Stewart Milne Group* [2011] CSIH 50.
23. See, e.g. *Dingwall v Burnett*, 1912 S.C. 1097.
24. Scottish Law Commission, *Report on Penalty Clauses* (HMSO, 1999), Scot. Law Com. No.171.
25. The charge imposed in *Parking Eye* was also unsuccessfully challenged under consumer protection legislation; see Ch.7.
26. Scottish Law Commission, *Report on Review of Contract Law* (HMSO, 2018), Scot. Law Com. No.252.
27. See, e.g. *GPP Big Field LLP v Solar EPC Solutions SL* [2018] EWHC 2866 (Comm) and *Cargill International Trading Pte Ltd v Uttam Galva Steels Ltd* [2019] EWHC 476 (Comm).
28. See, e.g. *Hochster v De La Tour* (1853) 118 E.R. 922 and *Miller Fabrications Ltd v J&D Pierce (Contracts) Ltd* [2010] CSIH 27.
29. G. Black, *Woolman and Black on Contract*, 6th edn (Edinburgh: W. Green, 2018), p.177.
30. See, e.g. *Clea Shipping Corp v Bulk Oil International (The Alaskan Trader)* [1984] 1 All E.R. 129, although note *Societé Generale, London Branch v Geys* [2012] UKSC 63, which is consistent with *White & Carter*.
31. See, e.g. *Salaried Staff London Loan Co Ltd v Swears & Wells Ltd*, 1985 S.C. 189.
32. *AMA (New Town) Ltd v Law* [2013] CSIH 61, per Lady Dorrian at [48], disapproving *AMA (New Town) Ltd v McKenna*, 2011 S.L.T. (Sh. Ct) 73.

9. TERMINATION OF CONTRACT

Early in Ch.1, it was noted that there is an essential and obvious requirement 9–01
to have at least two parties to a contract. These parties have reciprocal rights and duties, i.e. they are both debtor and creditor to one another. A "debt" is not only an obligation to pay money; it can equally be a duty to perform. So, if Mel agrees to sell goods to Nikki, we have the following situation. Mel is Nikki's debtor, in so far as Mel is due to deliver goods to Nikki. Mel is also Nikki's creditor, in so far as Mel is entitled to be paid by Nikki. Equally, Nikki is Mel's debtor, as she is due to pay for the goods, but Nikki is also Mel's creditor because she is entitled to have the goods delivered. This might seem confusing at first glance, but read through the example two or three times and it should become quite clear!

When these reciprocal arrangements are satisfied in full, the contract is terminated because it has been carried out in full, i.e. performed. Fortunately, the vast majority of contracts are terminated, uneventfully, by performance. However, there are many other ways in which a contract might come to an end.

TERMINATION BY METHODS PREVIOUSLY DISCUSSED

A number of reasons for a contract being terminated have already been 9–02
discussed in previous chapters. It may be, for example, that one party is in material breach, allowing the innocent party to rescind and claim damages; this will likely terminate the contract. The other party may have decided not to perform, i.e. to repudiate the contract. Unless it is one of the instances where specific implement is appropriate, the contract will be brought to an end in this case by the innocent party rescinding.

Strictly speaking, a void contract cannot be ended because it never existed. Nevertheless, a court may have to declare that the contract is void and make judgment as to the respective rights of parties; this will have the effect of terminating the contract. A voidable contract, as has also been demonstrated, continues to run unless or until it is set aside. If third parties acquire rights under a voidable contract in good faith and for value, that contract cannot be set aside and terminated in this way.

Other than as a result of the situations outlined above, there are still a number of ways in which a contract can be ended. These have a particular significance, in so far as none of them would normally give rise to any claim for damages. It is these ways that are now to be considered.

PERFORMANCE

As stated above, this is the obvious and the most common way of ending a 9–03
contract. Partial performance does not count as performance but there is a

legal maxim de minimis non curat lex (the law does not concern itself with trifles) which means that very minor discrepancies are not suitable matters for litigation, nor valid grounds for rescission. Quite frequently, of course, the missing element of performance is payment. Work is done, or goods are delivered, but payment is not forthcoming. Payment should be made in the proper manner, usually at the creditor's place of business or his residence, unless agreed to the contrary. A creditor can insist (again, unless agreed to the contrary) on being paid in what is called legal tender, which under the Coinage Act 1971 (as amended) is:

1. £1 or £2 coins up to any amount;
2. 20p and/or 50p coins up to a maximum of £10;
3. 10p and/or 5p coins up to a maximum of £5;
4. bronze up to a maximum of 20p.

In Scotland, no Bank of England notes are legal tender. Scottish clearing banks have the historic right to issue their own banknotes but they are not legal tender, even in Scotland. Certain "special issue" coins, such as £5 Crowns, are given the status of legal tender, although few of them pass into normal business coinage.

Payment by credit, charge or debit card is not legal tender, though of course these are very widely accepted, subject to conditions or limits. Payment by cheque is only a conditional payment of a debt. If the cheque is accepted, the money debt is extinguished, but it is revived if the cheque is dishonoured.[1] This is known as a resolutive condition. Recently, many businesses have implemented a policy of refusing to accept payment by cheque, due to the risks potentially involved.

In the case of *Charge Card Services* (1988), it was held that payment by a credit or charge card counts as absolute and not conditional payment. Here, consumers had been able to buy petrol from garages by means of a card. The finance company providing the card service went into insolvency. The garages were unable to recover their loss from individual card-holders. The cardholders, however, still had to pay any sums they were due to the liquidator of the insolvent company.

ACCEPTILATION

9–04 A debtor may have non-performed or part performed, or even defectively performed his part of the obligation, yet the creditor is prepared to accept this as though it was full performance. This is called acceptilation. Although not that common, there is one example of relevance; the giving of discount in price is, in fact, a form of acceptilation.

NOVATION

A creditor and debtor may agree that the debtor will substitute a new obligation 9–05
for the one originally undertaken. For example, Oliver orders a bag of red
apples from Pete. However, Pete only has green apples in stock, so he offers
these as a substitute. If Oliver is happy to do so, he can accept this "new"
obligation in place of the original. He does not *have* to, as the debtor has no
right to substitute a new obligation unilaterally. It is important that the original
obligation is expressly discharged, as there is a general presumption in law
against novation. Thus, there is always the danger that the debtor will find
himself with two obligations to perform.[2]

DELEGATION

Delegation involves the substitution of a new debtor, rather a new obligation, 9–06
in place of the original. It is similar to novation, although the distinction can
be important.[3] Delegation requires the express consent of the creditor and, in
any event, would clearly be inappropriate in a contract which has an element
of *delectus personae* (choice of person). For example, Olive engages the
services of Pippa, a well-known artist, to paint her portrait. Pippa finds that she
is too busy, so suggests that her apprentice paint the portrait instead. If Olive
wishes to accept this, she can do so—but this is perhaps unlikely since Pippa
is the well-known artist, not her apprentice!

There is a very general rule that an agent, because his appointment is a
matter of personal confidence, has no implied authority to delegate the
performance of his duties. This is summed up in the maxim *delegatus non
potest delegare* (the one to whom delegation has been made cannot delegate).
There are some notable exceptions to the general rule. It is well recognised that
a solicitor may delegate the searching of public registers to a professional
searcher. Similarly, in *Black v Cornelius* (1879), it was held that an architect
may delegate measurement of final plans to a surveyor.

CONFUSION

Confusion, occasionally known as "combination", operates where the same 9–07
person in the same capacity becomes both creditor and debtor in an obligation.
It is a basic principle of common law, to say nothing of common sense, that a
person cannot be his own debtor. If he finds himself in such a position, the debt
is normally extinguished *confusione* (by confusion). Examples are not all that
common, but there is one of relevance in the case of tenancy. Imagine that
Quentin is the tenant of a flat owned by Ronnie. Ronnie decides to sell the flat,
and Quentin buys it. Clearly, the contract of lease comes to an end as Quentin
will not have to pay himself rent.

Note that the situation would be different if Quentin was purchasing the
property as an agent, say as a director on behalf of a company; in that case,

confusion would not operate. However, such complications are really more a matter of company law and beyond the scope of this book.

COMPENSATION

9–08 This can be traced back to the Compensation Act 1592. In England, it is usually referred to as "set off". If one party is both debtor and creditor to the other party, he can offset (set off) one claim against the other, reducing or extinguishing the amount due.

For example, if Quinn owes Roberta £500 and Roberta owes Quinn £200, clearly Quinn will only pay Roberta the net sum of £300.[4] However, compensation can only operate if certain conditions are fulfilled:

1. Compensation must be pleaded in an action for recovery of the debt. It does not automatically reduce or extinguish the debt. Thus, in the above example, Roberta would be entitled to sue Quinn for £500. Quinn would then be able to plead compensation of £200, so the court would only grant decree for £300.
2. Unless both debts arise out of the same contract, or one of the parties is bankrupt, the debts must both be liquid, i.e. actually due and of an ascertained amount.
3. There must be *concursus debiti et crediti* (concurrence of debt and credit). The means that the parties must be debtor and creditor in the same capacity as well as at the same time. The case of *Stuart v Stuart* (1869) helps to illustrate this concept. Here, Col. S brought an action against his brother, Revd. S, for repayment of an alleged loan. Revd. S alleged that Col. S had received large advances from their late father and that, as executor of their father, he (Revd. S) had counterclaims against Col. S for more than the alleged loan. The court held that Revd. S could not plead the alleged counterclaims in compensation, there being no *concursus debiti et crediti*; the office of executor denotes a different capacity from the same person acting as a private individual.

PRESCRIPTION

9–09 Not all rights last forever (although some do, such as the right to recover stolen property). Many rights come to an end after a certain period of time, i.e. they "prescribe". Most obligations under contract prescribe after five years (called short negative prescription) and this includes the right to payment. Certain other rights, e.g. relating to land, are subject to the long negative prescription of 20 years, but that is not of concern at this point. Also, certain rights may be acquired by positive prescription, but this has nothing to do with termination of contract.

It is essential that the period of time is unbroken. If the period is interrupted, the running of the period is not only stopped, it goes back to "zero" and starts running again. An interruption can take place by a "relevant claim" (e.g. the creditor raises a court action or refers the matter to arbitration) or by "relevant acknowledgement" (i.e. the debtor has shown signs of performing or has admitted in writing that the obligation still exists).

An example of this in practice would be where, after a debt has been unpaid for two years, the debtor writes to his creditor, acknowledging that the debt is still owing. This puts the running of the period back to zero, because it is a "relevant acknowledgement". The creditor now has a new period of five years to extract his debt.

Prescription is of ancient origin, but the modern law is found in the Prescription and Limitation (Scotland) Act 1973, as amended. In some cases, a creditor may have personally barred himself (see Ch.3), e.g. by *mora* and taciturnity, from making a claim, although in practice such a plea is not common. A final important point to note here is that where the right to be enforced arises from a latent defect, the relevant period begins only when the defect becomes apparent.[5]

DISRUPTION TO PERFORMANCE

It is possible for a valid contract to be formed, but then for subsequent **9–10** supervening events outwith the power of both parties to materially disrupt performance. In such a situation, the parties may be freed from their obligations, usually with no damages being payable. However, it may be possible to recover monies paid over in advance of the supervening event.

It is essential that there has indeed been a qualifying supervening event. Not everything that acts to disrupt a contract will be accepted as such, even if the event is outwith the control of the parties. In *Robert Purvis Plant Hire Ltd v Brewster* (2009), an absence of planning permission which only became apparent after formation of a lease, and subsequent refusal of planning permission, was not accepted as a supervening event.

There are three possible circumstances in which performance might be disrupted:

1. impossibility;
2. illegality; and
3. frustration.

Impossibility
It is obvious that an obligation which has become impossible cannot be **9–11** enforced. However, the obligation must be literally impossible to perform, not merely inconvenient or more expensive. In addition, the impossibility must not be due to the fault of the non-performing party. In *The Eugenia* (1964), it was known that part of a ship's voyage from Genoa to India, namely the Suez Canal, was a war zone, but the charterer ordered it to proceed by that route. The ship was detained in the canal. The court conceded that performance was now impossible, but damages were still awarded since it was the charterer

who had been instrumental in causing the supervening event.

A common example of impossibility is *rei interitus* (destruction of a thing) where the subject matter of the contract is destroyed. *Taylor v Caldwell* (1863): a music hall had been hired for a concert. After the hire had been agreed, the hall was badly damaged by fire. This was not due to the fault of the owner. The contract was terminated, without damages, on the grounds of impossibility. Under s.7 of the Sale of Goods Act 1979, any contract for the sale of specific goods which perish, without fault of either party, before ownership passes from seller to buyer, is void.

There is a common law anomaly in a contract for the sale of heritable property in so far as the risk, as distinct from the ownership, passes to the buyer as soon as there is an agreement to buy. This rule applies even although the buyer has not taken entry, paid the price nor been given a legal title. In *Sloans Dairies Ltd v Glasgow Corp* (1977), agreement had been reached for the sale of some tenement property. Before the price was paid, the building was destroyed by fire. The full purchase price still had to be paid. In practice, it is common in contracts for the sale of heritable property to provide that risk remains with the seller until the buyer takes entry. The Scottish Law Commission recommended, some considerable time ago, the statutory reversal of the common law rule, but this has never been implemented.[6]

Sometimes subjects are not literally destroyed but, to all intents and purposes, they might as well have been. This is known as "constructive" destruction and has the same effect as actual destruction, as in *London and Edinburgh Shipping Co v The Admiralty* (1920), where a ship had been very badly damaged but had not actually sunk. In *Tay Salmon Fisheries v Speedie* (1929), a salmon fishing lease on part of the River Tay was terminated when the Government declared a stretch of the river an aerial bombing zone. Similarly, in *Mackeson v Boyd* (1942), the lease of a mansion house was terminated when the building was requisitioned by the military authorities.

It might also be impossible for a contract to be performed due to the condition of one of the parties. A common example would be breakdown of health, as in *Robinson v Davison* (1871), where a pianist was unable to fulfil a contract to play. Similarly, in *Condor v Barron Knights* (1966), a drummer in a pop group had contracted to play at a very heavy schedule of appearances. The contract was terminated as a result of a doctor's advice that his health would be put at risk if he attempted to adhere to the agreed schedule.

The fact that a contract has become more expensive or more difficult does not make it impossible to perform. *Davis Contractors v Fareham UDC* (1956): a builder had agreed to construct 78 houses within eight months for a fixed sum. Due to shortages of labour and material, bad weather and inflation, the builder found himself substantially out of pocket. However, as performance was not impossible, the builder was not entitled to have the contract terminated. Most building contracts routinely allow for rises in costs due to materials, wages, or inflation.

If the impossibility is due to the substantial neglect or default of one of the parties, the possibility of damages would be open. However, the courts will not grant a decree *ad factum praestandum* (see Ch.8) where an obligation is impossible, whether or not there is fault.

Illegality
The rule here is quite simple. If a valid contract is formed but a subsequent 9–12 change in the law, or political circumstances such as outbreak of war, make performance illegal, the contract is at an end. Indeed, it may be a criminal offence to continue with performance. In *Fraser & Co Ltd v Denny, Mott & Dickson Ltd* (1944), a contract for the supply of pine timber was terminated on these grounds; although stocks were available, supply had become illegal due to wartime restrictions.

Naturally, if a contract is illegal when it is formed, it is void *ab initio* (from the beginning) and does not require to be terminated, although the court may have to adjudicate on the relative positions of the parties.

Frustration
Frustration, from the Latin *frustra* (in vain), occurs where subsequent events 9–13 outwith the control of either party have made the end result of performance materially different from what the parties originally had in mind. Some texts use the term "frustration" to encompass *any* change in circumstances, including supervening impossibility and illegality. The three concepts have been separated here so as to better distinguish this final possibility, which is also sometimes referred to as "commercial frustration", though it should be appreciated that there is considerable crossover.

Frustration may sound complicated but the concept is actually quite simple and can be well illustrated by two cases, popularly known as the "coronation cases", because they arose from difficulties arising after the postponement of the coronation of Edward VII due to the King's illness.

In *Krell v Henry* (1903), a contract was formed for the hire of rooms in Pall Mall to overlook the coronation procession. This contract was disrupted when the coronation was postponed. In theory, it would have been possible for the contract to be performed, i.e. the hiring of the room, but the outcome (looking at the London traffic instead of the procession) would have been so radically different from what the parties originally had in mind as to frustrate the contract. By contrast, in *Herne Bay Steamboat v Hutton* (1903), there was a contract for the hire of a pleasure boat to watch the review of the fleet off Spithead by the King. Although the King was unable to attend, the fleet was still there and it was possible to enjoy the special outing; the contract was not frustrated.

Whether delay will constitute frustration depends on the particular circumstances. In *Jackson v Union Marine Insurance* (1874), a charterparty provided for a ship to proceed from Liverpool to Newport and pick up a cargo of iron for San Francisco. On its way to Newport, the ship grounded on a sandbank in Caernarfon Bay. It took several months to refloat her and carry out major repairs. Meanwhile, the charterer had put his goods on another ship. The original charterparty was held to have been frustrated; whilst it would still have been possible for the original ship to proceed to San Francisco, the outcome would have been very different, due to the long delay.

It should also be noted that frustration, like impossibility, does not terminate a contract merely because performance has become more expensive. Where a ship bound for Britain had to take the longer route round the Cape of Good Hope due to the sudden closure of the Suez Canal in 1956, the charterparty was not frustrated.[7]

Recovery of monies

9–14 In the case of impossibility, illegality or frustration, it is possible that money may have been paid over in advance, or other expenditure incurred in anticipation of the contract being performed. The issue of where any losses should lie is not an easy one, and in fact has more to do with the (very specialist) area of unjustified enrichment than contract law. As such, only brief commentary will be made here.

In general, any monies paid over require to be paid back. This is, strictly speaking, not under the law of contract but under an action for repetition (repayment) known as the *condictio causa data causa non secuta* (action applicable when consideration has been given and consideration has not followed). In *Cantiere San Rocco SA v Clyde Shipbuilding and Engineering Co* (1923), a Scottish company had agreed to supply engines to an Austrian company, payment to be by instalments. One instalment had been paid, but no engines were supplied as the outbreak of the First World War made performance illegal. After the war, the Austrian company was able to recover the deposit.

On the other hand, if a party has incurred expenses independently in anticipation of the contract's performance, this expenditure cannot be recovered. This is logical, since the basis of an action for repayment is that one party has been unjustifiably enriched at the expense of another, and where the expenditure does not benefit the other party, there has been no enrichment.[8]

As a final note here, it has been speculated whether the courts have the power to apportion losses between parties in the event of frustration.[9] Recent judicial commentary suggests that, while this might be possible, it would not be readily invoked and certainly not in cases where the disruption fell just short of frustration.[10]

---

1. *Leggat Bros v Gray*, 1908 S.C. 67.
2. See, e.g. *Blyth & Blyth Ltd v Carillion Construction Ltd*, 2002 S.L.T. 961.
3. See, e.g. *Budana v Leeds Teaching Hospitals NHS Trust* [2017] EWCA Civ 1980.
4. For a recent case see *Donnelly v Royal Bank of Scotland Plc* [2017] SAC (Civ) 1.
5. See, e.g. *Renfrew Golf Club v Ravenstone Securities Ltd*, 1984 S.C. 22 and *David T. Morrison & Co Ltd v ICL Plastics Ltd* [2014] UKSC 48.
6. Scottish Law Commission, *Report on the Passing of Risk in Contracts for the Sale of Heritable Property* (HMSO, 1990), Scot. Law Com. No.127.
7. *Tsakiroglou & Co Ltd v Noblee Thorl GmbH* [1962] A.C. 93.
8. *Watson & Co v Shankland* (1871) 10 M. 142, affirmed by the House of Lords: (1873) 11 M. (HL) 51.
9. *Robert Purvis Plant Hire Ltd v Brewster* [2009] CSOH 28.
10. *Lloyds TSB Foundation for Scotland v Lloyds Banking Group Plc* [2013] UKSC 3.

10. MATTERS OF ENFORCEMENT

Various problems associated with contracts, many of which have been 10–01 discussed in previous chapters, involve the issue of enforcement. A contract which is void or illegal, for example, cannot be enforced. The innocent party to a breach of contract might encounter difficulties whilst trying to enforce the contract. Circumstances might even occur which demand the termination of the contract altogether, after which, of course, enforcement is impossible.

Yet, there are a range of other matters which, whilst perhaps not as obvious as the abovementioned problems, still warrant consideration. For example, in order for a contractual right to be enforced, it must be possible to determine what that right actually *is*. There might also be a question of *who* the appropriate person to enforce the right is. These, and other matters, are the subject of this chapter.

INTERPRETATION

In practice, many written contracts in modern use are clear, unambiguous and 10–02 free from jargon. Nevertheless, problems of interpretation are bound to arise from time to time and certain basic rules have emerged, mainly through common law. There have also been statutory inroads, particularly through the Contract (Scotland) Act 1997 (see below).

The traditional approach

In areas of interpretation, words are generally given their ordinary and natural 10–03 meaning. In Ch.2, a quotation from a judgment of Lord President Dunedin was noted which demonstrates this:

> "Commercial contracts cannot be arranged by what people think in their innermost minds. Commercial contracts are arranged according to what people say."[1]

The starting point, then, is simple. It is assumed that parties say what they mean and mean what they say. Historically, the courts would be unwilling to deviate from this objective approach, mainly to avoid the risk of "surprises" which might unfairly impact on an unsuspecting party. An exception to this would be where the parties had already agreed to a departure from the ordinary meaning of a term.[2]

A concept connected to the above is the historical "parole evidence" rule. This, in fact, is a rule that no longer exists, but its long history and its subsequent abolition requires brief comment. At common law, the position was clear. Where a contract had been committed to writing, evidence, whether written or oral, from outside the document purporting to prove that the terms were other than those written, was not admissible. This rule was derived mainly from a House of Lords case,[3] but had been subject to many exceptions throughout the years, such as latent ambiguity or usage of trade. The Contract (Scotland) Act 1997 now provides a rebuttable presumption that a document contains all the express terms of a contract where it appears to do so. This presumption can be rebutted by contrary extrinsic evidence, i.e. from outwith the four corners of the document, that additional terms exist. This evidence may be either written or verbal. However, if the basic contract contains an express provision that it comprises the whole terms of the agreement (an "entire contract" clause), that provision is taken to be conclusive and thus extrinsic evidence cannot be admitted. These provisions also apply to unilateral promises.

Consideration of context

10–04 The traditional, objective approach to interpretation was taken in *Bank of Scotland v Dunedin Property Investment Co Ltd* (1998), when the court held that costs incurred "in connection with" a share agreement should be taken to mean any costs incurred which had a "substantial relation" to the agreement. That case also suggested, however, that the circumstances in which the words are used may also be taken into account, and indeed the importance of context has long been recognised.[4]

This latter issue attracts some controversy. The traditional Scots position is that context is only to be considered if the wording of the contract is ambiguous,[5] and even then the circumstances should only be taken into account for the purposes of establishing the factual background (rather than the parties' intentions).[6] However, a number of English cases, led by authority from the House of Lords, support the position that context should *always* be considered.[7] After a decidedly lukewarm reception from the Scottish courts, with a number of disapproving decisions,[8] it seems that this approach is now being followed consistently. In *Lloyds TSB Foundation v Lloyds Banking Group Plc* (2013), it was held that payments due as a percentage of pre-tax profits had to be calculated in light of the legal and accounting context in which the contract was agreed.[9]

Ambiguous wording

10–05 A related issue is that of ambiguous terms. Regardless of whether the courts are willing to examine the context or not, it might still be that there is more than one possible interpretation of a contract's wording. In such cases the courts tend to favour the interpretation that gives effect to the contract rather than the one that might nullify it.[10] Having said that, if the wording is just too vague, the contract may be unenforceable.

As with the court's approach to the consideration of context, there has recently been a degree of uncertainty regarding how strictly the language of a contract is to be construed. The general rule of common law, recently restated in a number of cases, is that courts do not seek to rewrite contracts for the parties,[11] and where unambiguous language has been used, the courts must give effect to it.[12] Despite some decisions supporting a relaxation of this where the outcome is contrary to "commercial common sense",[13] the prevailing view seems to be that departure from the natural meaning of words needs to be very well-justified by the circumstances.[14]

In addition to the common law rules, there are times when the court may have statutory power to vary an agreement. Examples include unfair credit agreements under the Consumer Credit Act 1974 (see Ch.5), and the power to vary a written document where that document fails to reflect what the parties actually agreed.[15]

The current position
The Scottish Law Commission has long recommended reform in this area. Its 2018 report provides an in-depth examination of how the courts' approach has developed, including extensive commentary on the issues highlighted above.[16] The report draws particular attention to the Supreme Court decision of *Arnold v Britton* (2015), in which it was authoritatively stated that the meaning of a contract had to be assessed in light of: **10–06**

1. the natural and ordinary meaning of the clause;
2. any other relevant provisions;
3. the overall purpose;
4. the facts and circumstances known to the parties;
5. commercial common sense; *but*
6. disregarding subjective evidence of any party's intentions.[17]

This approach was confirmed in *Wood v Capita Insurance Services* (2017), in which it was stressed that the courts should take a unitary approach to interpretation, encompassing various factors such as factual background and the language of the contract.

The Scottish Law Commission concluded in its report that, given the recent judicial development in this area, no legislative reform is recommended.

Other rules relating to interpretation
In addition to the general approach taken to interpretation discussed above, there are a number of rules to which the courts might make reference in appropriate circumstances. In fact, these are perhaps better described as guidelines than rules per se, since they are not invariably applied and would also require to be viewed in light of prevailing judicial development. **10–07**

The contra proferentem *rule*
To return to ambiguous wording, there are occasions in which, if a contract contains a term which is unclear, that term will be interpreted *contra proferentem*, i.e. against the party seeking to rely on it. This is most relevant where a contractual document has been prepared solely by one side, rather than being negotiated between the parties.[18] **10–08**

A common example is where the contract contains an exemption clause (see Ch.7), and in such a situation the rule will be vigorously applied. In *North of Scotland Hydro-Electric Board v Taylor* (1956), a sub-contractor to HE was required by his contract to indemnify HE against "all claims from third parties arising from the operations under contract". Due to the negligence of HE, one of T's employees was killed by electrocution. The obvious question was whether the clause covered claims arising from HE's negligence. As the clause was ambiguous on this matter, it was interpreted *contra proferentem* and T was not required to indemnify HE. In an older case of *Life Association of Scotland v Foster* (1873), there was ambiguity regarding a clause in a life assurance policy. The clause provided that the policy would be void if any statement in the proposal form turned out to be untrue. When the proposer completed the form, she was unaware of already suffering from a potentially terminal condition and stated that she was in good health. After her death, L attempted to avoid payment. As the clause did not make it clear whether the clause was restricted to illness known to the pursuer, it was interpreted *contra proferentum* and L was unable to withhold payment.[19]

Even if a contract term is clear, it seems that it can never protect one party from the consequences of a total breach of contract. This is sometimes referred to as the "doctrine of fundamental breach". In *Pollock v Macrae* (1922), P contracted to build marine engines for M. The contract stated:

> "All goods are supplied on the condition that we shall not be liable for any direct or consequential damages arising from defective material or workmanship, even when such goods are supplied under the usual form of guarantee."

This clause would have protected P if parts of the engine had been found to be defective. However, it gave no protection where there was a total breach of contract due to the delivery of unserviceable engines.

The ejusdem generis rule

10–09 Sometimes a contractual term will seek to provide a non-exhaustive list indicating things to which the term might apply, e.g. disruptions that might cause delay. These will often take the form of specific examples, followed by a general "catch all" phrase. The interpretation of such a phrase will be confined to items of the same kind (ejusdem generis) and characteristics as those mentioned in the indicative list.

A classic example is *Abchurch Steamship Co v Stinnes* (1911), where a contract of charterparty excluded liability for a range of delays such as floods, accidents, or "any other unavoidable cause". It was held that delay due to congestion at port was *not* covered by "any other unavoidable cause", since all the specified examples involved breakdowns of normal operations; congestion was not of the same kind as the specific example listed.

It is a fairly common practice nowadays to subvert the ejusdem generis rule with use of examples which vary widely in nature, or with a general phrase which makes it clear that the words are intended to have a very wide scope.

TITLE TO SUE

A basic point about a contract is that it is enforceable between the parties to **10–10** it. By and large the enforcement or otherwise is a matter only for these parties. This is known as the doctrine of *jus tertii* which, confusingly, translates as "right of a third party". In other words, it is saying that, in general, a third party, even if he has an interest in the contract, has *no* right to enforce it. To put it in more conventional legal language, the third party is said to have no title to sue. In English law, this rule was historically stricter than in Scotland and was known as "privity of contract". The Contract (Rights of Third Parties) Act 1999 made the rights of third parties under English law more or less the same as in Scotland at that time.

The general rule of *jus tertii* is well illustrated in the old case of *Finnie v Glasgow and South-Western Railway* (1857). A contract had been signed between two railway companies, agreeing the rate for the haulage of coal along a particular stretch of railway line. When one of the companies increased its charges, a customer sought, in effect, to enforce the original terms of the contract. The contract between the two railway companies was held to be *jus tertii* so far as that customer was concerned. There was no denying that the customer had an interest in the contract, but he had no title to sue.

Similarly, a misrepresentation (see Ch.5) gives no title to sue except to the person to whom it was addressed. In *Edinburgh United Breweries Ltd v Molleson* (1894), M agreed to sell a brewery to a Mr Dunn, the price being based on accounts which were fraudulent. Unaware of the fraud, D resold the business to E. Later, E and D raised an action to reduce the original contract between M and D. Since E had not been the victim of the misrepresentation, nor a party to the contract, they had no title to sue.

Scots law has permitted certain exceptions to the rule of *jus tertii*. Perhaps the most obvious is the creation of third party rights under what at common law was termed *jus quaesitum tertio*, now subject to a statutory regime. It is also possible for rights to be transferred to another person under a process known as "assignation". A number of other concepts are also worthy of brief comment.

Creation of third party rights

The rather grand-sounding phrase *jus quaesitum tertio*, literally translated as **10–11** "right accruing to a third party", was historically used to describe certain limited situations where the law does permit a third party to enforce a contract in his own right. Under common law the rules are very strict, requiring the third party (or "*tertius*") to show that the contract itself refers to him, either as an individual or as one of a class of people, and that the original parties to the contract intended him to benefit. This has proven to be a fairly onerous burden, but some parties have been successful. In *Lamont v Burnett* (1901), N agreed to purchase L's hotel and also undertook to pay £100 to Mrs L for her assistance when he had visited to inspect the premises. L accepted the entire offer but B failed to pay Mrs L the £100. She was held entitled to sue B separately for that sum. In *Morton's Trustees v Aged Christian Friends Society*

(1899) (considered in a different context in Ch.3), it was held that the Society could sue under the contract even though the Society had only been in formation when M had agreed with a steering committee to make certain annual payments to fund charitable pensions.

A further hurdle to be cleared relates to revocability. If it is possible for the contracting parties to vary or revoke the third party's benefits, this would generally *not* create a *jus quaesitum tertio*. How exactly the parties indicate their intention to be bound, and indeed whether they have done so, requires to be determined with regard to all relevant circumstances. Clarity of the term itself, registration of the contract, or intimation of the benefit to the *tertius* would all point towards creation. In *Carmichael v Carmichael's Executrix* (1920), a father paid premiums to an insurance company, i.e. the contract was between the father as first party and the insurers as second party. The contract stated that a sum of money would be paid to the son's executors on his death provided he lived to age 21 and took over the premiums. The son died testate, aged 21, but before paying the first premium or taking delivery of the policy. An aunt was his sole beneficiary. Although the son had never been a party to the insurance, he had acquired a *jus quaesitum tertio* and the aunt was entitled to the proceeds. Contrast that case with *Burr v Commissioners of Bo'ness* (1896). An official had his salary raised at a council meeting. At the next meeting, the council revoked the earlier decision. The official had no right, in law, to the increase since it had not been intimated to him.[20]

The Scottish Law Commission had long identified *jus quaesitum tertio* as a problematic area for the legal profession, and recommended its reform.[21] This was achieved with the passing of the Contract (Third Party Rights) (Scotland) Act 2017, which regulates all contracts formed on or after its date of coming into force, 26 February 2018. The common law rules continue to regulate older contracts unless the parties agree otherwise.

The statutory rules maintain the essence of the common law principles by stipulating that a third party right will be created when three conditions are met:

> 1. the contract must contain an undertaking that one or more of the contracting parties will do, or not do, something for the person's benefit;
> 2. it must be the intention of the contracting parties that the person should be legally entitled to enforce or otherwise invoke the undertaking; and
> 3. the person must be identifiable from the contract by being either named or described in it.[22]

Significantly, there is no requirement of irrevocability, a major departure from the common law. The contracting parties are free to modify or cancel the third party's rights, although the third party is provided with a range of protections. The third party's rights cannot be changed retroactively, and they cannot be modified or cancelled once the third party has been notified of them by a contracting party, or where the third party has already acted in reliance on the rights. It is worth noting that the statutory rules may be contracted out of if the parties wish.

Assignation
One party to a contract may well wish to substitute a third party in his place 10–12
while the contract is still running. It may be possible to delegate performance to a third party, with the consent of the original creditor (see Ch.9). Alternatively, it may be necessary to assign rights of performance to a third party as security for an obligation. An obvious example is a contract of insurance being used as a security for a debt. Say, for example, that Steven has an endowment life policy with TotalCare Insurance. He wants to assign it as security for a loan from Ultimate Finance. Steven is referred to as the *cedent* and Ultimate Finance is the *assignee*. Somewhat confusingly, TotalCare Insurance is traditionally referred to as the *debtor*, namely the party due to pay or perform under the contract of insurance.

Which contracts can be assigned?
If all that remains to be performed is payment for, or delivery of, a particular 10–13
item, that right to receive performance can be assigned without the debtor's consent, unless the parties originally agreed otherwise. This is known as an *executed* contract. However, in the case of an *executorial* contract, performance has still to take place. Whether executorial contracts can be assigned is a matter of fact as well as law and hinges on the crucial concept of *delectus personae* (choice of person), which was mentioned in Ch.9.

Choice of person can be inferred where one party enters a contract relying on the personal qualities of the other. Where there is an element of *delectus personae*, performance of the element relying on it cannot be assigned. The stereotyped examples are employment and partnership, painting a portrait or even writing a book like this! Usually, common sense is a good guide as to whether there is *delectus personae*. Occasionally, there may be an element of doubt, particularly in respect of delivery of goods. *Cole v Handasyde & Co* (1910): S sold H a quantity of black grease. S was an expert on the commodity, although he did not manufacture it. Before the grease could be delivered, S was declared bankrupt. H refused to accept delivery of the grease from C, S's trustee in bankruptcy, maintaining that he had only entered the contract in reliance on S's personal skill. The court held that C was entitled to take over the contract, as it did not rely on S's skill or experience in such a way as to make him *delectus personae*.

The effect of assignation
When a contract can be validly assigned, the assignee enjoys the same rights 10–14
as the cedent possessed. There is a legal maxim *assignatus utitor jure auctoris* (the assignee enjoys the right of his cedent). Less formally, it is said that the assignee "stands in the shoes" of the cedent. This means that the assignee acquires no better right than the cedent himself had. If there was some flaw or vitiating factor in the original contract, the assignee takes it subject to the possible right of challenge. *Scottish Widows' Fund v Buist* (1876): M took out

a policy on his own life with S but made false statements as to his health and, in particular, his drinking habits. He subsequently assigned the policy in security to B and others. When M died at age 30, S not only declined to pay the sum assured to B but also succeeded in an action to reduce the insurance contract on the grounds of the original false statements. Since the original contract was void as between S and M, it was also void as against B. Similarly, in *Johnstone-Beattie v Dalzell* (1868), a father put certain sums in trust through his daughter's marriage contract, these to be paid to her husband on the father's death. The husband assigned this money in security to his creditors, but on his subsequent divorce his rights to it were forfeited, as were the rights of his creditors.

Method of assignation

10–15 Under the Requirements of Writing (Scotland) Act 1995, it is not essential for assignations to be put in writing. Common sense indicates that, in practice, they will be written. Prior to the 1995 Act, assignations counted as one of the *obligationes literis* (see Ch.3). The writing may take the statutory form prescribed by the Transmission of Moveable Property (Scotland) Act 1862 although, in practice, less formal styles are frequently used. In *Brownlee v Robb* (1907), the written words "I hand over my life policy to my daughter" provided a valid assignation. The transfer of many of the more common examples of contractual and other rights may be governed by particular statutory provision, such as for insurance policies[23] or for stocks and shares.[24]

It is important to understand that even when a right is assigned, the assignee's right against the cedent is only personal. To make his right real, the assignee must intimate the assignation to the debtor. Any competing priority of right is governed by the date of intimation, not the dates of the documents of assignation. To go back to the earlier fictitious example, if Steven wishes to assign his insurance policy in security to Ultimate Finance, he signs and delivers an assignation in their favour. Ultimate Finance will then make their right real by intimating the assignation to TotalCare Insurance. This intimation should be made in writing. The normal practice is to send the intimation in duplicate with the request that one copy be returned, stamped as acknowledged. Occasionally, even if there has been no express intimation, the debtor may be personally barred (see Ch.3) from denying knowledge of the assignation if he has acted, or refrained from acting, in a particular way.

Negotiable instruments

10–16 A right under a negotiable instrument passes with the instrument itself and is not affected by the *assignatus* rule referred to above. These negotiable instruments include bills of exchange, cheques, promissory notes and banknotes. The "holder in good faith and for value" of such an instrument, such as someone who has had a cheque endorsed over to him, is not affected by a defect in title to that instrument earlier in the chain of negotiation, provided it was not originally void. Thus, a shopkeeper who, in good faith and in the course of business, accepts a banknote that turns out to have been stolen, is still entitled to retain it. If, however, the banknote is a forgery it is worthless ab initio (from the beginning) and the defect has not arisen in the chain of negotiation. Since the passing of the Cheques Act 1992, cheques that are crossed "A/C payee only" cannot be made negotiable. (As mentioned in Ch.9, many businesses no longer accept cheques as payment.)

Agency

If an agent, acting within his actual or ostensible authority, makes a contract on behalf of his principal (the person whom he represents), the principal will normally have a title to sue on that contract. Indeed, the general rule is that where an agent forms a contract on behalf of an undisclosed, i.e. unnamed, principal and the agent has acted within his authority, that agent is not personally liable to the third party provided he does disclose the identity of his principal when requested to do so. Even if it is arguable that, in all the facts and circumstances, the agent has a degree of personal interest, it is clear that either the principal or the agent (but not both) has a title to sue or be sued. In *Bennett v Inveresk Paper Co* (1891), B, an Australian newspaper owner and previously undisclosed principal, was entitled to sue for damage to a consignment of paper shipped to Australia on the order of B's London agent who had never disclosed B's existence to the paper supplier. Similarly, if the third party wishes to sue, he must elect between agent or principal. In *Ferrier v Dods* (1865), F bought a warranted mare from D, an auctioneer, but complained shortly afterwards that the mare was unsound. D invited F to return the mare to her original owner, B, whose identity had not been disclosed at the roup. F did so and later attempted to sue both D and B. It was held that, having returned the mare to B, F had made his election to sue B and could no longer sue D.

10–17

Death or bankruptcy

If either party to a contract dies, any title to sue will pass to his executor, unless the contract involves *delectus personae* (see above), in which case the contract dies with him. A similar rule allows a trustee in bankruptcy, whether acting under a trust deed or in a formal sequestration, to continue with contracts previously entered into by the debtor, assuming that the trustee elects to do so and is not precluded by *delectus personae*. The main distinction between the two situations is that if a trustee in bankruptcy elects not to proceed with a contract when he could do so, he may expose the estate to an action for breach of contract. Such an action would not be appropriate where a contract had been terminated by death.

10–18

Many leases contain a clause to the effect that should the tenant become bankrupt or insolvent, this will terminate or "irritate" the lease (see Ch.8).

Contracts that "run with the land"

It is possible to have contracts relating to land where the rights and obligations are enforceable (or undertaken) by the current proprietors of respective heritable properties. These rights and obligations are said to "run with the land" and will affect each successive heritable proprietor until the obligation is extinguished. Common examples of such rights are access, wayleave,

10–19

obligations as to maintenance or restrictions on use, and are generally referred to as real burdens and servitudes. It is critical that these are registered in either the Land Register of Scotland or the General Register of Sasines to make them "real" obligations (enforceable and defensible against the world in general) as opposed to "personal" obligations (enforceable and defensible only against specific parties); registration in the appropriate register ensures that the obligations attach to the land in question.

This area was altered as part of broader reforms involving the abolition of feudal tenure and the modernisation of Scots property law. Under the "new" system, primarily regulated by the Title Conditions (Scotland) Act 2003 (as amended), such a right must be created in a deed (of any form), which is registered against both the "benefitted" property and the "burdened" property. Previously, the form of deed was restricted and the right only required to be registered against the burdened property. The situation regarding enforcement of rights created under the "old" system, i.e. prior to the coming into force of the Abolition of Feudal Tenure (Scotland) Act 2000, depends on various factors outlined in the 2003 Act. This is a highly specialised area and, as such, is beyond the scope of this book.

Joint and several liability

10-20 This concerns liability when being sued rather than title to sue, but may be conveniently considered at this point. A contract may involve one of the parties being, in fact, more than one person. A particularly common example is partnership. Although a firm is a "person" under Scots law (see Ch.4), it is not entirely separated from the partners who make it up. Thus, if suing a firm for a money debt, the correct procedure is first to sue the firm, failing which the partners. However, it is not necessary to divide the debt amongst the partners. The creditor is entitled to pursue any one of the partners for the full amount. If that partner satisfies the debt, he may claim "relief", i.e. proportionate repayment from his fellow partners. Joint and several liability is common, either by implication of law or by agreement. As well as in partnership, it is found in the ownership of shared property (as in a tenement house) and in cautionary obligations.

CONTRACT (SCOTLAND) ACT 1997

10-21 Mention has already been made above of the abolition of the so-called "parole evidence" rule. This was one of "three bad rules" identified by the Scottish Law Commission[25] which were abolished by the Contract (Scotland) Act 1997. For the sake of completeness, the two other changes, which principally affect conveyancing practice, are now dealt with briefly.

Section 2 of the 1997 Act abolished a much-criticised rule that was developed through the decision in the case of *Winston v Patrick* (1980). This rule stated that missives for the sale of heritable property were superseded ("killed off") by the delivery of the disposition. (This became known as "the rule in *Winston v Patrick*", though its origins were actually far older.) The result was that any agreement or warranty made in the missives, but not expressly stated in the disposition, would be unenforceable. This was not an academic point, since modern missives are often complex documents bristling with conditions about the state of central heating, drainage and electrical wiring, to say nothing of demanding delivery of a bewildering selection of documents. In order to ensure that these missive conditions were kept "alive", notwithstanding the delivery of the disposition, it became customary for the missives to contain a clause continuing their effective life for a period of time, usually two years, after delivery of the disposition. This is called a "non-supersession" clause and, as a result of a plethora of conflicting sheriff court cases, it subsequently became almost universal practice to insert such a clause in the disposition itself. Since the 1997 Act came into force, this is no longer required; s.2 of the Act expressly states that any unimplemented term of a contract will not be superseded by virtue only of the execution of an implementing deed—though parties are free to agree otherwise.

Having cleared up this issue, however, there is still potential for problems. If an agreement made in the missives is *not* superseded by the disposition, then in theory a contractual obligation could continue to exist for an inordinate amount of time, perhaps even long after the transfer of the property has been completed. This is undesirable and so the practice has emerged among sellers' agents of inserting a "supersession clause" in the missives. This is a clause stating that after a period of time, usually two years, the buyer can no longer found on missive provisions and the disposition will (for the majority of matters) prevail. This avoids the problem of sellers having obligations extending over an unacceptably long period of time.

Finally, until the passing of the Act, it seemed that a buyer of heritable property or a business did not have a right in law to keep the property and claim damages if it turned out to be defective.[26] Either he had to keep the property and claim no damages or reject it and claim damages. Unlike a buyer of goods, who has the protection of the Sale of Goods Act 1979,[27] he did not have recourse to the *actio quanti minoris* which, very loosely translated, means "something off the price". Section 3 of the 1997 Act provides that a buyer who retains defective property may obtain damages for the seller's breach of contract. It used to be common practice for missives of sale to provide expressly for the *actio quanti minoris* to be implied into the contract. Such a provision is now unnecessary.

THE FUTURE OF CONTRACT LAW

As this book draws its commentary on contracts to a close, it is appropriate to **10–22** consider briefly what the near future might hold for contract law. Mention has been made often of areas which are under review, and the commendable work of the Scottish Law Commission has been referenced wherever possible.

It is, of course, impossible to say what will happen. Indeed, if a lesson can be drawn from the recent history of contract law, it must be that even speculating on what might happen is risky. As observed in Ch.1, since the early twenty-first century, the trend has been for an increase in harmonisation of contract law across EU countries. However, as if to underline the dangers of speculation, the future relationship of the UK (and so Scotland) with the EU is currently a matter of great uncertainty. The extent to which Scots law will continue to be influenced by EU developments, therefore, remains to be seen.

What can be said is that parties will continue to make contracts and that sometimes parties will break them. Such disputes, and the often spectacularly creative judicial approaches to resolving them, will no doubt keep lawyers, and law students, busy for the foreseeable future.

---

1. *Muirhead & Turnbull v Dickson* (1905) 13 S.L.T. 151.
2. *Houldsworth v Gordon Cumming*, 1910 S.C. (HL) 49.
3. *Inglis v Buttery* (1877–1878) 3 App. Cas. 552.
4. *Prenn v Simmonds* [1971] W.L.R. 1381.
5. *Credential Bath Street Ltd v Venture Investment Placement Ltd* [2007] CSOH 208.
6. See, e.g. *British Coal Corp v South of Scotland Electricity Board*, 1991 S.L.T. 302.
7. *Investor Compensation Scheme Ltd v West Bromwich Albion Building Society* [1998] 1 W.L.R. 896.
8. See, e.g. *Multi-Link Leisure Developments Ltd v North Lanarkshire Council*, 2011 S.C. (U.K.S.C.) 53.
9. See also *Luminar Lava Ignite Ltd v MAMA Group Plc* [2010] CSIH 1 and *Aberdeen City Council v Stewart Milne Ltd*, 2012 S.C. (U.K.S.C.) 240.
10. See, e.g. *R&J Dempster Ltd v Motherwell Bridge & Engineering Co Ltd*, 1964 S.C. 308.
11. *Bruce & Co v Ferguson*, 2013 G.W.D. 32–640.
12. *Patersons of Greenoakhill Ltd v Biffa Waste Services Ltd* [2013] CSOH 18.
13. *Grove Investments Ltd v Cape Building Products* [2014] CSIH 43; *Hoe International v Andersen* [2017] CSIH 9.
14. *@SIPP Pension Trustees v Insight Travel Services Ltd* [2015] CSIH 91; *AWG Business Centres Ltd v Regus Caledonia Ltd* [2017] CSIH 22.
15. Law Reform (Miscellaneous Provisions) (Scotland) Act 1985 (c.73) s.8.
16. Scottish Law Commission, *Report on Review of Contract Law* (HMSO, 2018), Scot. Law Com. No.252.
17. *Arnold v Britton* [2015] UKSC 36, per Lord Neuberger at [15].
18. *Credential Bath Street Ltd v Venture Investment Placement Ltd* [2007] CSOH 208.
19. For a recent Scottish case in which the rule was unsuccessfully invoked, see *Gammie v Abbey Legal Protection* [2011] 12 WLUK 469.
20. For more recent cases considering *jus quaesitum tertio* see *Marquess of Aberdeen v Turcan Connell* [2008] CSOH 183 and *Regus (Maxim) Limited v Bank of Scotland Plc* [2011] CSOH 129, later affirmed by the Inner House on other issues: [2013] CSIH 12.
21. Scottish Law Commission, *Report on Third Party Rights* (HMSO, 2016), Scot. Law Com. No.245.
22. Contract (Third Party Rights) (Scotland) Act 2017 s.1.
23. Policies of Assurance Act 1867 (c.144).
24. Stock Transfer Act 1963 (c.18).
25. Scottish Law Commission, *Report on Three Bad Rules in Contract Law* (HMSO, 1996), Scot. Law Com. No.152.
26. *Fortune v Fraser*, 1996 S.L.T. 878.
27. Sale of Goods Act 1979 (c.54) ss.15B and 53A.

APPENDIX: SAMPLE EXAMINATION QUESTIONS AND ANSWER PLANS

1. With reference to the law of contract, the law of Scotland places great store on "the essentials" of a valid contract. What are these essentials?

The only problem with a straightforward substantive question of this nature is that you have to answer it fairly fully. There is little opportunity for "on the one hand and on the other hand". Either you know the basic law or you do not. It is particularly important not to imagine that the examiner is going to read your mind. Assume that you are explaining the basic law to someone who is intelligent and quick on the "uptake" but has no previous knowledge of the subject. In that way, you should not go wrong.

So, be sure to cover the various essential elements of a contract:

Agreement about the same thing
You can cover the well-tried paths of *consensus in idem*, citing such cases as *Raffles v Wichelhaus* (1864). Take care in applying cases. Two factors that tend to irritate examiners are: (1) students who, by rote, merely repeat the facts of the case without showing its relevance; and (2) students who merely "name-drop" by saying "see the case of" and leave it to the examiner to fill in the details. What if you remember a case but, in the heat of the moment, cannot remember the names of the parties? It is better to say "in the case of A against B" or "in a settled case" than to omit it altogether, just because you have forgotten the name. Remember, you are out to achieve every mark possible and examiners do look for you to give authority for what you say. At the same time, examiners are looking to see if they can pass you. They are not searching for ways to ensure that you fail. There is normally no need to remember the dates of cases, unless the context shows otherwise.

At least two contracting parties
This part of the question should not take long. The need for there being at least two contracting parties may be painfully obvious, but it should still be stated. A surprisingly large number of students forget to state the obvious in examinations as though it were somehow beneath their dignity! It is probably worth mentioning that "party" can include legal persons, such as companies, but this is not a point to labour over.

Contractual capacity
You should explain the concept of capacity briefly and give some examples of persons whose capacity is restricted, e.g. young people. It is always a good idea to include statutory reference where possible, so cite the Age of Legal Capacity (Scotland) Act 1991.

Formalities

Again, this isn't something to spend too much time on. It is worth stating that most contracts are valid even if formed only verbally, but that proof might be a problem. Make brief reference to an example or two where the contract must be in writing, such as those relating to land under the Requirements of Writing (Scotland) Act 1995.

Enforceable obligations

There should be plenty of material here. Outline those agreements which are clearly illegal due to immorality, criminality, public policy or statutory provision. There are other agreements that are perfectly legal but which the courts will not enforce, such as social agreements. Lastly, it would be appropriate to discuss the development of *sponsiones ludicrae* (sportive promises), i.e. that traditionally gambling and wagering contracts would not be enforced, but that this principle has now been abolished by the Gambling Act 2005.

2.(a) *What is the distinction between a contractual offer and a willingness to negotiate? Why is the distinction important?*

(b) *Joan is a hard-up student; she goes into a Summerways Supermarket and fills up a trolley with groceries. She wheels it to the checkout and states to the operator that she intends to buy the entire contents of the trolley for £10, although the market value is around £20. Comment on the legal issues involved.*

(c) *George discusses the possible sale of his car to Mildred, although they are unable to come to an agreement. Somewhat frustrated, George writes to Mildred stating that he will sell the car for £3,000 and concludes the letter "If I do not hear from you by Friday, I shall treat the deal as concluded." Comment on the legal issues involved.*

This question involves a small part of substantive law and then invites comment on two possible scenarios.

(a) Difference between offer and willingness to negotiate

This is a well-tried but crucial area, namely formation of contract. An indication of willingness to negotiate is exactly what it says. Parties have not got beyond the preliminary stages and may still be thinking of making or receiving an offer. A familiar area is that of shops, which do not offer to sell items to the general public (*Pharmaceutical Society of Great Britain v Boots Cash Chemists* (1952)). An offer, on the other hand, is open for acceptance and once it is accepted without qualification, a binding contract is formed. A willingness to negotiate, by contrast, can never be accepted, because it is not an offer. Thus, a shop cannot be forced to sell any item if it does not wish to. A further important point is that an offer must always come before an acceptance.

How is it possible to tell the difference? Every case has to be considered on its own merits. As well as goods in shops, advertisements, goods in

Appendix: Sample Examination Questions and Answer Plans   111

catalogues and estimates are usually considered to be willingness to negotiate. Offers may be made expressly (verbally or in writing) or by implication. A good case on an unusual offer is *Chapleton v Barry UDC* (1940). Contrasting cases identifying mere willingness to negotiate and firm offer are *Harvey v Facey* (1893) and *Philp & Co v Knoblauch* (1907) respectively.

A brief mention could also be made of offers to the general public (*Carlill v Carbolic Smokeball Co* (1893), etc.) but be careful not to get sidetracked into a good story and let your pen run away with you!

(b) Problem number 1
An easy problem, but take time to explain it logically. The legal points at issue are the status of goods in shops (i.e. that they are a mere willingness to negotiate), who makes the offer and at what point in time. Using the facts from the *Boots* case (see part (a) above), it is clear what the status of goods is. It is also clear that it is the customer who makes the offer when he takes the items to the point of sale. Accordingly, even although goods are price marked or bar-coded, any customer is entitled to make his own offer for any item or collection of items. Obviously, the checkout operator is unlikely to accept, in which case the customer's offer falls.

(c) Problem number 2
It is possible to have both an offer and acceptance by implication but the law generally takes a dim view of offers being unilaterally imposed on anyone. Sometimes an acceptance can be implied by a failure to reject, but this can only arise if there have been similar dealings between the parties in the past. As there is no evidence of similar dealings in the present case, there is no contract. You could also mention the statutory provisions of the Unsolicited Goods and Services Act 1971.

3. John has worked for six years for an employment agency which has offices in most of the cities and large towns in the United Kingdom. He has been offered a promoted post with another equally large agency and wishes to accept. His prudent employer points out that he cannot take up such a post within one year of leaving, due to a clause in his contract. This clause provides that he may not take up a post with any other employment agency "in order to prevent disclosure of the employers' system of work, presentation of the service to the customer and, in particular, the fee charging policy". Is this clause enforceable against John, in your reasoned opinion?

This is the type of question that comes up in 101 different guises but basically asks the same thing and is popular with examiners.

It is important to be aware that there is not one obvious answer and that the problem needs to be addressed in such a way as to highlight the main legal issues. You should certainly come to your own conclusion based on your interpretation of these issues. A fair-minded examiner—and the vast majority are very fair minded—should not penalise a candidate merely because a different conclusion from his own is drawn provided the candidate argues his case well. Indeed, an examiner will probably prefer a conclusion with which he disagrees to the totally open-ended conclusion, "it could be this but on the other hand it could be that". Of course, there are two sides to any question but it is part of a lawyer's forensic training and skill to identify the strengths and weaknesses of both sides.

Identify the main area of law

What John is faced with is a restrictive covenant, which restricts a person's freedom to work where he pleases, for whom he pleases and in what line of business he pleases.

The general rule of law

As a very general rule, a restrictive covenant is only going to be upheld if it passes the test of being reasonable. It is reasonable to protect trade secrets and to prevent customers being enticed away. It is not reasonable to prevent fair competition.

The interpretation of what is reasonable

The courts tend to interpret "reasonable" rather more strictly where the contention is between employer and employee than they do as between the buyer and seller of a business—so this is already a point in John's favour.

Factors taken into account

As well as relying on the notoriously elusive concept of reasonableness, the court will take other factors into account, such as the type of the business, the radius or customer area it serves, where it is located, e.g. city, large town, small town or rural and the status of the employee. Make sure you cite cases. Established favourites are *Mason v Provident Clothing* (1913); *Fitch v Dewes* (1921); and *Bluebell Apparel v Dickinson* (1980), but there are others quoted in the text. A great deal will depend on the status of John within the agency and we cannot assume what we are not told. If he occupies a fairly ordinary position, then that is in his favour. The agency appears to operate on a countrywide basis and it is clearly a blow that any employee will go to work for the arch-rival. The question is whether that move could reasonably threaten trade secrets or customer base. Trade secrets need not be of a purely industrial or manufacturing basis. The present writer would suggest that, in context, the clause is enforceable. Of course, only a court can ultimately decide. It is probably worth pointing out as a parting shot that the courts will only uphold or strike down clauses of this nature and will not alter them.

4. *(a) In which circumstances is a party entitled to treat a contract as having been breached?*

(b) Give a reasoned opinion of the remedy available to the aggrieved party in each of the following situations:

(1) Cecil has been having a new bathroom suite installed by Loobylose Bathrooms. The centre of attraction was to have been the marble effect sunken bath with its gold-plated taps. The bathroom was satisfactorily completed apart from the bath—and it is now six weeks overdue.

(2) Blue Marmalade, a famous pop group, have signed up to give a concert at the Saturn Centre in Edinburgh. On the night of the concert, they fail to appear.

(3) Sid, a self-employed taxi driver, has put his vehicle into a garage for servicing. The work has been done but Sid is experiencing cash-flow problems and cannot pay the bill. Sid is insisting that the garage return the vehicle as he needs it to earn the money to pay for the service.

(a) Breach of contract

A party is in breach if he fails to perform the contract. This may be total non-performance, partial performance or defective performance. Unless a party fulfils his obligations in full, he is, at least technically, in breach. It may be important, in practice, to establish whether or not a breach can be treated as material, as the remedy of rescission is only available in such cases. At least in theory, any breach of contract can give rise to a claim for damages. The other point to be addressed is whether the breach has already taken place or whether it may take place in the future, i.e. anticipatory breach. If it is the latter, the innocent party has two choices: he may treat the contract as having been repudiated there and then and proceed accordingly in an action for damages (*White & Carter (Councils) Ltd v McGregor* (1962)); alternatively, he could presume that the contract is still alive and wait until the set time for performance. If the performance does take place, then clearly there has been no breach. If performance does not take place, then clearly an action for damages may be raised. In this case, the damages may well be substantial.

(b)(1) Delay in performance

Delay is a common and problematic breach of contract. What the innocent party should do is probably as much a matter of pragmatism as of law. However, the crucial area in law is whether "time is of the essence" of a particular contract. If it is of the essence, Loobylose are in material breach which would open the possibility of Cecil rescinding. It is futile to rescind a contract when the innocent party wishes performance. It may at least be unwise to try to rescind a contract where restitutio in integrum is not possible. The delay in fitting the bath may be annoying but, unless the parties have agreed that time is of the essence, mere delay will, at best, only give rise to damages for trouble and inconvenience (*Webster v Cramond Iron Co* (1975)). You might argue that, by implication, time is of the essence of this contract. It would certainly be inconvenient, though not impossible, to live without a bath for such a long period of time. Even if you could muster an argument that time is of the essence, and that the contractor is in material breach, there is little point in rescinding the contract immediately, since restitutio cannot be given. However, prudent advice to Cecil might be to give Loobylose an ultimatum to the effect that work must be completed within a reasonable time. If it is not, Cecil will pay Loobylose for what work has been done on a *quantum meruit* basis and the bath will be supplied and fitted by other contractors. Cecil will seek damages from Loobylose for additional costs involved plus a sum to compensate for the inconvenience involved. It is just possible that Loobylose have a valid reason; war may have broken out with the country in which the supplier of this type of bath is manufactured! Whilst this is unlikely, it is important, in giving advice, to ensure that any party in breach has an opportunity to explain himself. This is no more than natural justice.

(b)(2) Total non-performance

This is a simple question and you can answer it briefly, but not too briefly. It is as clear an example as you will find of breach by total non-performance. There is no point in advising the promoter to attempt specific implement. It is a waste of time to ask the court to grant a decree *ad factum praestandum* as the time of the concert is past. Performance is impossible and such a decree would not be awarded. Blue Marmalade have, by their non-appearance, repudiated the contract. The promoter can claim damages, which could well be substantial.

(b)(3) The defensive measure of lien

The garage is perfectly entitled to exercise a right of lien over the vehicle, pending payment of the bill. Sid has no right to insist that the vehicle be returned, although common sense dictates that a taxi driver does not have much opportunity of earning money without a taxi at his disposal. If, however, the garage agrees to return his taxi on the understanding that he will earn enough money to pay the bill, you would be duty bound to point out that they have now lost their right of lien. If Sid does not pay the bill, the garage cannot unilaterally repossess the taxi as a right of lien does not run with the goods (*Hostess Mobile Catering v Archibald Scott Ltd* (1981)).

5. (a) *Give an account of the application and effect of impossibility, illegality and frustration on a contract.*

   (b) *A firm of builders undertake to build a number of flats for a Housing Association at a fixed price of £750,000. Due to shortage of building materials and skilled labour, to say nothing of inclement weather, the job takes many months longer than expected and costs the builder almost £1 million. Comment on the legal issues involved.*

   (c) *Muthill United FC sign up Oscar Deadeye, a very promising striker from another club. Not long after his joining the club, there is a terrible blizzard which leads to a power cut, causing the central heating in Oscar's house to fail. His goal-scoring foot, which is protruding from under the duvet, becomes frost-bitten and the striker has to have a toe amputated. Oscar's days as a striker are over. Discuss the legal issues involved.*

(a) Impossibility, illegality and frustration

It is important to notice that if a contract is terminated by any of these three possibilities, damages are not payable. Obviously, anyone in breach of contract will want to consider whether any one of these three "cards" could be played. If the reason for impossibility, illegality or frustration is the substantial fault of the party who is unable to perform, he cannot escape potential liability for damages. In addition, the cause for the inability to perform must be "supervening", i.e. it must have arisen since the contract was formed due to some external factor over which the parties have no control.

Impossibility means what is says: the contract must be impossible to perform, not merely inconvenient, expensive or based on an error of judgment. An easy example of impossibility is *rei interitus*, where specific property essential to the contract is destroyed (*Taylor v Caldwell* (1863)) or constructively destroyed (*Mackeson v Boyd* (1942) or *Tay Salmon Fisheries v Speedie* (1929)). Depending on the number of marks allocated to this question, you could also make brief mention of the fact that there is a common law rule which provides that a buyer of heritable property assumes the risk as soon as missives are concluded (*Sloans Dairies Ltd v Glasgow Corp* (1977)), unless expressly provided to the contrary. In the case of moveable property there is a statutory provision (Sale of Goods Act 1979 s.7) that where specific goods perish, without fault of either party, before ownership passes to the buyer, the contract is void. It might also be impossible to perform a contract due to the ill health of one of the parties, if *delectus personae* was a factor (*Condor v Barron Knights* (1966)).

Illegality, as a means of terminating a contract, occurs when the obligations were perfectly legal at the time of formation but supervening elements, beyond the control of the parties, have made performance illegal (*Fraser & Son v Denny* (1944)). This is quite different from illegality at the outset. In the latter case, the contract would be void ab initio.

Frustration takes place where a contract can, at least in theory, be performed but because of supervening events outwith the control of the parties, performance produces a quite different outcome from what the parties had originally intended. It would be hard to resist citing the two contrasting "coronation" cases of *Krell v Henry* (1903) and *Herne Bay Steamboat v Hutton* (1903).

(b) The builder's problem

Obviously, this builder is learning a hard lesson. The fact that a contract has become difficult or expensive to perform does not make it impossible. A case very much in point is *Davis Contractors v Fareham UDC* (1956).

(c) The striker's problem

Even the most litigious lawyer would be hard pressed to blame a blizzard on any particular person (other than God?). It is agreed that there was a power cut. Is there any mileage in suing the electricity supply company? You could look at remoteness of damage—*Hadley v Baxendale* (1854) and related cases, including particularly *Balfour Beatty v Scottish Power* (1994).

The conclusion would be "no". You could try to prove that Oscar had failed to take proper care of his precious foot by leaving it sticking outside the duvet. The contract could be terminated on account of impossibility of performance (as in *Condor v Barron Knights* (1966)), but the Club could try to claim damages from Oscar as he has contributed to his own injury. Whether they would succeed is another matter.

INDEX

Acceptance
consensus required, 2–11
counter-offers, 2–11
electronic communications, 2–19
exemption clauses
generally, 7–05
implied acceptance, 7–05
generally, 2–11
implied acceptance, 2–11
method, 2–13
offer as a whole, 2–11
offers to general public, 2–06
postal rules, 2–15—2–20
qualified acceptance, 2–11
standard terms, 2–12
withdrawal, 2–14
Acceptilation
termination of contract, 9–04
Acquiescence
see **Mora taciturnity and acquiescence**
Actio quanti minoris
title to sue, 10–21
Action for payment
breach of contract, 8–11
Advertisements
offers, 2–06
Agency
title to sue, 10–17
Agents
actual authority, 4–12, 10–17
apparent authority, 4–12
capacity, 4–12
disclosure of principal, 10–17
formation of contract, 4–12
ostensible authority, 4–12, 10–17
Agreement
formation of contract, 1–04, 2–02, 7–01
elements of contracts, 1–04, 2–02, 7–01
exemption clauses, 7–01
Alien enemies
capacity, 4–07
Aliens
capacity, 4–07
Anticipatory breach
breach of contract, 8–18
law reform, 8–18
Arm's length transactions
caveat emptor principle, 5–20
contract negotiations, 5–20
disclosure of material facts, 5–22

exemption clauses, 7–09
fiduciary relationships, 5–23
full disclosure required, 5–21
insurance contracts, 5–22
partnership contracts, 5–22
utmost good faith, 5–22
Assignation
assignable contracts, 10–13
assignee, 10–12, 10–14
cedent, 10–12, 10–14
debtor, 10–12, 10–15
delectus personae, 10–13, 10–18
effect, 10–14
generally, 10–12
insurance contract, 10–12, 10–15
method, 10–15
negotiable instruments, 10–16
security for obligation, 10–12
substitution of third party, 10–12
writing requirement, 10–15
"At least two contracting parties"
formation of contract, 1–06, 3–01, 9–01
Bankruptcy
offer, 2–10
title to sue, 10–18
Battle of forms
see **Standard terms**
Betting
legal obligations, 1–08
Bilateral error
generally, 5–07
Breach of contract
action for payment, 8–11
anticipatory breach, 8–18
damages
see **Damages**
defective performance, 8–02
foreseeable loss, 8–16
illegal contracts, 8–07
partial performance, 8–02
payment of sums of money, 8–04
performance impossible, 8–07
performance of obligations, 8–01
personal relationship contracts, 8–05
remedies
see **Remedies (breach of contract)**
remoteness of loss, 8–16
repudiation of contract, 8–08
subject matter of contract, 8–06
Capacity
agents, 4–12
children, 4–02—4–04

contractual capacity, 1–07
corporate bodies, 4–08
enemy aliens, 4–07
heritable property, 4–04
intoxicated persons, 4–06
introduction, 4–01
limited liability partnerships, 4–11
mental illness, 4–05
minors, 4–02— 4–04
necessaries, 4–03—4–04
partnerships, 4–10—4–11
requirement, 4–01
statutory limitations, 4–01
unincorporated bodies, 4–09
validity of contract, 5–01
young people, 4–02— 4–04
Causation
damages, 8–14
Caveat emptor
contract negotiations, 5–20
Children
capacity, 4–02—4–04
Common error
generally, 5–07, 5–09
Common law
fraudulent misrepresentation, 5–18
generally, 1–02
illegal agreements, 6–04
interdict, 8–03
interpretation of contract, 10–02
rectification, 5–06
restraint of trade, 6–06—6–08
silence or concealment, 5–20
Companies
capacity, 4–08
Compensation
damages, 8–12
termination of contract, 9–08
Competition law
illegal agreements, 6–09
Concealment
misrepresentation, 5–20
Confusion
termination of contract, 9–07
Consensus ad idem
see **Agreement**
Consideration
requirement, 3–02
Consumer contracts
exemption clauses, 7–11—7–13
Consumer Rights Act 2015
enforcement, 7–13
introduction, 7–11
protections, 7–12
Consumer contracts
exemption clauses, 7–11—7–13

Consumer protection
fraudulent misrepresentation, 5–18
Contra proferentum
interpretation of contracts, 10–08
Contract
agreement about the same thing, 1–04
at least two contracting parties, 1–06, 3–01
breach of contract
see **Breach of contract**
definition
generally, 1–03
enforcement, 1–08
see also **Enforcement of contract**
EU law, 1–02, 10–22
formation of contracts
see **Formation of contracts**
future development, 10–22
gratuitous contracts, 3–02, 3–03
harmonisation, 1–02
implied contract, 2–22
introduction, 1–01—1–08
legal obligations, 1–08
legislative competence, 1–02
moral obligations, 1–08
reciprocal nature, 3–01
statutory control, 1–02
written agreement, 3–01
Contracts of employment
changes to agreement, 6–07
employer protection, 6–07
exemption clauses, 7–08
restrictive covenants, 6–07
severable clauses, 6–07
wrongful dismissal, 6–07
Contracts of hire
exemption clauses, 7–08
Contracts for services
exemption clauses, 7–08
Contractual capacity
see **Capacity**
Conveyancing
delivery of disposition, 10–21
heritable property, 10–19
missives, 10–21
non-supersession clauses, 10–21
supersession clauses, 10–21
Corporate bodies
capacity, 4–08
Courts
role of the courts, 1–02
Damages
anticipatory breach, 8–18
calculating damages, 8–13
causation, 8–14
compensation, 8–12
fraud, 5–18

generally, 8–12
liquidated damages, 8–17
misrepresentation, 5–16—5–19
mitigation of loss, 8–15
punitive damages, 8–13
remoteness of loss, 8–16
repudiation of contract, 8–08
Death
  offer, 2–10
  title to sue, 10–18
Delectus personae
  assignation, 10–13, 10–18
Delegation
  termination of contract, 9–06
Distance selling
  consumer protection, 2–21
  withdrawal from contract, 2–21
Ejusdem generis
  interpretation of contracts, 10–09
Electronic communications
  distance selling, 2–21
  offer and acceptance, 2–19
  validity of contract, 3–03
Employment contracts
  see **Contracts of employment**
Enforcement
  generally, 10–01
  illegal contracts, 10–01
  legal obligations, 1–08
  moral obligations, 1–08
  verbal promises, 3–02
  void contracts, 10–01
  written agreements, 3–01, 3–02
Entry to property
  exemption clauses, 7–08
Error
  bilateral error, 5–07
  common error, 5–07, 5–09
  error of expression
    examples, 5–06
    incorrect offer, 5–06
    meaning, 5–06
  error of fact, 5–05
  error of intention
    bilateral error, 5–07
    common error, 5–07, 5–09
    contract void, 5–09—5–15
    introduction, 5–07
    mistake, 5–07
    mutual error, 5–07, 5–10—5–15
    unilateral error, 5–07, 5–08
  error of law, 5–05
  essential error
    see **Essential error**
  ignorance of the law, 5–05
  incidental error, 5–10, 5–17
  legal effects, 5–05

misrepresentation, 5–01, 5–16—5–23
  see also **Misrepresentation**
mistake, 5–07
  see also **Mistake**
mutual error
  contract void, 5–10—5–15
  essential error, 5–10
  identity, 5–13
  incidental error, 5–10
  introduction, 5–07, 5–10
  nature of contract, 5–15
  price, 5–12
  quantity, quality, extent, 5–14
  subject matter, 5–11
rectification, 5–06
unilateral error, 5–07, 5–08
unjust enrichment, 5–05
validity of contract, 5–05, 5–29
Essential error
  identity, 5–13
  innocent misrepresentation, 5–17
  nature of contract, 5–15
  price, 5–12
  quantity, quality or extent, 5–14
  subject matter, 5–11
Estimates
  offer, 2–05
EU law
  harmonisation, 1–02, 10–22
Ex turpi causa
  illegal agreements, 6–02
Exclusion clauses
  acceptance of conditions
    generally, 7–05
    implied acceptance, 7–05
  adequate attention to conditions, 7–04
  bargaining power, 7–01, 7–10
  consumer rights, 7–11—7–13
    see also **Consumer Rights Act 2015**
  enforcement, 7–13
  introduction, 7–11
  protections, 7–12
  examples, 7–01
  exclusion of liability, 7–01
  generally, 7–01
  knowledge of condition, 7–02
  notice displayed, 7–01, 7–03
  post–formation conditions
    generally, 7–02
    tickets, 7–03
  standard form contracts, 7–09
  tickets
    adequacy of notice of condition, 7–01, 7–03
    arm's length transactions, 7–09
    attention drawn to notice, 7–04
    exclusion clause, 7–03

introduction, 7–01
post-formation conditions, 7–02—7–06
receipt or voucher, 7–03
types, 7–01
Unfair Contract Terms Act 1977, 7–08—7–10
see also **Unfair Contract Terms Act 1977**
Expression of intention
offer, 2–05
Extortionate terms
validity of agreements, 5–28
Facility and circumvention
validity of agreements, 5–25, 5–32
Fiduciary relationship
relationship of trust, 5–23
solicitor and client, 5–23
undue influence, 5–26
Force and fear
validity of agreements, 5–27, 5–31
Formation of contract
acceptance
see **Acceptance**
agreement about the same thing, 1–04, 2–02, 7–01
at least two contracting parties, 1–06, 9–01
bargaining power, 7–01, 7–10
distance selling, 2–21
electronic communications, 3–03
employment contracts, 2–02
error
see **Error**
evidence of agreement, 1–05
formalities, 1–05
heritable property, 1–05
implied contracts, 2–22
industry standards, 2–02
intention of the parties, 2–22
introduction, 2–01
legal obligations, 1–08
objective approach, 2–02
offer
see **Offer**
oral agreements, 1–05
postal rules, 2–15—2–20
prescribed form, 1–05
price, 2–02
reciprocal rights and duties, 9–01
written agreements, 1–05
Fraud
damages claims, 5–18
mere carelessness, 5–18
restitutio in integrum, 5–18
Fraudulent misrepresentation
common law, 5–18
company prospectus, 5–18
consumer protection, 5–18
damages, 5–18
dishonesty, 5–18
generally, 5–16
heritable property, 5–18
restitutio in integrum, 5–18
statement of opinion, 5–18
trade puffs, 5–18
void contract, 5–18
voidable contract, 5–18
Frustration
apportionment of loss, 9–14
materially different outcome, 9–13
performance disrupted, 9–13
performance more expensive, 9–13
termination of contract, 9–13
Gambling
legal obligations, 1–08
Gentleman's agreement
legal obligations, 1–08
Gratuitous contracts
enforcement, 3–02
gratuitous unilateral obligation, 3–02, 3–03
Heritable property
capacity, 4–04
conveyancing practice, 10–21
defective property, 10–21
formation of contract, 1–05
fraudulent misrepresentation, 5–18
Holding out
personal bar, 3–05
Homologation
personal bar, 3–04
Ignorance of the law
error of law, 5–05
Illegality
agreements
buyer and seller of business, 6–08
contrary to public policy, 6–05
employers and employees, 6–07
joint agreements (manufacturers or traders), 6–09
cartels, 6–09
common law, 6–04
competition law, 6–09
ex turpi causa non oritur actio, 6–02
generally, 6–02
immoral contracts, 6–02
pacta illicita, 6–01
parties not equally at fault, 6–02
restraint of trade contracts, 6–06—6–08
see also **Restraint of trade**
restrictive covenants 6–06—6–08

see also **Restrictive covenants**
  solus agreements, 6–10
  statutory illegality, 6–03
  termination of contract, 9–12, 9–14
  unenforceable contracts, 6–01
Implied contracts
  generally, 2–22
Impossibility
  performance impossible, 8–07
  termination of contract, 9–11, 9–14
Incidental error
  generally, 5–10
  innocent misrepresentation, 5–17
Innocent misrepresentation
  absence of fraud, 5–17
  contract void, 5–17
  contract voidable, 5–17
  essential error, 5–17
  incidental error, 5–17
  restitutio in integrum, 5–17
Insanity
  capacity, 4–05
  offer, 2–10
Interdict
  specific implement compared, 8–03
  breach of contract, 8–03—8–07
Interpretation
  ambiguous wording, 10–05, 10–08
  common law, 10–02
  context, 10–04
  contra proferentum, 10–08
  ejusdem generis, 10–09
  generally, 10–02, 10–03
  objective approach, 10–03
  ordinary and natural meaning, 10–03
  parol evidence, 10–03
  reform, 10–06
Intoxicated persons
  capacity, 4–06
Invitations to treat
  offer, 2–07
Jest
  legal obligations, 1–08
Joint and several liability
  title to sue, 10–20
Jus quaesitum tertio
  title to sue, 10–11
Leases
  termination of contract, 10–18
Legal obligations
  elements of contracts, 1–08
Liens
  breach of contract, 8–10
Limited liability partnerships
  capacity, 4–11
Liquidated damages
  amount recoverable, 8–17

  breach of contract, 8–17
  building contracts, 8–17
  law reform, 8–17
  penalty clauses, 8–17
  pre–estimate of loss, 8–17
  public policy, 8–17
Mental illness
  capacity, 4–02—4–04
Minors
  capacity, 4–02—4–04
Misrepresentation
  arm's length transactions, 5–21—5–23
  concealment, 5–20
  damages claims, 5–16—5–19
  effect, 5–05
  essential misrepresentation, 5–10
  extortionate terms, 5–28
  facility and circumvention, 5–25
  fiduciary relationships, 5–23
  force and fear, 5–27
  fraudulent, 5–18
  see also **Fraudulent misrepresentation**
  innocent, 5–17
  see also **Innocent misrepresentation**
  meaning, 5–16
  negligent misrepresentation, 5–19
  see also **Negligent misrepresentation**
  silence, 5–20
  statements of opinion, 5–18
  title to sue, 10–10
  "trade puffs", 5–18
  undue influence, 5–26
  utmost good faith
    contracts, 5–22
  validity of contract, 5–01, 5–30
  verba jacantia, 5–18
Mistake
  nature of contract, 5–07
  price of goods, 5–05
  subject matter, 5–07
Mitigation
  damages, 8–15
Mora taciturnity and acquiescence
  personal bar, 3–04, 3–07, 3–08
Moral obligations
  elements of contracts, 1–08
Mutual error
  essential error, 5–10
  generally, 5–07
  identity, 5–13
  incidental error, 5–10
  introduction, 5–07, 5–10
  nature of contract, 5–15

price, 5–12
quantity, quality, extent, 5–14
subject matter, 5–11
Negligence
duty of care, 5–19
Negligent misrepresentation
contract voidable, 5–19
damages, 5–19
duty of care, 5–19
generally, 5–19
reliance, 5–19
Negotiable instruments
assignation, 10–16
Negotiation
offer, 2–04—2–07
Notice
personal bar, 3–10
Novation
termination of contract, 9–05
Offer and acceptance
advertisements, 2–06
bankruptcy, 2–10
communication, 2–03
counter-offers, 2–11
death, 2–10
duration, 2–09
electronic communications, 2–19
estimates, 2–05
express offer, 2–03
expression of intention, 2–05
implied offer, 2–03
incorrect offer, 5–06
insanity, 2–10
intention to be bound, 2–03
introduction, 2–03
invitation to treat, 2–07
lapse of offer, 2–09
negotiation, 2–04— 2–07
online shopping, 2–07
postal rules, 2–15—2–20
quotations, 2–05
standard terms, 2–12
subject to contract, 2–11
tender, 2–05
willingness to negotiate, 2–04— 2–07
withdrawal, 2–08
Offers to general public
acceptance, 2–06
Pacta illicita
illegal agreements, 6–01
Parol evidence
interpretation of contracts, 10–03, 10–21
Partnerships
capacity, 4–10— 4–11
Performance
breach of contract, 8–01

defective performance, 8–02, 8–08
impossibility, 8–07
partial performance, 8–02, 9–03
repayment, 9–03
termination of contract, 9–03
Personal bar
acquiescence, 3–04, 3–07
fairness, 3–04
generally, 3–04
holding out, 3–05
homologation, 3–04
mora and taciturnity, 3–08
notice, 3–10
rei interventus, 3–04
representation, 3–06
statutory form, 3–04
voidable contracts, 5–04
waiver, 3–09
withdrawal from contract, 3–04
writing requirement, 3–04
Postal rule
accepting offers, 2–16
excluded contracts, 2–19
generally, 2–15
offering offers, 2–16
reform, 2–20
scope of rules, 2–19
withdrawal of acceptance, 2–18
withdrawal of offer, 2–17
Prescription
termination of contract, 9–09
Privity of contract
title to sue, 10–10
Promises
enforceability, 3–02
gratuitous unilateral obligation, 3–02
presumption against donation, 3–02
Proposals to do business
offer, 2–05
Public policy
agreements contrary to public policy
covenants in restraint of trade, 6–06—6–08
generally, 6–05
joint agreements, 6–09
solus agreements, 6–10
Puffs
misrepresentation, 5–18
Quotations
offer, 2–05
Reasonableness
solus agreements, 6–10
Unfair Contract Terms Act 1977, 7–10
Recovery
generally, 9–14

Rectification
  common law, 5–06
  statutory procedure, 5–06
  validity of contract, 3–03
Rei interventus
  personal bar, 3–04
Remedies (breach of contract)
  action for payment, 8–11
  anticipatory breach, 8–18
  damages
    causation, 8–14
    compensation, 8–12
    generally, 8–12
    liquidated damages, 8–17
    mitigation of loss, 8–15
    remoteness of loss, 8–16
    repudiation of contract, 8–08
  decree *ad factum praestandum*, 8–03, 8–05
  fines, 8–03
  imprisonment, 8–03
  interdict, 8–03—8–07
  introduction, 8–01
  lien, 8–10
  rescission, 8–08
  retention, 8–09
  specific implement
    generally, 8–03
    illegal contracts, 8–07
    payment of sums of money, 8–04
    performance impossible, 8–07
    personal relationship contracts, 8–05
    subject matter of contract, 8–06
    unjust to grant remedy, 8–03
Remoteness of loss
  damages, 8–16
Repayment
  termination of contract, 9–03, 9–14
Repetition
  error, 5–05
  repayment of money, 9–14
Representation
  personal bar, 3–06
Rescission
  defective performance, 8–08
  generally, 8–08
  material breach required, 8–08
  repudiation of contract, 8–08
  respective contractual obligations, 8–08
  restitutio in integrum, 8–11
  right to irritate, 8–08
  termination of contract, 8–08, 9–03
  timing of performance, 8–08
Restitutio in integrum
  fraudulent misrepresentation, 5–18
  innocent misrepresentation, 5–17
  rescission, 8–11
  voidable contracts, 5–04
Restraint of trade contracts
  agreements between manufacturers, 6–09
  common law, 6–06
  contract for sale of business, 6–08
  employment contracts, 6–07
  illegal agreements, 6–04
  restrictive covenants, 6–06
  solus agreements, 6–10
Restrictive covenants
  buyer and seller of business, 6–08
  employers and employees, 6–07
  generally, 6–06
  restraint of trade, 6–06
  trade secrets, 6–07
Retention
  breach of contract, 8–09
Rule in *Winston v Patrick*
  title to sue, 10–21
Sale of goods
  exemption clauses, 7–08
Sanity
  capacity, 4–05
Scottish Parliament
  legislative competence, 1–02
Signatures
  electronic signatures, 3–03
  exemption clauses, 7–05, 7–06, 7–09
  validity of contract, 3–03
Silence
  common law, 5–20
  contract negotiations, 5–20
  duty to disclose, 5–20
  half-truths, 5–20
  misrepresentation, 5–20
  statutory protection, 5–20
Social agreements
  legal obligations, 1–08
  validity of agreements, 1–08
Social workers
  legal obligations, 1–08
Solus agreements
  illegal agreements, 6–10
  meaning, 6–10
  period of restriction, 6–10
  reasonableness, 6–10
  relative bargaining position, 6–10
Specific implement
  generally, 8–03
  illegal contracts, 8–07
  interdict compared, 8–03
  payment of sums of money, 8–04
  performance impossible, 8–07
  personal relationship contracts, 8–05

subject matter of contract, 8–06
Sponsiones ludicrae
   legal obligations, 1–08
Standard form contracts
   exemption clauses, 7–09
   UCTA 1977, 7–09
Standard terms
   battle of forms, 2–12
   offer and acceptance, 2–12
Statements of opinion
   misrepresentation, 5–18
Taciturnity
   see **Mora taciturnity and acquiescence**
Tenders
   offer, 2–05
Termination of contract
   acceptilation, 9–04
   compensation, 9–08
   confusion, 9–07
   delegation, 9–06
   expenses incurred, 9–14
   frustration, 9–13, 9–14
   generally, 9–02
   illegality, 9–12, 9–14
   impossibility, 9–11, 9–14
   material breach, 9–02
   money paid in advance, 9–14
   novation, 9–05
   performance, 9–03
   prescription, 9–09
   repayment, 9–03, 9–14
   repudiation, 9–02
   rescission, 9–02, 9–03
   right to irritate, 8–08
   void contracts, 9–02
   voidable contracts, 9–02
Tickets
   acceptance of conditions
      generally, 7–05
      implied acceptance, 7–06
   additional conditions, 7–02—7–06
   arm's length transactions, 7–09
   exclusion clauses, 7–03
   introduction, 7–03
   notice of conditions
      adequacy of notice, 7–04
      attention drawn to notice, 7–04
   receipt or voucher, 7–03
Title to sue
   actio quanti minoris, 10–21
   agency, 10–17
   assignation, 10–12—10–16
      see also **Assignation**
   bankruptcy, 10–18
   contracts "run with the land", 10–19
   death, 10–18
   delectus personae, 10–13, 10–18
   generally, 10–10
   joint and several liability, 10–20
   jus quaesitum tertio, 10–11
   jus tertii doctrine, 10–10
   misrepresentation, 10–10
   parole evidence, 10–03
   privity of contract, 10–10
   rule in *Winston v Patrick*, 10–21
Trade secrets
   employment contracts, 6–07
Uberrimae fidei
   see **Utmost good faith**
Undue influence
   validity of agreements, 5–26, 5–32
Unenforceable contracts
   validity of agreements, 1–08
Unfair Contract Terms Act 1977
   introduction, 7–08
   reasonableness test, 7–10
   standard form contracts, 7–09
Unincorporated bodies
   capacity, 4–09
Unilateral error
   generally, 5–07, 5–08
Unjust enrichment
   recovery of money, 5–05
Utmost good faith
   misrepresentation, 5–22
Validity of contracts
   annexations, 3–03
   capacity
      see **Capacity**
   concealment, 5–20
   electronic communications, 3–03
   error, 5–05, 5–29
      see also **Error**
   extortionate terms, 5–28
   facility and circumvention, 5–25, 5–32
   force and fear, 5–27, 5–31
   fraudulent execution, 3–03
   illegality
      see **Illegality**
   introduction, 1–08
   misrepresentation, 5–30
      see also **misrepresentation**
   rectification, 3–03
   signature, 3–03
   silence, 5–20
   social agreements, 1–08
   statutory provisions, 3–03
   subscribed by the granter, 3–03
   undue influence, 5–26, 5–32
   unenforceable contracts, 1–08
   void contracts, 5–03
   voidable contracts, 5–04

writing requirement, 3–01, 3–02, 3–03, 3–04
Verba jacantia
   misrepresentation, 5–18
Void contracts
   enforceability, 10–01
   error of intention, 5–09
   essential misrepresentation, 5–10
   force and fear, 5–27, 5–31
   fraudulent misrepresentation, 5–18
   innocent misrepresentation, 5–17
   lack of capacity, 5–03
   lack of consensus, 5–03
   mutual error, 5–10
   third parties, 5–03
   termination of contract, 9–02
   validity of agreements, 5–03
Voidable contracts
   contract set aside, 5–04
   defect ignored, 5–04
   facility and circumvention, 5–25
   fraudulent misrepresentation, 5–18
   innocent misrepresentation, 5–17
   personal bar, 5–04
   restitutio in integrum, 5–04
   termination of contract, 9–02
   third parties, 5–04
   undue influence, 5–26
   utmost good faith, 5–22
   validity of agreements, 5–04, 5–32

Wagers
   legal obligations, 1–08
Waiver
   personal bar, 3–09
Willingness to negotiate
   offer, 2–04—2–07
Withdrawal
   acceptance, 2–14
   distance selling, 2–21
   offer, 2–08
   personal bar, 3–04
   postal rules, 2–17—2–18
Writing requirement
   agreement of the parties, 3–01
   creation of trust, 3–03
   electronic communications, 3–03
   generally, 1–05, 3–01, 3–03
   gratuitous unilateral obligations, 3–03
   interests in land, 3–03
   personal bar, 3–04
   promises, 3–02
   validity of agreements, 3–03
Young people
   capacity, 4–02—4–04